Teacher Education and the Development of Practical Judgement

Also available from Continuum

Subject Knowledge and Teacher Education   Viv Ellis
Teaching Teachers   Angi Malderez and Martin Wedell
Teacher Development   Qing Gu
Philosophy of Educational Research   Richard Pring

Teacher Education and the Development of Practical Judgement

Ruth Heilbronn

continuum

Continuum International Publishing Group

The Tower Building   80 Maiden Lane
11 York Road   Suite 704
London   New York
SE1 7NX   NY 10038

www.continuumbooks.com

British Library Cataloguing-in-Publication Data
A catalogue record for this book is available from the British Library.

ISBN: 978-18470-6032-7 (hardcover)

Library of Congress Cataloging-in-Publication Data
The Publisher has applied for CIP data

Typeset by Aptara
Printed in the United Kingdom by Biddles, Norfolk

To Ruby and John

'What the best and wisest parent wants for his own child, that must the community want for all its children'.

(Dewey, J. *The School and Society*, p. 5)

Contents

Preface

This book is mainly concerned with the formation of teachers at a pre-service level in England. However, much of the discussion around practical judgement and professional learning is relevant to all stages of teacher development and to other high-skilled vocational practices in other countries in which similar preoccupations over standards and targets dominate. The history and context of teacher training and education in England raise questions about what teachers need to know in order to teach, which in turn is based on a view about what teaching is about and the nature of its relationship with learning. In this debate, teacher training in England cannot be separated from broader questions about the education of children.

In the political context it is clear that over the past 25 years, both the school curriculum and teacher training courses have come under an increasing set of control mechanisms and that a conflict between two apparently oppositional views has emerged. In the first and dominant view, teaching is construed as in some sense the technical role of a functionary and teachers are seen largely as 'deliverers' of a predetermined curriculum. Performance is prioritised within an overall target-setting culture, for both pupils and teachers. The second perspective views teaching as a professional practice or set of practices and values the autonomy of the practitioner to make choices about curriculum, methodology and modes of working. Both these views imply an underlying epistemology, a view about the kind of knowledge and understanding embodied in teaching and required to be gained by trainees. In the current model of teacher formation in England, teachers gain Qualified Teacher Status (QTS) by going through training and assessment based on a number of 'standards'.

These are descriptive statements intended to articulate aspects of good teacher behaviour, which the trainee needs to be able to demonstrate.

The first part of the book explores how far standards may give general guidelines for both teacher formation and assessment and where they may fall short of accounting for the complexity of the practice of teaching. Practical teaching involves 'craft knowledge', which is always exercised in situations that are in some sense unique. This 'craft knowledge' may be called 'practical judgement'. The first part of the book examines how practical judgement is developed and what 'training' might mean in the context of practical judgement.

Dewey's version of the acquisition of practical knowledge and understanding yields insights into the question of teacher development. Dewey's analysis of Cartesian rationalism illuminates the nature of practical judgement, which is exercised in the expert application of practical knowledge. Three concepts are particularly useful in this analysis: 'experimental empiricism', 'operational definitions' and 'intelligence'. These concepts can be applied to the experience of teachers dealing with complexity in situations with many variables, and help to elaborate a publicly accessible, theoretical basis for this knowledge and understanding. Dewey indicates how we may undertake a process of reflection, which can lead to articulation of theoretical knowledge. This articulation can further develop the knowledge and understanding of the trainee.

In England and Wales trainees currently spend two-thirds of their time in placements in schools. The book provides an account of teacher education and training, which combines the idea of 'apprenticeship' with the idea of 'partnership', involves highly skilled tutors, in different sites of learning – schools and higher education institutions (HEI) – and a shared responsibility for the trainee's acquisition of theoretical and practical knowledge. The term coined to express this high-skilled, dual- or multi-site vocational training is 'Practiceship'. When a trainee teacher enters into practiceship, schools are sites of supervised and supported practice in the unpredictable situations of real classrooms and a university department of education, an institution of higher education, carries the primary responsibility for trainees acquiring requisite theoretical knowledge and for providing opportunities for simulated roleplay training situations. 'Practiceship' involves communities of practitioners who have expertise in the theory and practice of the craft knowledge, and the mentoring capacity to enable it to be learnt. Such learning requires trust between mentor and learner and a reflective, guided engagement with the process of teaching. The second part of the book discusses each of these elements to show how they all need to be in place to enable practical judgement to develop and flourish.

At its core the book is about the development and exercise of practical judgement. In analyzing practical knowledge it is sometimes difficult to avoid applying language embodied in the discourse of technical rationality when actually attempting to explain some if its limitations. Nouns that are current in everyday usage, such as 'training' or 'knowledge', and adjectives such as 'effective', and particularly 'good', are tricky. Using them risks undermining any attempt to explain that, and how, in any manifestation of expert and fluent practice of craft expertise, of finely tuned decisions about courses of actions, we exercise practical judgement. The difficulty over terminology exists because in talking about practical judgement we would not want to say that what happens when we exercise this judgement is somehow unutterable (that it is akin in some sense to magic), which can only be learnt by shadowing the master craftsperson for a long period of time. As Bronowksi's example has pointed out, in Japan the making of a samurai sword involved complex processes to temper the sword to the required degree of both strength and flexibility. Once the study of chemistry had developed a scientific formula for the heat of the furnace, a thermometer had been made to measure the heat and a timekeeping device was used to measure the period of any particular process, the sword maker no longer needed to rely on recognising the exact moment when a fine and subtle colour change in flame and metal meant that a particular procedure needed to be followed, for a particular time span (Bronowski, 1973, pp. 131–33). The study of chemistry and the technical expertise in reading written instructions, such as chemical formulae, now provides the theoretical knowledge, which can be applied to the sword-making practice. The theory can be learnt, and when applied in the practice the results can be discussed. Was the sword brittle? Was it strong? How did we know?

What does this mean for future successful practice in making a new sword? There is rationality in the process of reflecting on the practice and the success of the practice depends on building up expert knowledge out of which theory can be explicated and develop. What cannot be completely articulated is the working of judgement in each individual case as to what to do when.

Differences between concepts of education and teacher training are exemplified to some extent in the way in which different writers use the terms 'teacher training' and 'teacher education' (Smith, 1992; Carr, 2003). 'Training' is frequently used with a narrower application than 'education' and seems to beg the question about the role of theory, the definition of teaching and the teacher's role. I use the term 'initial teacher training and education' (ITET) to avoid this apparent conflict. To note that it is possible to conceive of teacher formation as a form of high-skill vocational training (Winch, 2006), since it might also be argued that the current conception of training is wrongly associated with low-skill occupations.

Less contentiously, throughout the book I refer to 'new teachers' or the official term 'trainees' (DfES & TTA, 2002) for those working towards qualified teacher status in England and Wales (QTS). I use 'newly qualified teachers' (NQTs) for those in their first teaching year, generally undertaking induction, and 'teachers' with a general application.

Three major questions for the book therefore are:

- Are current ITET concepts based on a notion of technical rationality?
- If so, does this matter?
- What would an alternative conception look like?

Part 1

The Nature of Teacher Capacity and Judgement

Chapter 1

Setting the Scene

Over the past 25 years the story of educational change is complex (but may be captured in one underlying principle) that of control replacing autonomy in both the general education sector and teacher training. Centralised directives replace the autonomy of both schools and teacher training institutions to devise their own curricular and programmes. This control is exercised through the introduction of a statutory curriculum for pupils as well as for trainee teachers, in tandem with an assessment system involving targets for pupils and standards for teachers. The two curricula are necessarily tied together: both have assessment and reporting mechanisms from which quantifiable outcomes may be drawn. The national curriculum (NC) for pupils has attainment target levels, with statutory reporting ages. The NC for teacher trainees is expressed in standards. The standards relating to teaching and learning are tied in with pupil learning. Where this pupil learning has already been defined in terms of the attainment targets of the NC, the performance of pupils is measured against whether they achieve certain teaching and learning objectives. These objectives are largely determined by the scheme of work to which individual teachers must work. Although in theory these schemes of work may be produced by teams of people within a school, there are tight limits placed on how they may develop. This is because the schemes of work are to a large extent assessment led, in that the outcomes to be achieved by the teachers must result in the highest possible achievement of the attainment target levels. The schemes of work are designed to ensure that pupils cover all the things they need to know to achieve at each attainment target level. These attainment levels are then plotted for each school against national targets. The achievement of each school against a national target impacts on every teacher in the school. Teachers' experiences of teaching in their schools are heavily determined by how the school is defined in this process. Teachers in those schools deemed to be 'good' by the Department for Children, Schools and Families (DCSF) have a different perception of their roles and are 'managed' by their senior managers in a different way to those teaching in schools deemed to be 'failing' on this process. The discourse of technical rationality pervades all aspects of school life, so although this chapter discusses recent history of growing control over these two areas in separate sections, they are inextricably linked together.

General Educational Context

Differing views about the purpose of education and the role of the teacher can be traced in educational policy and practice over the last 50 years (Corbett, 1968; Wright, 1983; Chitty, 1990; Goodson, 1990; Whitty et al., 1992; Davies, 1994; Gardner, 1996). The 1970s were a significant decade of challenge to an apparent consensus about the role of the autonomous education professional. The roots of this consensus lie in the 1944 Education Act, with its lack of prescription about curriculum and pedagogy (Benn & Simon, 1972; Chitty, 1990; Hirst, 1996). Chitty has characterised the period as a 'cosy era of ... teacher autonomy' (1990, p. 5) and it is generally agreed that by the 1960s a 'post-war consensus about the general good that education pursues was ... clearly set out' (Hirst, 1996, p. 167; see also Corbett, 1968; Peters, 1965; Peters & White, 1969). So although there was no centralised control over the curriculum, there was a consensus about many aspects of educational practices, in which education was generally seen to provide 'the foundations of a good life for everyone, through the promotion of their development as rationally autonomous individuals' (Hirst, 1996, p. 167). There was also consensus that the matters at stake in education could be debated in 'the rationalist climate of the time' (ibid.).

The good life was seen as the rational life, the product of each individual applying in her or his own context, the ever increasing knowledge and understanding provided by the physical sciences, the social sciences ... and so on.

(ibid.)

This conception of education is one in which 'education has a value for the person as the fulfilment of the mind, a value which has nothing to do with utilitarian or vocational considerations' (Hirst, 1974, p. 31)[1].

Alongside this view of education, other conceptions also emphasised the individual learner at the heart of education (Newsom, 1963; Plowden, 1966).

At the heart of the educational process lies the child. No advances in policy, no acquisitions of new equipment have their desired effect unless they are in harmony with the nature of the child.
(Plowden, 1966, vol. 1, chapter 2, section 9, p. 7)

Plowden emphasised individualised approaches to learning, the centrality of play (at primary level), the use of the environment and curriculum flexibility. The report recommended that teachers should not assume 'that only what is measurable is valuable' (Gillard, 2005). The terms 'progressive' and 'child centred' education cover a broad field of educational thinkers such as Dewey, Piaget and Bruner, whose views cannot be crudely conflated. Nevertheless the terms came to be shorthand for the kind of approach favoured by Plowden. Proponents of Plowden and Newsom found a rationale for the introduction of comprehensive schools and the abolition of secondary selection in the two reports (Gillard, 2005; Kogan, 1987). While it is true to say that various types of schools and views on education could be found at the time, a 'dominant discourse' has been identified in which the teacher was viewed by many as a committed idealist, and a charismatic and inspirational figure (Moore, 2004, p. 33). Many teachers were attracted into teaching in this setting (Corbett, 1968, p. 26). It is worth noting that although there were differences between liberal philosophy of education and progressive education, the two shared a belief in the value of individual autonomy. Subsequent control mechanisms, which are discussed in this chapter, attacked both alike.

Comprehensive Schools

Social equity was a strong value underlying educational debate in the early 1970s and writers such as Benn and Simon argued for the establishment of comprehensive schools on social equity grounds (Benn & Simon, 1972, pp. 491–507). Other writers concurred:

> Education for democracy ... precisely describes the nature of our concern for education at the present time. We want more and better education of a type appropriate to a democracy, and leading towards a much more democratic society than we have at present. Education for democracy, not for aristocracy, meritocracy, plutocracy, or any other kind of elitist system.
>
> (Daniels, 1970, p. 9)

It is not too strong to state that a view of the liberal aims of education, as defined by Hirst, came to be associated by some teachers and writers on education, with a view of education as a socially liberating, egalitarian force and that this view in turn was rejected by others as an ideological justification for a certain kind of school and curriculum. The Plowden report for example has been accused of 'seeking refuge in ideology, by dipping eclectically into ... the pluralistic, often self-contradictory field of progressive education' (Gillard, 2005).

Significant, fundamental disagreement about the aims of education from the political right, particularly in the Black Papers, emerged to challenge contemporary educational practices, sowing the seeds of the current debate about teaching and teacher education and training. The views of some teachers about the socially transformative value of education, coupled with the desire to establish non-selective schools, in which children of all social classes and abilities were to be educated as individuals, came to be attacked as undemocratic and even revolutionary:

> If informed, civilised, mature and well-balanced citizens are wanted ... we must scrutinise most carefully those educationalists who teach hatred of authority and contempt of tradition; who nurture ignorance and self-indulgence as a point of principle ... and disregard the claims or indeed the realities of the social world.
>
> (Cox & Boyson, 1971, pp. 16–17)

Cox and his co-writers of 'the Black Papers', claimed that educational standards were falling and that this was a direct result of progressive education and educators (Cox & Boyson, 1971, p. 17; Cox & Dyson, 1971). A government initiated 'Great Debate in Education'[2] highlighted a climate of 'assertive teacher-power' (DES, 1976, p. 17) and initiated a process of government scrutiny of curriculum and pedagogy that reached a significant stage under the government of Margaret Thatcher, when the Black Papers authors began to influence educational policy (Furlong, 2002, p. 23). Flew, for example, published a pamphlet for the Centre for Policy Studies promoting education for 'examinations, excellence and elites', in which he challenged the egalitarian slant of the comprehensive school movement, in favour of a system to promote 'excellence' and its inevitable formation of an elite class.

> To achieve excellence in any sphere is to become a member of an elite; as such one is no longer, in whatever maybe the relevant respect, equal to those who have not achieved that particular form of, or perhaps any, excellence.
>
> (Flew, 1982, p. 23)

It has been said that Cox and Flew grossly misrepresented educational practices in the early 1970s as

> comprehensivism, secrecy, curricular erosion and teachers trained behind closed college doors on sociological pap.
>
> (Davies, 1994, p. 21)

We can claim then that by the later 1980s there is evidence of considerable debate about the aims of education and the proper role of teachers and teacher training, with some writers perceiving an attack on the professionalism of teachers, their autonomy of judgement on curriculum and pedagogy:

> 'teacher-power', if it ever existed, was to be first eroded, then destroyed – at least in theory.
>
> (Chitty, 1990, p. 10)

A National Curriculum

Part of the story of control exercised over schools and teachers lies in the introduction of the first national curriculum (NC) through the 1988 Education Reform Act (ERA), which was seen as a narrowing of the curriculum by some contemporary critics. White, for example, pointed out that it contained:

> nothing about the prerequisite understanding of socio-economic structure, or the principles of democracy, about fostering the virtues necessary in democratic citizens, about equipping people for critical reflection on the status quo, or about building the imperfect democratic structures we have now into something more adequate.
>
> (White, 1990, p. 37)

It was framed within the confines of subject divisions, rather than across subjects, and this made it difficult to sustain some of the earlier curriculum initiatives, which teachers were free to introduce without centralised direction. An example is the fate of the various projects on 'language awareness', such as Garson et al. (1989) on linguistics, which was taught across the subjects of Modern Foreign Languages (MFL), English and Humanities. In theory, such initiatives were not condemned, but in this case the NC for Modern Foreign Languages, with its ladder of attainment levels and targets, took specific and statutory curriculum time.

The NC was devised to cover specific curriculum subjects; to apply to four key school stages, from ages 5 to 16, to match pupil achievement against ten levels, and to accompany an assessment and testing regime, designed to raise standards of achievement. The rationale for both the choice of NC subjects and the testing regime was questioned (Davies, 1994) and two years after the introduction of the NC Goodson remarked that:

> The first thing to say about this whole exercise is that it unwinds 80 years of English (and Welsh) educational history. It is a case of go back to go.
>
> (Goodson, 1990, p. 49)

The genesis of the so-called 'deregulator' view of education and other areas of social policy in England at this time has been located in a particular historical context, the 1973 oil crisis and subsequent 1974 major world recession. Bernbaum (1979) believes that when an economy ceases to be characterised by high rates of growth, 'the assumptions that growth is closely related to the benefits obtained through large-scale educational enterprises are more readily challenged' (p. 12). Chitty (1990) has speculated that the oil crisis and the recession led to a crisis of confidence in the notion of progressive economic expansion, and a challenge to the concomitant liberal beliefs of the 1960s, including the liberal philosophy of education.

During the period, changes in ITET run parallel with, or follow swiftly on from changes in general educational policy (Hewett, 1971). This is to be expected in that ITET is 'a contingent service', which cannot exist in its own right 'but is there to further the development of children and young persons by its supply of manpower and by the quality of its teacher education' (Millins, 1971, p. 38).

ITET in the Period

This section notes some major stages in the reorganisation and reconceptualisation of teacher education, to reveal the roots of a profound conceptual rift between the DCSF's view of ITET, which is further developed in Chapter 2, and that of a significantly different view, further discussed in Chapter 3. (Key dates appear in the Appendix.) The genesis of the current ITET debate emerged as early as 1944, in the McNair committee investigation into the formation of teachers, particularly concerning two related, pertinent topics, one on the role of the universities and the other on the definition of an appropriate relationship between theory and practice in ITET[3]. McNair's committee was divided on the role that the universities should play in teacher training, and 'adopted the unusual procedure of presenting two alternative scenarios in the main body of the Report, each supported by five members of the committee' (Turner, 1990, p. 41). One group prioritised practice over theory to the degree that it recommended that the colleges should continue to work with the existing Joint Boards, which had been established in 1929 and functioned only for the purposes of certification[4]. There is evidence that this view was seen as 'foreshadowing the anti-intellectualism of many subsequent writers on teacher education' (Turner, 1990, p. 43). The other group recommended that the universities should take over responsibility for teacher training and should establish Schools of Education, which could militate against ITET coming under the direct control of a single centralised service.

> We reject anything approaching permanent central control over the training of teachers. Centralisation of power and authority has potential dangers in every sphere of education and nowhere are those dangers so great and subtle as in the training of teachers. We believe that in years to come it will be considered disastrous if the national system for the training of teachers is found to be divorced from the work of the universities or even to be running parallel with it.
>
> (McNair, 1944, para. 169)

Post-McNair, most of the existing teacher training colleges opted to become part of the university Schools of Education, almost all of which called themselves Institutes of Education[5]. In so doing, they created the opportunity for aspects of the ITET curriculum to remain independent of central government. As university departments, the opportunity to retain or develop a strong theoretical basis to the ITET curriculum existed. The McNair Report has been described as 'surprisingly prescient' in this regard (Turner, 1990, p. 42).

> It recognised ... the importance of collaboration between various kinds of specialist colleges and the universities.
>
> (ibid.)

In Chapters 5 and 6 the importance of 'communities of practice' in supporting teachers' work is discussed. The universities at this time supported such communities, in the form of teacher development networks, which worked independently of the DES and evolved their own particular committee structures (ibid., 44–45)[6].

The HEI Role in ITET

The higher education institutions (HEI) role in ITET during the past 40 years has undergone significant changes. First, following the Robbins Report on Higher Education (HE) in 1963 the HEI ITET role was strengthened; teacher training colleges were renamed Colleges of Education; the B.Ed degree was developed, and in 1972 teaching became an all graduate profession (Robertson, 1971, p. 47; Turner, 1990, pp. 48–49). Turner believes that

> the concept of a higher education institution which co-operated with and influenced a wide range of different institutions within its own area, even when these institutions were not of full degree level, was a far-sighted one and one which has been adopted in number of other countries.
>
> (Turner, 1990, p. 49)

While *The Training of Teachers Regulations of 1967* consolidated previous regulations and amendments and widened the range of powers exercised by the DES (DES, 1967), in practice the training institutions had considerable freedom over what and how they trained teachers. In 1971 Millins reported that:

> academic and professional syllabuses, patterns of practical teaching, rationalisation of resources, inter-college collaboration, examinations and standards of performance are all left almost entirely to the institutes of education.
>
> (Millins, 1971, p. 37)

Significantly, Millins states that the DES 'does not ask searching questions about the quality of future teachers' (ibid.). He ponders that this 'might betoken either indifference or confidence in the deeprooted and dependable liberalism of the vast body of teacher training' (ibid.). He cites research to support his statement that the DES seems to prefer to leave much to individual and local initiative; to be told what people would like to do, rather than to evolve fundamental priorities and to co-ordinate endeavours within their framework.

(ibid., pp. 37–38)

Individual and local initiatives allow for a diversity of approach to ITET. They also suffer from a disadvantage in not providing an overall, nationally recognisable coherence in terms of assessment criteria. This function was fulfilled largely through the inspectorate (Her Majesty's Inspectorate [HMI]), which reported on standards achieved and issued advice and guidance. Following some HMI reports, various 'piecemeal improvisations' in teacher training (Millins, 1971, p. 39) were implemented, until the 'watershed document' (Turner, 1990, p. 51) of the James Report (DES, 1972)[7] was published. The importance of this report has been widely conceded (Furlong & Hirst, 1988; Turner, 1990; DfES, 2002a). It made a large number of recommendations, covering the whole ITET field. Significantly, it focused attention on the possibility and need for a greater school contribution to training. This training was to take place in partnership with HEIs, within a staged process, from degree level, through initial training and into continuous professional development. This was to be achieved through a radical reorganisation of teacher training into three 'cycles', the first two broadly accepted by the DES (Patrick, 1986). The first two-year cycle was to be a general higher education course and the second cycle a year of professional studies, with a further year as a 'licensed teacher'. Successful completion of these cycles was to lead to a BA (Ed.) qualification, with teacher status. The third cycle was to be professional development, amounting to the equivalent of at least a term every seven years for all teachers in post, an aspiration still to be achieved.

In the early 1970s a political attack on a perceived role of educational theory, as taught by HEI ITET providers, was based on what were seen as declining educational standards, premised on the theoretical basis of much university teacher training. This perception directly fuelled recommendations for 'on the job' training (O'Hear, 1988; Lawlor, 1990), leading Carr to claim that 'O'Hear and Lawlor deny we need any theory at all' (Carr, 1993a, p. 253). There are also the complexities surrounding the political dimension, one of which may be that political questions are sometimes muddled with other issues, such as funding or teacher shortage. This is an area outside the current discussion however.

HMI's account of some shortcomings in teacher training were more substantial, and were related to the changing nature of schools, particularly the rise of the comprehensive school. Reporting on a national secondary school survey undertaken between 1975 and 1978, HMI pointed out that secondary education had undergone changes from a largely selective to a largely comprehensive system in around 12 years, at a time of rapidly increasing pupil numbers (DES, 1979). Teacher training was concurrently reviewed because of

> the coincidence of many different pressures, some of them in con-
> flict with one another. Most schools were faced with the simultane-
> ous demands of expansion and internal change and some had to
> meet them with a high proportion of inexperienced teachers.
>
> (DES, 1981, p. 3)

At this time HMI looked for professional development for those teachers challenged by a change to a new kind of school:

> A recognisable system of secondary education for all has emerged,
> but it is one where the curriculum and the style of teaching have
> in general failed to change in line with changing expectations and
> changing circumstances, despite the presence within many schools
> of flexibility, experiment and innovation of very high quality. If,
> however, there is a tendency towards conservatism in our schools
> then it must be acknowledged that teacher training has failed to
> make an impact on it.
>
> (ibid.)

It is clear then that the perspective of the Black Paper authors around this time differed from that of HMI. The Black Papers criticised teach-
ers, teacher training and comprehensive schools on grounds of a lowering of standards, and the loss of educational selection for the creation of an educated 'elite'. HMI sought to encourage different

ways of working in the comprehensive schools and to stimulate a debate about ITET around the idea of comprehensive education.

> The role of teacher training must be seen in relation to a system of secondary education which has undergone marked changes in some fundamental respects ... but has remained largely unaltered in others.
>
> (ibid.)

For HMI some teachers were not suited to the new comprehensive ideal, had a tendency to 'subject chauvinism' (ibid., p. 4), and needed a rounded view of the curriculum as a whole (ibid., p. 9). HMI believed that changes in the organisation of schools entailed a need to reassess the curriculum, which in turn required a change to the ITET provision, difficult to achieve when the ITET providers worked independently. At that time, in the late 1970s and early 1980s, there were four-year B.Ed programmes and one year PGCEs, in a variety of settings, HEI, polytechnics and colleges of education (Hirst, 1979; DES, 1980; Alexander & Whittaker, 1980; Patrick et al., 1982). So the desirability of gaining some kind of coherent overview of ITET was much debated and in this account of the increasing control of central government over ITET, the formation of the Council for the Accreditation of Teacher Education (CATE, 1984) is significant. CATE was mandated to centralise, for the first time, the content and many of the procedures of teacher education, which anticipates to some extent the centralisation of the school curriculum four years later by the Education Reform Act (McNamara, 1996).

In 1994, new arrangements for ITET were established through the 1994 Education Act, including setting up the Teacher Training Agency (TTA), to replace CATE, taking over and enlarging on the former body's functions. Now called the Teacher Development Agency (TDA) this body has responsibility for accrediting and funding all ITET courses in England. The past decade has been significant in establishing the statutory framework and regulatory and funding procedures in which new teachers are trained. One aspect of ITET that was changed was the amount of time trainees were to spend in school.

School-Based Training

We come now to a highly significant factor in current ITET, and one which forms the background to much of the subsequent chapters in this book, the provision of a large element of school-based training for new trainee teachers. This emphasis on school practical experience as the major part of the trainees' curriculum time began in the early 1990s (DFE & Welsh Office, 1992 and 1993). Once a substantial amount of time was to be spent in school, ITET programmes were significantly altered, as the site of learning about teaching shifted from mainly HEIs to largely in schools. It then became debatable what the particular role of the HEIs might now be in developing a scholarly approach to teaching and providing access to and sites for research and scholarship in education.

Schools in general are busy places and by and large teacher trainees in them focus almost exclusively on practical matters. However, what is a 'practical matter? The fact that henceforth ITET was managed in partnerships between HEIs and schools, significantly throws into question the nature of practical knowledge. A view that the HEI taught 'theory' and the school was the site of 'practice' is thrown into question if, as is the present case, 70 percent of the Post Graduate Certificate of Education (PGCE), leading to QTS now takes place in school. In the Graduate Teacher Programmes (GTP) this may rise to between 90 and 100 percent of trainee time, with no HEI input. What view of teacher knowledge and understanding underpins the ITET model of mainly school-based training, including the taught and the assessed elements? These questions are discussed in detail later in the book – Chapters 2–5 discuss fundamental questions about the nature of practical knowledge, such as is manifest in teaching, and create an account of practical knowledge pertinent to teaching and learning to teach. Chapters 6–9 apply this account to specific matters in ITET and create a description of an appropriate ITET model.

Not surprisingly, there was considerable criticism from HEIs, teachers and teacher organisations, of many of the proposals for new ITET arrangements made through the 1994 Education Act (Menter & Whitehead, 1995). An NUT (National Union of Teachers) survey of staff in schools and HEIs, for example, found considerable concern about several aspects of partnership school-based training, including the sufficiency of funding available to cover school mentors' time, school mentors' workload, the lowering of entry standards to the profession and the downgrading of primary teachers' qualifications in comparison with secondary teachers. The NUT concluded that the proposals sought to 'de-professionalise teaching by lowering entry standards and reducing the personal and theoretical study required of trainee teachers' (ibid., p. 49).

Reducing the amount of time, and hence influence of the HEI in ITET was viewed with some apprehension. It could be said with some justification that university teacher trainers, by and large, seek

> to remain custodians of an educational tradition which respects the freedom of thought based on scholarship and research.
>
> (Pring, 1996, p. 10)

It might seem somewhat bold to say that the creation of the TTA

> removed at one stroke the buffer between government funding and university autonomy – the protection against government interference in the freedom of enquiry and of teaching.
>
> (ibid., p. 13)

However, in the ITET story the role of HEI is significant: in operating independently of central government control they offer the possibility of diverse viewpoints about what constitutes good teaching and good ITET practice.

Currently assessment of teachers for the award of QTS is based on the achievement of certain standards, for which evidence is required (TDA, 2007). These standards can be, and are, largely evidenced on practical teaching experience in schools. Chapter 2 provides an account of how these standards embody a view of practice that is fundamentally technicist, based on a reductionist view of practical knowledge, which Schön has called 'technical rationality' (Schön, 1983, 1987). Assessment using the QTS standards is tied to this particular view of practice. This raises an issue about the scope for thinking about teaching, preparing for teaching, reflecting on teaching that can be supported by university tutors. The second part of the book suggests how these functions and perspectives can be allowed to flourish (Chapters 7–9).

The general educational context also places limitations on ITET providers in the pursuance of breadth and depth of perspective. First, Ofsted inspections of ITET courses tend to generate an assessment-led model, dictated by quality assurance criteria. Secondly, ITET tutors need to cover the statutory standards agenda, the National Curriculum (NC), the various strategies and policy priorities, such as the current Children's Agenda (DfES, 2004a, 2005a), in a reduced time frame. The NC's assessment regime requires schools to report on pupil performance against the NC attainment levels and national examinations. In a crude way it could be possible to map teachers' 'performance' against their pupils' performance in tests and examinations. The technicist discourse is an economic one, of measurable outcomes and the kind of ITET assessment mechanism which developed in the 1990s is linked to the idea of appraising teachers in relation to target setting for raising NC attainment. Teacher appraisal was introduced in 1991 and one of the aims of the appraisal process at the time was to link pay with performance (DfE, 1991). It therefore became important to define 'performance' for appraisal purposes. It follows that developing a work-based assessment system for teachers, which might be used by appraisers 'on site', becomes an important step for reporting on teacher performance.

The appraisal story is linked to a current tension in ITET and teacher development. On the one hand some LEAs (Local Education Authorities) rejected the link between pay and performance and used statutory appraisal to implement their own staff development programmes, interpreting the regulations broadly, with teachers able to set their own developmental agenda. This approach favours the professional autonomy of teachers to decide their own developmental needs and routes and weakens appraisal as a control mechanism, in terms of higher pay or disciplinary procedures. An example was Camden LEA:

> Camden's approach to appraisal is founded on the principles that appraisal is a developmental process which should reflect a professional partnership between appraisers and appraisees, and that it should not be related to pay or discipline, or be subject to improper interference by parents or governors.
>
> (Camden LEA, 1991, p. 2)

On the other hand a performance agenda for appraisal is clearly discernible in the period. HMI evaluating appraisal between 1991 and 1996 found it had not achieved its potential to 'improve school effectiveness' (Ofsted, 1997; BBC, 1999, 2000):

> The key challenge for school management over the next few years is to exploit the potential of appraisal and self-evaluation. Appraisal in many schools has lacked rigour. The conclusions of the appraisal process have not been followed through into management action which benefits the appraisee and the school.
>
> (Ofsted, 1997)

We can see then that those critics of appraisal who took a 'professionaliser' view saw appraisal as a 'deregulator's' tool for management and control of the teaching work force. Appraisal was replaced by an 'annual performance management' (APM) from September 2000, in which the link between pay and 'performance' was established, allowing successful teachers to pass over a 'threshold' of higher pay. The mode of threshold assessment is standards-based. Standards are used within the whole picture of NC assessment, recording and reporting, national league tables and judgements about individual schools' performances. The question to be asked is how well standards can account for good teaching. The next chapter looks in detail at competencies and standards as a mode of assessment for teaching.

Notes

1. See particularly Chapter 3, 'Liberal Education and the Nature of Knowledge' (Hirst, 1974, pp. 39–54).
2. 'The Great Debate in Education' was launched in a speech in October 1976 by Prime Minister James Callaghan, following a confidential government report, known as the Yellow Book (DES, 1976).
3. At the time there were voluntary teacher training colleges, such as those maintained by Christian foundations, and colleges maintained by the LEAs. Teachers went through a college route, gaining

the Teacher's Certificate, or went straight into school with an honours degree, and underwent a period of probation.

4. The Joint Examining Boards were established in 1929 as a result of a 1925 Board of Education Report, which concluded that only trained teachers should be accepted for service in elementary schools and that the training colleges and the universities should jointly take over the examination for the Teacher's Certificate from the Board of Education (Hewitt, 1976, p. 20).

5. Homerton, Froebel and Goldsmiths remained independent.

6. There were originally seventeen Area Training Organisations: fourteen were integral parts of universities or university colleges and four were directly funded by the Ministry of Education (Turner, 1990, p. 39).

7. A decision to review teacher training was taken in 1970 (Turner, 1990, p. 50). A letter of February 1970 to the Area Training Organisations (ATOs) from the Secretary of State for Education of the Labour Government of the day, called for a ' comprehensive inquiry' and asked that the ATOs undertake a self review, particularly examining their structure 'from the point of view of involvement of the teaching profession itself' (Turner , 1990, pp. 56–57). However, the ATOs did not have time to undertake this process, which was overtaken by political events. The succeeding Secretary of State for Education in the new Conservative government, Margaret Thatcher, commissioned an enquiry into teacher training and probation, with comprehensive terms of reference (DES, 1972).

Chapter 2

Competencies and Standards in ITET

A significant development in ITET was an extended requirement for school-based practice, through which trainees engaged in real teaching episodes for the majority of their ITET course. This required an assessment mechanism appropriate to the ITET curriculum taking place largely and in some cases totally in schools. Issues for any accreditation system for ITET may be summed up under three major areas. First, learning to teach requires knowledge and understanding in a number of areas, as well as the development of expertise in the craft of teaching (Marland, 1975). The nature of this knowledge and understanding is complex as is discussed in the following three chapters. Managing, promoting, supporting and assessing such learning needs to account for the inherent complexity. Questions such as the nature of technical, theoretical and practical knowledge and the relation between them need to be understood and articulated, in order for a curriculum and accompanying assessment to be developed. (See particularly Winch, 2000, pp. 100–103 and the substantive discussion in Chapters 3–6).

Secondly, any ITET assessment instrument needs to be capable of clarity in use, to enable all involved, trainees, tutors, mentors and assessors to use them with confidence in both development and assessment. Thirdly, it needs to generate reliable assessment judgements for entry into the profession. Defining requisite teacher 'knowledge and understanding' in terms of assessment criteria, which are unambiguous, standardisable and reliable is a requirement of any system of national accreditation. (Further implications for assessment are discussed particularly in Chapter 8.) These three criteria may, for convenience, be termed the complexity, clarity and warrant criteria.

In the early 1990s a non-statutory, competency-based ITET model was developed, which attracted considerable criticism. This chapter considers the competency model and the development and context of the current QTS standards, which replaced the competency approach. Some conclusions about the nature of teaching are developed that relate to the fundamental question of whether a version of technical rationality underpins the current QTS standards.

Competencies As Teacher Assessment Tools

Any assessment of practical teaching needs to be capable of application by assessors in the practice base, across a range of different schools and conditions. Competencies were introduced into ITET in the early 1990s in an attempt to provide such an assessment mechanism (DfE & Welsh Office, 1992, 1993). They were not statutory, but many institutions attempted to work with them (N. Ireland Working Group, 1992; Kerry & Mayes, 1995; Menter & Whitehead, 1995). The new teaching competencies were based largely on a particular model of vocational training, the General National Vocational Qualifications (GNVQ) (NCVQ 1991; DfE & Welsh Office, 1992, 1993). The GNVQ model of competency assessment relies on analysis of discrete, observable, measurable, verifiable 'pieces' of behaviour, functioning in specified ways as performance indicators (Houston, 1990; Lively, 1992).

There were political objections to competencies as a form of managerial control 'entrenched in the official discourse of policy making' (Carr, 1993a, p. 254). The term 'competence' was used without a clear definition in much of the debate about teacher education in the 1990s. Discussions about competencies in teacher assessment were plagued by 'inconsistency, ambiguity or incoherence' (Lum, 1999, p. 404). The term suffered from 'instability of sense' (Carr, 1993a, p. 255) and needed to be clarified (Carr, 1993a; Lum, 1999). The feasibility of competency based assessment for ITET was questioned on grounds of clarity and warrant:

> how can a system which claims to be based on precise standards and explicit outcomes be allowed to get away with such confusion about the basic terms, which are at the heart and foundation of the whole process?.
>
> (Hyland, 1994, p. 21, quoted in Lum, 1999, p. 404)

The key idea in Competence Based Education and Training (CBET) is the work-based nature of the assessment, relying on testing or verifying the candidate's ability to perform a variety of tasks in the workplace. One of the claimed virtues of CBET is that 'it focuses on what workers need to do in the workplace and not on superfluous extras' (Winch, 2000, p. 88). The competence that is assessed is based on performance 'defined in a circumscribed way, namely the ability to perform a task according to certain specification on a particular occasion' (ibid.).

Teaching is a high-skilled occupation. To provide warrant for assessment the competency model needs unambiguous assessment criteria, capable of standardised application in individual work situations. To this end many competency models design statements to describe the skills required in the workplace situation in terms of what a candidate can do. An individual performance indicator in any competency model of assessment constitutes both a descriptor of one specific 'piece' of behaviour and the criterion for assessing the achievement of that behaviour. On this model, after verifying that the behaviour has taken place, the assessor should be assured that the particular competence defined in the criterion has been verified. How satisfactory is the application of this model of assessment to ITET?

The answer revolves around the question of what we mean when we say: 'X is a competent teacher'. We can readily understand that some aspects of competency can be demonstrated in a 'piece' of behaviour and we can construe 'competence' as having modest connotations of practical effectiveness or efficiency ... (which) tends to invite quantitative, statistical explanations. (See Carr, 1993a, pp. 253–54 for an extended discussion of this point).

For example, we could invent a competency criterion for the use of the overhead projector (OHP) such as:

OHP Criterion 1: The teacher can use the overhead projector safely in the classroom.

This statement could be verified by anyone, in any school, by observation and judgement, in the context of electrical equipment around children and current safety legislation (HMSO, 1999). The notion of safety is implicit in the OHP criterion, and safety criteria need to be formulated, promulgated, known and understood, in order both for performance and verification to occur. These 'base-line principles' regarding safety must embody at least clarity, comprehensiveness and appropriateness. So warrant for the OHP criterion lies in criteria external to the stated competency criterion itself, since the baseline principles exist prior to the formulation of the competency statement and underline its appropriateness as an assessment descriptor or criterion. Further, safety cannot be the only factor in judging a teacher's competence in the use of the OHP, as its safe use to show holiday slides to friends, while showing competence with the equipment, does not guarantee it being used appropriately or well in the context of the lesson for the benefit of the pupils' learning. To establish this dimension of competency a further competency statement is needed such as:

OHP Criterion 2: The teacher can use the OHP pedagogically well (or 'with good pedagogical affect').

Baseline principles for 'pedagogically well' or 'good pedagogical affect' are also a necessary condition for performance and verification. Arguably here there may be many factors to take into consideration, some of which will be relatively easy to verify and some that will not. We could easily tell if the equipment was not used particularly well if the teacher stood in front of it and the pupils could not see the demonstration or illustration made. Although if the transparency in question was not pedagogically useful, it might have confused the pupils, so that masking the screen might be a good thing. So context specific information is important to making a judgement about achievement of the criterion. Questions about teaching are less easy to answer in such an immediately reductive manner as are questions of safety. We would need to understand the precise context of the classroom and many of the variables of the teaching situation. It might also be difficult to extrapolate factors relating to teaching and learning in general from factors relating only to the use of the OHP. We could attempt to devise a raft of criterion referenced statements, relating to the safe, efficient and good use made in teaching of the OHP. If it were possible to make unambiguous, descriptive statements about verifiable behaviour for each of these aspects of use, we would need a separate criterion referenced statement and separate, comprehensive, baseline principles for each statement. The baseline principles involve propositional knowledge and understanding, such as technical information relating to a specific skill, and possibly in addition some theoretical knowledge, for example, about theories of child development.

It follows that if we wish to verify even a relatively straightforward notion concerning the use of the OHP in teaching using competency criteria, we probably need several different competency statements. Therefore, while it is possible that competence criteria might be formulated for some teaching skills we need to ask how useful and how appropriate such competency statements are. Some teacher competencies might amount to little more than pieces of behaviour, while for others there is a hinterland of propositional knowledge and understanding required to achieve them, which may not be evident in any particular manifestation of behaviour. We would need some additional verification mechanism, such as questioning the trainee or the mentor. The use of the OHP in the above example directs us to think of 'the complex issues surrounding workplace learning' (Winch, 2000, p. 2), which are further discussed in Chapters 3–6.

There are also logistic objections to using competency criteria in ITET assessment. Even if we were to grant at this point the possibility of formulating competency criteria for many aspects of a teacher's job, how manageable would such a system of assessment be? A teacher might 'achieve' the competency criterion for some skills but fail some others. The question then arises of overall pass or fail for Qualified Teacher Status (QTS). We could make a final assessment based on aggregated results as some early models of competency did (Burke, 1989; Jessup, 1991; Houston, 1990; Lively, 1992). It is possible to create an assessment procedure in which scores are given against assessed descriptors, which are then aggregated to give a pass or fail grade. However, given that each element of a competency statement needs to cover a discrete, observable aspect of competence and that a teacher's job is extensive and complex, the number of competence statements is likely to be large. One such scheme in use in the 1990s covered five large volumes, requiring ticks against around 2,000 boxes (INTASC, 2006)[1]. So even were one to concede that competency criteria can be safely used to arrive at secure judgements on trainee teachers' performance in the sense of purely demonstrable skills, any system likely to be subtle enough to capture their performance in use is also likely to fulfil the clarity criterion, being too unwieldy to manage.

Professional Values and Competence

We use the term 'a competent teacher' to mean more than competence with certain technical skills. When a teacher stops a class because she has overheard a racist remark, which she tackles sensitively, knowledgeably, successfully, while upholding the value of tolerance, we would say she dealt competently with the situation, drawing on her own values and her experience. Carr has identified this as one of the meanings of the use of the term 'competence':

> Capacities entail the voluntary and deliberate exercise of principled judgement in the light of rational knowledge and understanding ... Capacities are knowledge-driven.
>
> (Carr, 1993a, p. 253)

Can we formulate competency criteria in the capacity sense, such as when judging the teacher's competent professional responsibility to 'children and to society and to the profession's purposes and characteristics'? (Thompson, 1997, p. 1). It is possible to formulate some general statements relating to observable professional expectations, such as 'the teacher generally arrives on time to all school commitments'. This statement relies on a notion of teacher reliability that is not difficult to cash out. It is more difficult to formulate some kinds of specific statements to cover some universally recognised values. Suppose it were possible to identify and define different values in such a way that they gained universal acceptance, such as integrity for example. Integrity is not a skill, the sort of thing we tick off once we have seen it in action. Integrity is a virtue that is exhibited non-sporadically and non-arbitrarily over time and is not reliably exhibited in a single action or piece of behaviour. Compare this to the quality of reliability as shown by a builder for which we can amass specific empirical evidence, such as viewing references, examples of his work, discussing his plans and so on. This kind of evidence is not difficult to interrogate and can build up into a belief in the builder's reliability. We do not seek to amass the same kind of evidence of integrity.

Having professional values and living by them in practice are an essential part of being a practitioner involved with others, and the capacity for trustworthiness is fundamental to teaching. This is very evident when one is acting pedagogically within the parent-child relationship (van Manen, 1991) for example. Any model of teacher assessment needs to be able to account for the teacher's values in some sense. (See detailed examination of the notion of trust in Chapter 6 on mentoring).

The project to conceptualise teaching in competency terms fails to meet the complexity criteria. Many areas of teacher behaviour cannot be isolated in such a way as to be capable of formulation in simple descriptive statements. Teaching skills, knowledge and understanding are 'dispersed' across contexts and competency criteria cannot account for the normative nature of teaching. It fails the clarity criteria, because an accumulation of competency statements causes difficulties for assessment processes and for overall assessment grading. It might be possible to formulate some general competency statements around specific technical skills, but in practice these skills are used within a specific pedagogic situation, multi-dimensionally, such as the example of OHP use, which entails safety and pedagogic criteria. Even if a competence-based ITET assessment system could be comprehensive enough to embody teacherliness in its entirety it would be unmanageable.

In this respect learning to teach is one example of workplace learning involving various kinds of skills, which need to be understood in their complex interactions. The argument against the possibility of comprehensively capturing the trainee's knowledge and understanding through a narrowly competence-based mode of assessment, where different kinds of skills and their inter-relations are not well defined, applies in other kinds of complex learning environments. Winch has identified various inter-related types of skills as:

'polyvalent skilling, in which a worker possesses a related group of skills that can be applied in a variety of different tasks in the workplace, deep skilling, where a worker acquires fundamental principles of a trade or craft, which can be augmented as different applications of the fundamental principles emerge, and redundant skilling, where the worker applies skills that may be required in circumstances that do not yet obtain'.

(Winch, 2000, p. 87)

Winch believes that competence-based education and training

is . . . symptomatic of a commitment to identify vocational education and training with forms of low-level training, rather than formation. The reason is that the emphasis rests on the behavioural characteristics of an individual rather than a more holistic measure of ability.

(ibid., p. 89)

Nevertheless, in ITET, various HEIs began to develop ways of working with competencies[2], even though an NUT survey of teachers and others engaged in education found general agreement that

the competencies against which student teachers must ... be assessed had not been developed with the involvement of the profession and consequentially were mechanistic and did not satisfactorily articulate the attitudes and qualities which must be combined with knowledge and understanding in defining a teacher.

(Menter & Whitehead, 1995, p. 5)

The adequacy of competencies as the basis of assessment for teaching was widely questioned (Whitty & Willmott, 1991; Thompson, 1992; Carr, 1993a; 1993b; Hyland, 1993), never became a statutory requirement and were abandoned in favour of standards.

Standards for the Award of QTS

The attempt to develop competency criteria for ITET was replaced by a national curriculum for ITET, articulated in statutory standards (DfEE, 1997, Annex A; DfEE, 1998b; TTA, 1998; DfES & TTA, 2002; TDA, 2007). Standards were a key element in the control mechanism introduced to regulate the awarding of QTS and were intended to ensure consistency over provision and to develop a national assessment mechanism, given the variety of diverse routes into teaching. To note also the possible influence of standards being developed in other countries, particularly Australia and Canada (Hextall & Mahony, 2000).

Currently, teachers in England and Wales are subject to standards-based assessment at all points in their career (TDA, 2007), moving from QTS, through statutory induction into continuing professional development (CPD) and annual performance management procedures (DfES, 2001; TDA, 2007). From September 1997 only those trainee teachers who successfully completed an accredited course and met all the QTS standards were awarded QTS (DfEE 1997). In writing the standards the TDA worked with a network of 'people from local education authorities (LEAs), higher education institutions (HEIs), teachers and headteachers' (op.cit.). The initial draft of the framework for the standards came from concurrent work in business management by the Management Charter Initiative, published in 1997 as the National Occupational Standards for Management, which have been subsequently updated (TTA, 1998, p. 1; Reynolds, 1999, p. 247). These management standards were designed as a national benchmark of good management performance, to be used for a wide variety of purposes, including defining roles and determining standards of performance, for both individual and organisational development[3].

This first set of standards was criticised for its managerial basis, for being outcomes based, and ignoring the normative dimension of teaching (Reynolds, 1999; Martin & Cloke, 2000). The whole endeavour of the formulation of teaching in terms of standards was seen as misguided and limiting experiences in relation to the development of a professional dialogue about the practice (Emery, 1998, p. 286). In general they did not achieve wide professional agreement that they had met what has been termed in the introduction to this chapter, the complexity, clarity or warrant principles (Spindler & Biott, 2000). The standards were viewed as difficult to use:

> What precisely the TTA means by standards, how precisely teacher trainers are to interpret the new standards and the implications they have for current interpretations of what we mean by successful practice are not clear.
>
> (Reynolds, 1999, p. 249)

The 1997 QTS standards were used for 5 years with a variety of explanatory instruments, policies and procedures accompanying them in various ITET courses and were reviewed and updated from September 2002 (DfES, 2002b). The 2002 standards attempted to overcome difficulties identified in the earlier framework. Professional values, which in the 1997 standards had been summarily defined in a final standards category of 'Other Professional Requirements' (DfEE, 1997), were highlighted. A number of standards were inserted largely based on the *Statement of Professional Values and Practice for Teachers*, which had been drawn up by the General Teaching Council for England (GTCE) after a large-scale consultation with teachers.

A framework of forty-two QTS standards, 'functioning as outcome statements that indicate what trainee teachers must know, understand and be able to do in order to achieve QTS' was developed (TTA, 2004, p. 4). The framework was designed to function as 'a rigorous set of expectations and set out the minimum legal requirement' (TTA, 2004a, p. 4). Trainees had to provide evidence that they had met all the standards, which were grouped under three headings: *Professional Values and Practice, Knowledge and Understanding, and Teaching*. The QTS standards in this version were an assessment instrument, framed as descriptions of aspects of competence and warrant to teach at QTS level. In attempting to define standards pertaining to professional values there was an attempt to construe the teaching role in terms of a professional practice and not on narrow competency lines and to account for the essentially normative nature of teaching.

The complex nature of teaching also seemed to be recognised in the formulation of the QTS standards as a 'framework' in which

many of the standards are inter-related and single assessment opportunities are likely to produce evidence for a wide range of Standards.
The Standards relating to professional values and practice underpin
all the rest: trainees should be able to show that they meet these Standards in everything they do. In the same way, the Standards relating to knowledge and understanding are closely related to those
on planning, teaching and assessment, and successful trainees will
demonstrate them in the classroom as well as through their academic attainments.

(TTA, 2004b, p. 5)

TTA guidance was subsequently published to illustrate how the
related Standards might be used. It suggested ways in which they
could be grouped together other than under their numbered framework categories (TTA, 2003). This begged the question as to why
the three headings were chosen and the usefulness of the framework
construction.

In contrast to the attempt to account for competence in teaching across complex contexts, some standards required propositional knowledge of curricular and statutory responsibilities and
guidelines[4]. Around 10 percent of the standards related to professional relationships and a further 10 percent related specifically to
pastoral issues, both spread across the categories of the framework[5].

Values and Teaching

The 2002 QTS standards attempted to account for the normative
nature of teaching but difficulties in using them became apparent.
Standard 2.2 for example required that trainees 'know and understand ... the values, aims and purposes in the National Curriculum
Handbook, relating to the values of society and the kind of society we
want to be' (DfEE & QCA, 1999(a), p. 10)[6]. 'We' and 'society' were
undefined and the lack of clarity meant that in practice it proved
impossible to validate this standard other than superficially. To do
so would be quite unlike checking teachers mark books to validate
their understanding of recording and reporting under the assessment

standards, required a relational engagement with the trainee and time and circumstances to pursue discussion.

A further example is Standard 1.1 requiring that trainees 'have high expectations of all pupils; respect their social, cultural, linguistic, religious and ethnic backgrounds; and are committed to raising their educational achievement'. While at first sight a non-controversial statement of commitment to social and cultural equality, clarity and warrant is not achieved. Under scrutiny, what is to count as a 'high expectation'? Evidently teachers should not have low expectations of pupils' potential achievements. Respecting pupils' backgrounds seems equally uncontentious, as a fundamental ethical injunction on teachers, which 'goes with the territory'. As an assessment criterion, however, it fails the clarity criteria. For example what happens if a pupil's family belongs to the National Front and the child brings leaflets to school with text or visuals that do not respect other pupils' religious and ethnic backgrounds? This points to the difficulty of standards assessment to meet individual cases. The words 'respect' and 'values' have been used in these standard statements but the endeavour to articulate what they mean in practice, in individual cases, fails. The endeavour is based on a notion of technical rationality, rather than rationality of another sort. What this other kind of rationality might entail is discussed in later chapters in this book, particularly Chapters 3–6.

Wherever the 2002 QTS framework attempted to account for the essentially relational nature of teaching, it hit the buffers of clarity and warrant. For example, Standard 1.4 required that trainees could 'communicate sensitively and effectively with parents and carers recognising their roles in pupils' learning and their rights, responsibilities and interests in this'. Although formulated like a competency 'can do' statement it is unclear what the teacher might do which an assessor could verify? 'Communicate' is straightforward as an assessor could see letters written and received from a parent or carer or could attend a parents' evening. But would this evidence show that the teacher had recognised the role of the parent or carer in the pupil's learning? As there are no sets of standards for parents there is no published uncontroversial definition of what this role is. Some parents think that their responsibility to their child's learning consists solely in sending the child to school to be taught by teachers. At the other end of the scale are parents whose understanding of their responsibilities involves them in providing and sometimes force-feeding their children with extra tuition and coaching. Should the teacher remonstrate with parents who do not see eye to eye with the teacher on what their respective roles should be? If not, what does 'recognise' mean? It might mean that the teacher should 'respect the parent'. Common sense might provide a guideline on what is meant by the parent's role in this standard, but without a clear definition of what should be expected, there is ambiguity in interpretation. 'Rights' and responsibilities are less difficult to grasp as they are defined by statute. The final injunction to recognise the parents' 'interests' in their children's learning seems redundant since they are defined by 'rights and responsibilities'. If 'interests' means more than rights and responsibilities this needs to be defined. For example, parents who are ill-treating a child can have their rights overridden by legislation regarding children's rights. This case indicates how some of the underdefined areas in the standards hindered their use in assessment. Rather, the standard embodied an overarching statement about a teacher respecting a child's home background. In practice the vagueness meant that there was no clear guideline for correct action either.

Trying to Meet the Complexity Criterion

It is clear from the foregoing discussion that there was an attempt in the 2002 QTS standards to meet the complexity criterion, which impacted on the ability of the framework of standards to meet the clarity criterion, particularly in relation to values and attitudes. General and fundamental statements relating to teachers' values and attitudes appeared under all the heading categories and in twelve different standards and this impacted on clarity and warrant. It might also be said that it indicated a doomed endeavour from the outset[7].

Similarly, the fundamental notion of teachers being able to teach such that pupils could learn, the indivisible nature of teaching and learning, was dispersed among many standards. This type of dispersal of notions is a necessary consequence of the structural nature of the framework, the recognition of the complexity and subtlety involved and the attempt at a tight competency type definition in each standard, to meet the warrant criterion. Under the category 'Knowledge and Understanding' trainees needed to show that they knew 'a range of strategies to promote good behaviour and establish a purposeful learning environment' (Standard 2.7). This could not be evidenced and lacked both clarity and warrant in use, since one can know strategies in an academic way, without being able to deploy them. In accepting the notion of complexity in teaching and learning to teach, the 2002 QTS framework of standards conceptualised individual aspects of teacher behaviour, knowledge, understanding and attitudes under category areas that were difficult and sometimes impossible to use as guidelines in formative assessment, for example when observing a lesson. The standard had to be taken in conjunction with Standard 3.3.1, which required trainees to 'establish a purposeful learning environment'. However, this standard also linked the ability of trainees to establish such an environment, with pupils feeling secure and with a classroom 'where diversity is valued', thereby broadening out the scope of 'behaviour management'.

In fact, it is not possible to know if the pupils feel secure, rather than seem to be so to an observer. Apart from difficulties in experiencing what the pupils experience, matters may not be under the control of the teacher, so matters of equity of opportunity to create a secure atmosphere arise from one school to another. In a school where mayhem reigns in corridor and playgrounds, a teacher may be able to create a purposeful learning environment, yet many of the pupils may carry a sense of insecurity from elsewhere. The standard also introduced the notion of valuing diversity, which had previously been part of Standard 1.1 and therefore seemed redundant.

Managing pupil behaviour is mentioned again under the Category 3.3.9, which required that successful trainees 'set high expectations for pupils' behaviour and establish a clear framework for classroom discipline to anticipate and manage pupils' behaviour constructively, and promote self-control and independence'. Again this formulation needed to be interpreted according to the context of the school, illustrating further that individual circumstances influence performance and hence the notion of standardised assessment. Lessons may be taught equally successfully by trainees in schools where the school does not promote pupil independence as schools where it does. In the former case the classes may be set by ability and teacher-led. In the latter the school may value independent and interactive learning, fitting the intent of the last word of the 2002 Standard 3.3.9. In order to accurately gauge whether that standard had been achieved an assessor needed to invoke her professional judgement of how the particular context impacted on what she has seen, and she needed to gauge the teacher's use of her professional judgement, over time. (Chapters 4 and 5 explore these themes in more depth).

Context for Assessment

It is evident that the need to re-visit across standards and standard categories, notions such behaviour management and more importantly management of pupil learning, raised difficulties for clarity and warrant, while attempting to answer the issue of complexity. The 2002 QTS standards attempted to deal with complexity and warrant, but at the expense of clarity. The framework's organisation suggested that by 'interrelating' the several and many issues and matters under investigation, the complexity of teaching could be respected, while retaining a standards-based framework. This stretched the notion of standardisation. Some of the standards were under-defined, some concepts undefined, and ambiguities and confusions abounded in use. The criterion for warrant was not met, namely that the 2002 QTS standards could give reliable and valid judgements, over national contexts, in such a high-skilled vocational context, which also has a relational, normative dimension.

Validation of registration with the General Teaching Council for England, and hence of entry into the teaching profession, requires passing both QTS and induction. Newly qualified teachers must raise their 'performance' to pass standards for teachers on the main teaching pay scale ('classroom standards'), after they have achieved QTS (TDA, 2007). Their induction period could be viewed as 'a bridge from initial teacher training to effective professional practice' (DfEE, 1999, para. 1). However, the schools in which both initial teacher education and induction take place can vary enormously and this poses a problem for assessment, in that there are too many variables across contexts for the assessment in question to be truly standardised. Some, but by no means all, of the factors that contribute to this variety of contexts are the values and commitment of the headteacher and senior team; the support given to their teaching staff; the understanding of what the standards mean in practice; the behaviour of their students; the levels of achievement of their students; their parental, community and wider support, and the amount of funding they can draw upon.

In such varied contexts it is useful to have a document that lays out a baseline for allowing trainees to qualify and to consolidate a period of probation. This can be helpful to trainers and useful for achieving consistency, in so far as the document lays out the parameters and gives broad brush strokes in the areas of required workplace competence, knowledge and understanding. However, trainees and new teachers are to some extent participants in a lottery, since gaining QTS and passing induction in one school can be very different from passing in another. An analogy could be made between passing a driving test in a quiet country area or in the middle of an urban area. Since contexts vary, the question should be posed as to what standardisation means. The standard length of a metre of cloth measured against a metre rule is the same wherever in the world cut and whatever fabric it is. Clearly 'standard' in the context of teacher assessment does not mean the same as 'standard' in the context of a metre of cloth. Certainly, moderation of assessments and assessor training is useful and important to create some kind of localised standardisation. Nevertheless, the variation in contexts poses the question as to whether teacher assessment is standardised assessment of the kind required to generate reliable information on teacher 'performance', which is a principle underlying the assessment policy.

There are also many aspects to variability in school contexts. In a recipe, for example, the term 'Gas Mark 6' is read as a standard measurement of the heat of the oven. Variations in performance across individual mechanisms such as ovens do vary and are context specific to a certain extent. Cooks who know their own oven's variations are able to transfer instructions to adjust for their own conditions. There are few factors which create the variability. Once these are understood, adjustments can be made, such as a lower temperature setting for an oven which constantly 'over-heats'. The term 'the classroom' cannot have such a predictable transference process because there are too many variables. Therefore the standards relating to managing pupil learning cannot be applied in the same way in all contexts, since it is not always up to the individual teacher how well she is able to manage her pupils and the resources at her disposal.

A case study of a teacher trainee illustrates this variability. She was assessed against the QTS standards on two occasions, in two different schools, not far from each other geographically. She reported on the different ethos in each school, and on how this had a direct effect on her 'performance' in the classroom. The pupil intake was from the same catchment area and from a similar range of educational, ethnic and social/economic backgrounds. Her two schools had 'a very different approach to educational philosophy and this was strongly reflected in their ethos' (Institute of Education, 2004a). The first was a mixed, independent school of around 400 pupils, in small classes (12–15 pupils), in which she found classroom management difficult. She reported that each teacher was expected to form 'informal friendly personal relationships with the pupils' out of which it was assumed that:

> learning takes place without the need for precise rules framing expectations of behaviour and discipline. The idea is that there is no need for rules and that the pupils will automatically behave in an appropriate way if they are engaged in a lesson which they feel is somehow special to them.
>
> (ibid.)

She found that a lack of consistency from class to class was exploited by the pupils 'as every department, and within these, every individual teacher, has a different view of what is a suitable behaviour within these informal parameters'.

Her second school, a girls' grammar school, of around 1,000 pupils had class sizes of between 25 and 32 and clearly defined rules of behaviour, which the trainee teacher reported was applied to the pupils across all the classes consistently. She stated that the rules had been 'defined by the Head, who has a very involved approach to management and shows great professionalism at all times in ensuring that the team as a whole consistently apply the rules'. As a result the larger classes were easier to manage and she believed that more work was done, because of:

> clarity and consistency of expectations. I believe that the head acts as a leader who knows that there is a correct way to behave and that this frees the teachers and the classroom of permanent conflicts and lets them concentrate on learning.
>
> (ibid.)

She concluded that

> the expectation of behaviour from the pupil is what affects class-room management the most. A teacher cannot as an individual expect more than the school ethos allows that teacher to expect. Consequently, if expectations are low or unclear classroom management becomes a constant negotiation. Negotiations are emotionally draining and they are time-consuming: this is not suited to teaching pupils.
>
> (ibid.)

She went on to reflect on the school as a community and the effect this had on her own performance as a teacher, including her ability to manage the classroom (and hence meet the standards relating to this area of her work as a trainee[8].

> The second school has a view of the school as an entity with one head and one body, we are all one community: the need of the community is greater than the needs of individuals. The needs of individuals can only be addressed if the community as a whole is working towards a shared goal. All the teachers at all times ensure that the pupils (the ones they teach and every other one in the school) follow the rules; we have a responsibility to the school. There is a great sense of belonging and working together. Expectations of the pupils are very high.
>
> (ibid.)

The conditions within which teachers work greatly affect their teaching. The case study trainee illustrates this in her experience of trying to manage a classroom in the two different schools:

> The first school had the view that the school is made of a multitude of separate entities, which need to be approached differently at all times. This revealed itself to be highly impractical and deeply unfair as the loudest or more articulate ones got away with despicable behaviour. The notion of individuality was the predominant one and the school did not seem to work towards a shared goal.
>
> (ibid.)

She concluded that she found it paradoxical that

> through being one entity we actually care more about individuals as we can find the time for them. We are not diluting our efforts repeating and negotiating rules at every lesson. A "laissez faire" attitude is most tiring and it leads to all kind of disruptive behaviour, the most common being to question the relevance of the teaching . . .
>
> (ibid.)

Significantly, those who assess teachers for the award of QTS do take variability of context into account. Otherwise the failure rates from schools in 'problematic' areas, would be significantly higher than those in relatively 'easy' schools, which is not the case. (Ash et al., 2004)[9].

New Standards in 2007

A revised framework of professional standards for teachers replaced the 2002 QTS standards from September 2007. The policy decisions behind the revision were largely driven by the need to update the standards to come into line with new legislation and policy around children, a remodelled teaching work force and the economic and skills demands of globalisation. The introduction to the framework makes clear that these motors have substantially driven the revisions:

All the standards are underpinned by the five key outcomes for children and young people identified in Every Child Matters and the six areas of the Common core of skills and knowledge for the children's workforce. The work of practising teachers should be informed by an awareness, appropriate to their level of experience and responsibility, of legislation concerning the development and well-being of children and young people expressed in the Children Act 2004, the Disability Discrimination Acts 1995 and 2005 and relevant associated guidance, the special educational needs provisions in the Education Act 1996 and the associated Special Educational Needs: Code of Practice (DfES 2001), the Race Relations Act 1976 as amended by the Race Relations (Amendment) Act 2000, and the guidance Safeguarding children in education.

(DfES, 2004a; TDA, 2007, p. 13)

It is to be expected that revisions need to account for relevant legislation, which has come into force since the publication of previous standards, but how far this objective dominates the standards needs consideration. The current version has eliminated many of the problems in the use of the former standards in assessing trainees, by its streamlining into three categories instead of four and its reduction of the number of standards from 42 to 33. The technical changes in organisation under new headings and the rationalisation and tighter definition in wording in the 2007 QTS standards help to meet the deficit on clarity in the 2002 QTS standards. In general, many of the ambiguities in the 2002 QTS standards have been ironed out: the standards are less ambitious in their attempt to create a framework of inter-connections, which might in some way be capable of reflecting the complexities in teaching. There is more clarity and precision about what each standard purports to assess. While easier to understand, the 2007 QTS standards have abandoned the attempt to conceptualise teaching as a fundamentally complex endeavour. While these technical changes have helped to meet the deficit on clarity in the 2002 QTS standards, the new policy initiatives have introduced new ambiguities, most notably around the notion of personalised learning.

'Personalised learning' (PL) is a major theme in education policy documents, evidenced in the white paper on education, Higher Standards, Better Schools for All (DfES, 2005b) and the wide agenda for change in children's services in Every Child Matters (DfES, 2004a, 2004b). The principle of personalised learning was launched by the Prime Minister in his speech to the Labour Party Conference on 30 September 2003 and expanded by David Miliband, the Minister of State, in his speech to the National College for School Leadership in October 2003. The political and policy context of the promotion of personalised learning has emerged from social and economic needs and technological possibilities.

(DfES, 2004b, 2006; Paludan, 2006)

The notion has been guardedly embraced by some in education (Pollard & James, 2004; NCSL, 2006). A variety of concerns have been raised about the concept, including difficulties of interpretation; scepticism about its purpose and function and its place in an economic rather than an educational agenda; its seeming challenge to the teaching of specific content in subject areas; underlying moral assumptions, and anxiety about the rise of individualism over the social (for example see Lambert, 2005, ATL, 2006, Smith, 2006). Even Paludan (2006) from the perspective of the Organisation for Economic Cooperation and Development (OECD), while promoting personalised learning for necessary future skills development and the 'life-long learning project' also confesses that:

A more personalised education is not without its downsides. It becomes more difficult to estimate what the individual student gains from his studies. At the same time concerns that a more discontinuous education will undermine society's cohesiveness may grow. A personalisation that concentrates on easing the individual student's way through the system will therefore be much less controversial than one that also personalises the content of the education.

(Paludan, 2006)

It seems clear that the requirement to personalise learning in the 2007 standards relates to the target setting agenda, in terms of the achievement of key skills, key stage attainment targets, and target level examination results. The introduction to the 2007 standards clearly states that personalisation is not about differentiation, and meeting the individual needs of the child if these needs are not first defined in terms of the national standards and skills agenda:

> The term 'personalised learning' means maintaining a focus on individual progress, in order to maximise all learners' capacity to learn, achieve and participate. This means supporting and challenging each learner to achieve national standards and gain the skills they need to thrive and succeed throughout their lives. 'Personalising learning' is not about individual lesson plans or individualisation (where learners are taught separately or largely through a one-to-one approach).
>
> (TDA, 2007)

Finally, in reflecting on the 2007 QTS standards it is worth examining how far they are able to account for the normative nature of teaching. The 2002 QTS standards were prefaced with a stated requirement that 'those awarded qualified teacher status must understand and uphold the professional code of the General Teaching Council for England ...' The 2007 standards has replaced the 2002 standards category of 'Professional Values and Practice' with 'Professional Attributes'. Some possible definitions of an attribute, depending on context might be a characteristic, a trait, a distinction or a feature, such as the possession of a gregarious personality. One could have a gregarious personality, show an attribute for getting on well with people, and also hold professionally unacceptable values. People fitting this professional profile are not unknown in other spheres, such as politics and business.

It is fair to say that the first two standards of the 2007 list refer to some of the values inherent in teaching and therefore to a limited extent attempt to account for the evaluative dimension in demanding 'fair, respectful, trusting, supportive and constructive relationships' with young people (TDA, 2007, Q1) and the need to 'demonstrate the positive values, attitudes and behaviour' expected from children and young people (ibid., Q2). Nevertheless, although the 2007 QTS standards gain in clarity and applicability over the 2002 standards, they suffer from many of the drawbacks of their predecessors. They fail to account adequately for the essential norma-tive dimension and the impact of the uniqueness of each individual teaching situation upon the growing competence of trainee teach-ers. They are a product of political and economic demands on the education system, and while they are a useful gauge of some aspects of teacher competence within the contemporary conditions in which they are evidenced, they are ultimately a technically rational instru-ment, and as such suffer limitations in 'capturing' and accounting for teaching and for learning in a full and adequate way.

A Portrait of a Teacher?

The 2007 QTS standards define some of the qualities required of a teacher in the current context: Indeed, school has an 'organic con-nection ... on the social side, with the life without' (Dewey, 1980, p. 48). Teachers must have a number of important 'professional attributes' (Q1–9) as cited in the previous section. A teacher's ability to learn and develop is foregrounded and made to account for suc-cessful teaching by being linked to 'professional needs'. New teachers need to:

> Q7 (a) reflect on and improve their practice, and take responsibility for identifying and meeting their developing professional needs.

In relation to being able to learn from experience, teachers must have a 'drive' to want to reflect, look back, make sense of it all and to do the best for their pupils. The standards are strong in defin-ing where areas of knowledge and understanding relate mainly to subject specialist expertise; child development; aspects of learning theory related to pupils' individual learning needs; health and safety and other legislative frameworks, and the curriculum and the con-texts within which the curriculum is situated and taught. A teacher gaining QTS needs to understand, for example, school and national policies and strategies, as well as the individual school organisational framework and the values promulgated. Some of these contextual fea-tures are easy to understand, providing the appropriate information is given to the trainee, but some rely on 'savvy', on the teacher being alert to her role in an organisation, to organisational politics. We might even talk about the skill of being both alert and comfortable in the social role of a teacher (Hewitt, 1976). These observations suggest that the skills, knowledge and understanding required of a teacher might be conceptualised on a different model from that of the standards, starting with the practitioner herself, the person embedded in the practice, rather than de-contextualised descriptors. Does the current conceptualisation and the current ITET context restrict the growth of teacher knowledge and understanding, by dissociating the agent who develops professional knowledge and understanding from the source of this knowledge and understanding in experience?

Constraints, Standards and National Strategies

It might be also be argued that an ITET curriculum articulated in standards discourse limits trainees' autonomy to experiment with teaching methods and styles. Also, the current context for trainees is one in which there are significant pressures to achieve particular types of outcomes, within particular demands of time and resources, while being assessed and inspected on these outcome criteria. As a result, there is limited time and some discouragement for new teachers to experiment with methods or ideas in teaching. In a sense, a definition of what constitutes 'good teaching' begins to emerge, which is influenced by the demands made on the time and resources of the school, by national statutes, strategies and 'high-stakes' Ofsted assessment. Even though in theory teachers in English schools can develop their own methodology, teachers must fulfil statutory demands and teach the National Curriculum; respond to examination pressure and teach the examination syllabuses; fulfil school and LEA demands to follow the various national strategies, such as the various primary strategies, or the Key Stage 3 Strategy (DfES, 2001). These strategies reflect particular methodologies and exclude a diversity of approach.

An illustration is one of the key documents, the Framework of Objectives for Teaching Modern Foreign Languages (MFL), which is part of the Key Stage 3 National Strategy (DfES, 2003). The framework is not a statutory document but heavily promoted as a successful method of raising pupils' achievement in MFL. The framework is aimed at pupils in the first 3 years of secondary schooling and designed to ensure progression in MFL learning across these 3 years. Like the QTS standards the framework is a detailed document: it contains 103 objectives organised under five categories, called 'strands'. The categories chosen are: words; sentences; texts – reading and writing; listening and speaking; cultural knowledge and contact. Examining the framework in detail does not reveal any underlying theory about language acquisition, and no rationale for why or how the objectives will help pupils to become 'language learners'. Formulating teaching as a progression from 'word', to 'sentence' to 'text' level implies a specific view of language acquisition not backed up by research cited in the framework itself (Mitchell, 2003, p. 21; Mitchell & Myles, 1998). The progression route through words to sentences and texts is schematically simplistic. This is to some extent acknowledged by the statement that some of the objectives 'may need revisiting over time', which is similar to the attempt in the 2002 QTS standards to create an inter-relational framework. It is also not at all clear how this cyclical curriculum model matches with the notion of progression expressed through the 'ladder' levels of the Attainment Targets of the National Curriculum. These two notions of progression seem at odds with each other, so that despite providing tables which aim to relate each of the objectives, under each of the strands, to the correspondingly numbered objective in each of the 3 years of study, it is difficult to begin to analyse how successfully the framework tackles learner progression, which is its main aim. More seriously, it is also difficult to understand the structure of the framework itself.

The lack of a research base to justify the framework is hardly surprising, since applied linguistics cannot provide an undisputed evidence base to recommend the most appropriate model of language which should underpin a MFL pedagogic grammar; the detailed selection and sequencing of grammar items to be taught; the usefulness of metalinguistic understanding for MFL learning; the most useful forms of corrective feedback (Mitchell, 2000, p. 297). Rather than acknowledging the difficulties in reaching an overarching explanation of the right way to teach 'grammar', the framework suggests a taxonomy and a technical mode of delivery, with the teacher as a delivery technician. Yet what texts will the teacher choose to illustrate the various framework objectives? What will govern her choice? On what basis will she choose how to 'deliver' the objective to her particular class, in a particular way? Being a modern foreign languages teacher is not merely a matter of competency, of having competent command of a foreign language and of following a strategy, or a plan to 'deliver' it to others.

The example is indicative of the way in which current educational policy uses strategies and frameworks to create an apparent taxonomy of skills, as though the job of being a teacher, in this case a teacher of a foreign language, were reducible to merely having a great deal of technical knowledge, such as knowing the grammar; knowing what order in which to teach the various 'bits' of grammar by consulting a pre-designed framework. In practice, teachers need to adapt what they teach to their own individual circumstances, which is a matter of judgement. There is a much wider base of propositional knowledge required, about language learning theories and factors that affect learning for example. In the end, however, the 'right' way to teach can only be judged in the particular circumstances. The framework may be useful to some teachers in some circumstances. It is set out, however, as a definitive example of 'good practice', which carries weight in the climate of Ofsted inspections.

In July 2007 the Qualifications and Curriculum Authority (QCA) issued a new secondary curriculum. One of its aims was to introduce more flexibility into the curriculum, to overcome criticisms regarding time constraints:

> The new programmes of study have been designed to give teachers a less prescriptive, more flexible framework for teaching, creating more scope to tailor the curriculum to meet the needs of each individual student. The change of focus within the curriculum will provide a foundation for education post-14, and includes specific transitional material to ensure smooth progress to key stage 4 and beyond.
>
> (QCA, 2007)

How far the curriculum change will enable more place for individual curriculum initiatives and how much time can be spared from the revised programmes of study at secondary level, is to be discovered.

Conclusion

The QTS and Induction Standards represent an initial and early years teacher training curriculum; a developmental programme and a 'wish-list', the statement of what a teacher should be, do and think. This is a far cry from the 'can do' competence statements of the vocational competency movement. In moving away from simple competence statements into standards there is an acknowledgement that teaching is not reducible to a set of performance indicators. However, the standards do attempt to provide a guideline of minimum requirements in relation to specific skills and to prescribed propositional knowledge, about the subjects taught, the national curriculum, policies and legal requirements.

The value of the standards lies in their being a point of reference for all involved in ITET but the contexts within which teachers work are varied. Even if contexts could somehow be standardised and reproduced the nature of practice is such that no standardised assessment could account for its complexity. Having a list of descriptive statements as a basis for discussion is useful for trainers and trainees alike and helps to develop consistency across different contexts. However, the list cannot be taken at face value and no mere list could ever add up to a description of what a good teacher does, or what good teaching is all about. Ultimately, the endeavour to grasp teaching within their net fails to account for the normative nature of teaching and the individual nature of teaching. Moreover the sheer weight of technical content in the National Curriculum and national strategies militates against explorations of alternative views about teaching. So the standards limit, narrow and confine the conception of what a good or even competent teacher might be, do, know and understand.

Notes

1. This was the Florida State New Teachers' Assessment Instrument, which has since been updated and simplified. Reference to the updated version is made in the References section of this book.

2. Such as Roehampton Institute with Surrey County Council (1993) and The Open University (1994).
3. See http://www.management-standards.org/.
4. Such as Standard 2.1.d., on progression pathways and curricular requirements. Standard 1.8 on knowledge of the statutory frameworks was likewise context specific, as were four relating to the National Curriculum (2.1; 2.2; 2.3; 3.2.3).
5. These were 1.4 ('parents and carers'); 1.5 ('the corporate life of schools'); 1.6 (support staff and other professionals'); 3.3.13 ('work collaboratively with ... other colleagues') and 1.2 ('treat pupils with respect and consideration'); 3.1.5 ('out of school activities'); 3.3.1 ('high expectations ... build successful relationships); 3.3.14 ('equal opportunities issues ...').
6. See also DfEE and QCA (1999b).
7. See Standards 1.1; 1.2; 1.3; 2.4; 2.6; 3.1.1; 3.1.2; 3.2.1; 3.2.2; 3.2.3; 3.2.4; 3.3.1.
8. See also MacGilchrist et al., 1997.
9. Variability of context has been pointed out in various pieces of research (DfES, 1992; Earley, 1993; Earley & Kinder, 1994).

Chapter 3

The Reflective Practitioner

Chapter 2 established the limitations of the QTS standards to comprehensively describe the nature of good teaching. Nevertheless, it ought to be possible to define some *prima facie* desirable features of good teaching without a concomitant claim to complete comprehensiveness. The concept of 'the reflective practitioner' is frequently used to counter inadequacies in competencies and standards-based assessment. It is underpinned by a notion of teaching as a 'practice' and the good teacher is conceptualised as exemplifying the skills and values of the practice (MacIntyre & Dunne, 2002; Dunne, 2003; Noddings, 2003). The concept of the reflective practitioner relies to a large extent on the importance of personal experience as a basis for the development and exercise of expertise. The notion of reflective practice is well established (Schön, 1983, 1987; Eraut, 1994), and embedded in many courses of initial teacher education (Benton, 1990; Whitty et al., 1992; Garrison, 1997). Reflection is widely vaunted in fields as diverse as nursing (Johns, 2004), government (Schall, 1997), animation (Bruns, 2005), management and training (Swenson, 1999), conservation and ecology (Davis-Case, 2001), computer science (Hazzan, 2002) and sports coaching (McShane, 1999). Dewey and to some extent Piaget and Vygotsky, who all developed a theory relating the primacy of experience to learning, might be said to underpin Schön's influential conceptualisation of the nature of professional expertise, although it is Dewey's *Logic the Theory of Inquiry* that Schön acknowledges as his primary influence (Schön, 1992).

Schön's Formulation of Reflection

Schön (1983, 1987) views the reflective practitioner as an expert performer, capable of skilful action, which 'reveals a knowing more than we can say' (Schön, 1983, p. 51), which (citing Polanyi) is the professional's 'tacit knowledge' (ibid.). He states that experienced practitioners acting in their everyday practice demonstrate what he calls 'knowing-in-action' (Schön, 1987), which is the sort of knowledge that highly skilled practitioners come to depend on to perform their work apparently spontaneously. Examples of highly skilled practices exist in many areas, such as sport, medicine, music, art and teaching. In his development of the concept of reflective practice Schön attempts to create an epistemology of practice (Gilroy, 1993; Eraut, 1995, p. 12). He criticises the kind of reductionist view of practical knowledge and understanding which Chapter 2 has established characterises the competency and standards based view of ITET assessment. Schön calls this view 'technical rationality' and concludes that 'we need to think ... about knowledge ... in a different way' (Schön, 1971, p. 49). Schön stated in an article written some years after his influential book, *The Reflective Practitioner* (1983) that he had taken Dewey's theory of inquiry and developed it to cover the kind of situations in which expert practitioners practise their 'craft' and explicated and expanded it with practice-based case studies. Schön claims that Dewey's theory of inquiry only fits problematic situations, which limits its use as an explanatory tool in ordinary, expert practice where no problematic situation is present (Schön, 1992, pp. 121–23).

Schön also argues that 'knowing-in-action' is not limited to expert practice but is also manifest in everyday situations, such as in our habitual performance of everyday routines, for example, when we are able to act spontaneously, without apparently thinking, and 'the situation of action is not problematic; the smooth flow of action is not interrupted by surprise' (Schön, 1992, p. 124). Schön says that in such cases 'knowing-in-action' is revealed by action and it is tacit, in that it cannot be described (Schön, 1983, pp. 49–50, 53–54). It is 'the knowing we manifest in the doing' (Schön, 1987, p. 230). He states that 'knowing-in-action' might commonly be called 'intuition' or 'instinct' and is evidenced for example in the successful performance of physical skills such as crawling, walking, juggling, or when engaging in ordinary social interactions and conversations (Schön, 1992, p. 124). 'Knowing-in-action' for Schön is the first and simplest component of reflective practice. Two more complex constituents of reflective practice are 'reflection-in-action' and 'reflection-on-action' (Schön, 1983 p. 61).

Schön defines 'reflection-in-action' as reflecting on practice, whilst 'in the midst of it' (Schön, 1983, p. 61). 'Reflection-in-action' occurs during the activity, without interrupting it, as the practitioner, the person 'practising', responds to the moment, adjusting and reshaping behaviour, performance and action, while it is underway. There is a constant adjustment to what is happening, a constant interaction between the acting, practising person and the environment, such as in Schön's example of a jazz musician improvising. 'Reflection-in-action' takes place in the moment and is 'bounded by the "action-present"' (Schön, 1983, p. 62). It occurs when 'practitioners surface and criticise ... tacit understandings ... and can make new sense of the situations of uncertainty or uniqueness' (Schön, 1983, p. 61).

Schön believes that 'reflection-in-action' is a crucial component in what he terms the 'artistry' of competent practitioners (Schön, 1992, p. 125) and that someone engaged in 'reflection-in-action' is able to become 'a researcher in the practice context' (Schön, 1983, p. 68) and, through this process, break free of 'the dichotomies of Technical Rationality' (ibid. p. 69). Gilroy has claimed a logical impossibility of reflection-in-action in Schön's formulation, due to an 'abyss of an infinite regress' (Gilroy, 1993, p. 138) in that

> the 'knowledge' produced by reflection can only be recognised by further reflection, which in turn requires reflection to recognise it as knowledge, and so on.
>
> (ibid.)

It seems that Gilroy takes 'reflection-in action' too literally, as though the term meant the same thing as 'thinking', whereas the concept seems more akin to a particular kind of thoughtful, acting, which van Manen has seen as one way of describing what goes on in the act of 'tactful' teaching, which 'locates practical knowledge not primarily in the intellect or the head but rather in the existential situation in which the person finds himself or herself'.

(van Manen, 1995, pp. 45–46)

'Reflection-in-action' does not mean going through some staged process of thinking through logical steps in an argument. Schön's use of the term 'reflection' in relation to acting in the moment might be more accurately seen in its relation to 'flexible', rather than in relation to 'thinking'. Practitioners need to be flexible in order to practice competently, in response to the contingencies of the moment. However, there are two principle reasons why the concept of 'reflection-in-action' is not particularly useful in ITET. First, teachers do not work in isolation from others and when learning to become a competent practitioner teachers engage with others and learn the 'craft knowledge' of the practice in collaboration with other people. Winch's comment on workplace learning in general is applicable to ITET, in that the concept of 'reflection-in-action' does not take account of 'the social contexts in which learning very often takes place' (Winch, 2000, p. 106). Although many of Schön's examples relate to coaching and mentoring in the workplace, the concept of 'reflection-in-action' tends to rely on an individual practitioner's going through a particular kind of acting, grounded by her own 'tacit' or 'intuitive' knowledge, which suggests that when a practitioner 'reflects-in-action' she is on her own. Taylor and White (2000) in relation to nursing noted a 'solipsistic' tendency, which seemed to privilege the practitioner's perspective above that of others involved in the practice. This could be as undesirable as an uncritical privileging of technical rationality in the approach to practice.

Secondly, it is in the nature of the teaching situation that one responds to the contingencies of the moment. There may be a wealth of propositional knowledge that underpins what is done and in this sense it could be possible to say (as Schön does) that the teacher has some kind of 'theory-in-action', or 'theories-in-action', but the terms 'reflection' and 'theory' when coupled with the phrase 'in-action' are misleading, and ultimately not useful to the ITET discussion. As van Manen has stated:

one should even say that, ironically, in the active or dynamic situation of teaching one cannot help but be 'unreflective' in the curious sense that the classroom teacher must constantly act on the spot and cannot step back and postpone acting in order to first reflect on the various alternatives to this action and consequences of the various alternatives.

(van Manen, 1995, p. 35)

For these reasons the term 'reflection-in-action' is not considered in the following discussion about reflective practice and its relation to ITET. However, the question about the nature of the knowledge and understanding, which is manifest in the practice of teaching remains open. Schön's adaptation of Dewey in the notion of 'reflection-in-action' can now be abandoned and we can return to some aspects of Dewey's *own* analysis of the nature of practical knowledge in Chapter 4. There still remains Schön's illuminating idea that 'reflection-on-action' is necessary for the development of the competent practitioner.

The Wider Uses of the Term 'Reflection'

For Schön, 'reflection-on-action' happens either following or by interrupting an activity, so involves thinking about it after it has occurred, not in the full flow of activity. 'Reflection' in its more generalised use in relation to ITET tends to involve evaluation of teaching or other activities that have already taken place, and thinking about teaching or teaching situations which are yet to happen, in the light of those which have already taken place, using various modes and means. So it might be possible to talk of 'reflection-on-future-action'. Significantly these reflections may include how the practitioner feels about the matter in hand, and meta-analysis of these feelings. The practitioner, in reflecting on, thinking about how she felt, why she chose to do what she did in particular circumstances, engages with a particular facet of her experienced practice rationally, and in a personalised way which is rooted in her own experience and as such engages with the kind of person she is, her values and her personal character.

General Definition

There is no generally agreed definition of the term 'reflection' in the context of ITET: accounts of what 'reflective teaching' is and how to do it are numerous and varied and the term is used inconsistently (Fenstermacher, 1988; Eraut, 1994; Zeichner, 1994; Bengtsson, 1995; McLaughlin, 1999; Newman, 1999). 'Reflection' has not been adequately defined (van Manen, 1995), and needs to be developed and situated 'within a richer account of the nature and requirements of teaching and teacher training' (McLaughlin, 1999, p. 9). Lack of rigour in definition devalues reflective practice as a defensible ITET model. To some extent Rogers is right in asserting that

> over the past 15 years, reflection has suffered from a loss of meaning. In becoming everything to everybody, it has lost its ability to be seen because no one knows what to look for.
>
> (Rogers, 2002, p. 842)

How is it possible to know if a particular instance of reflection leads to valuable insights or valid conclusions, if we have an imprecise notion of the desired aims, in terms of the scope and range of any specific instance? One can reflect on specific, routine happenings at one level, and on general principles at the other, and differing levels of reflection invite different forms of reflection (McLaughlin, 1999). When we have an adequate definition we may be able to distinguish good reflection from bad. 'Bad' reflection, among other things, might not get at the nub of the practice under scrutiny, or might start from wrong assumptions, or jump to non-valid conclusions.

Bad reflection may be 'ritualistic' reflection (Moore, 2004), reinforce current thinking and perceptions and become

> a shelter within which to hide from more challenging explanations of circumstances and events.
>
> (Moore & Ash, 2002)

An example might be given of the practice of some school-based mentors who appear to follow reflective processes with their trainees in weekly meetings, which are in fact ritualistic. These mentors collaboratively identify 'targets' for their trainees' development; hold weekly discussion meetings, and seem to be engaged in a reflective, developmental process. However, many such meetings are viewed as occasions to tick off various QTS standards, without deep engagement with the actual practice of the trainee.

The trainee too may not be genuinely engaged in a critical, reflective process. An example is a sympathetic and competent school mentor and a ritualistically engaged trainee. The mentor went through a process of explanation, modelling, narrating how the trainee's pupils needed signposts, bridges and 'scaffolding' for what was taught. Weekly mentoring meetings were held; lessons were analysed, and suggestions for future lessons were made. The trainee took part in this reflective process and said that she would implement the suggestions made. However, the suggestions were poorly understood and implemented and the trainee failed to engage the pupils. The mentor took the trainee through a reflective process but could not get the trainee to understand how to create lessons in which the children were able to engage with the learning tasks. The trainee attempted to put the advice into place but was unable to understand the pupils' viewpoint. The pupils become restless through lack of engagement with the lesson and presented the teacher with challenging behaviour. The trainee acknowledged that the lessons were not successful but blamed the pupils, making comments such as 'what can you expect with children like these', or 'they're thick aren't they?' Despite repeated attempts on the mentor's part to enlighten the trainee, she persisted in her belief that the pupils' lack of intelligence determined their failure to follow her lessons.

A further difficulty even where ITET programmes conceive reflection in a robust manner may be the trainee's 'pseudo-reflection' (Moore & Ash, 2002), going through the motions with no real engagement and hence no gains in understanding. For example a trainee teacher I worked with early on in his first teaching practice had trouble with a badly behaving pupil. When asked for more details about that pupil, the teacher had only a sketchy understanding of that pupil's prior attainment in relation to the rest of the class. The information was available: pupils' reading ages particularly were issued to all teachers for that particular class. In fact, the pupil had a reading age of 9 in a class of 14-year-olds, but the teacher did not know this. The teacher knew a great deal about Freudian analysis, which he had undertaken for a few years. When we began to talk about the difficulties he was experiencing with this particular pupil's behaviour he reflected on the various occasions of bad behaviour he had experienced, but he did not make the connection between the pupil's behaviour and the tasks set, specifically the reading demands involved. He explained the pupil's behaviour in psychological terms, with no understanding of possible learning difficulties relating to the pupil's inability to read the material presented in the lesson. The teacher told me that the pupil had a bad relationship with her mother, and that she was playing out a typical case of transference, in that she had transferred onto him, the teacher, features of this bad relationship. The teacher had constructed an explanation in psychological terms to explain his pupil's behaviour. This wrong diagnosis of the pupil's problematic behaviour led the teacher to respond inappropriately to the pupil's behaviour, which in fact exacerbated the situation.

I asked the trainee teacher to find out more about the pupils' prior achievements and we subsequently discussed the importance of applying this data to the planning of lesson objectives and tasks. The teacher began to take the individual pupil's specific learning needs into account and then began to make progress in 'managing' the difficult pupil's behaviour. The reflection process was initially ineffectual and led to false conclusions, suggesting that all the significant factors within a situation need to be taken into consideration. The teacher did not reflect on all the relevant data, and went off on his own on a false trail, but was unaware that this was the case. This indicates first how helpful it is to work with another more experienced colleague when reflecting on practice and secondly, that it is also helpful to consider a number of different hypotheses, as various, significant factors may inter-relate in a number of different ways. Chapter 6 discusses how important a mentor becomes in the process of reaching illuminating and 'valid' understandings through the process of reflection.

Without a clear definition of what is meant by reflection it is difficult to distinguish when there has been 'constructive' reflection, which actively seeks to problematise situations and to challenge existing views, perspectives and beliefs, promoting or leading to development or change in terms of work-related understandings and/or outlooks.

(Moore & Ash, 2002)

The three examples cited above show that there are a variety of ways in which reflection on practice may not be productive. It cannot therefore be a panacea for ITET practice.

The lack of a clear and agreed definition of reflective practice has three main drawbacks. First, it is difficult to talk about: sharing of good practice cannot occur with any degree of security where definitions are fuzzy. Secondly, with a slippery and contestable notion of what reflective practice is it is difficult to research the effects of reflective teacher education and professional development on teachers' practice and students' learning. Thirdly, in the wake of the first two disadvantages, it is also difficult to develop reflective practice: it is difficult to find ways to develop 'well-grounded reflection', reflection that develops new understandings, capable of leading to more competent practice, such as is defined by the success of the application of the new understandings, in terms of the practitioner's ability to grow more expert and confident in the practice.

Is it necessary for teachers to be reflective, in the sense of 'able to reflect in a well-grounded way'? This question revolves around the nature of teaching as an enterprise, in which teachers and pupils are engaged, within classrooms, in nested contexts of school, local authority and national and policy contexts. Much empirical research on pupil achievement defines various approaches to teaching in relation to various successes in learning (Novak & Gowin, 1984; Watkins, 2000, 2001; Watkins & Carnell, 2002). Evidently teaching is linked to learning, as we would not say that someone has taught something if no one had learnt it, whereas we could say someone had cooked even if the food was burnt or no one had eaten it. In this sense 'teaching' is an 'achievement word' rather than a 'process word' or a 'task word' (Ryle, 1963, pp. 143–47)[1]. The concept of teaching requires someone who teaches and someone who learns. We do not need to look to the context of formal education to know that there is a broad, universally recognisable notion of teaching and learning exemplified by animals teaching their young, including the human animal. We can conclude from this that the content of what is taught is culturally specific but the notion of teaching and learning is not. Teaching is one of those concepts which Wilson (2003) has said refer to 'enterprises which given the human condition, seem inalienable or inevitable' (p. 106).

One can also learn without being taught, as when we have a tooth abscess we learn not to drink hot or cold liquids, because they cause pain. In this case we may learn quickly an appropriate response. One can learn to do something by trial and error, such as how to programme a video, or unfreeze a non-responsive computer. This experimental method of learning takes time, as it is extremely rare to hit on the correct solution immediately, and even when happily the correct solution occurs it is sometimes difficult to retrace exactly how it came about. One can also use a manual to learn how to do these kinds of tasks, which may accelerate the learning, depending on the manual's intelligibility and the user's skills.

It seems reasonable that the process of learning how to programme the video or unfreeze the computer may be accelerated if someone who already knows how to do these tasks shows us how to do them. Teachers act in some sense as an intermediary between the learner and what is to be learnt in a 'zone of proximal development' (Vygotsky, 1978), so teaching is a 'triadic relationship between a person, another person and something taught' (Martin, 1969, p. 3). It is useful to define teaching more specifically. A primary sense of 'teaching' is tied up with the teaching-learning relationship, in which

the notion of learning which is not the learning of some particular X is as vague as the notion of going somewhere but nowhere in particular.

(Hirst, 1974, p. 109)

There can be immediate and remote ends in teaching. An immediate end might be to get the other person to know or to understand, or to be able to do something she could not do before. A remote end might be to enable someone to gain a qualification and hence get into university. The immediate ends must be the same for the teacher and the learner for any specific objective of learning to take place. If a teacher taught a lesson involving analysing a sonnet and the pupil chose to spend the lesson listening to her Walkman, it is unlikely that the pupil did learn to analyse the sonnet, but she may have been learning something else at the time. The remote ends do not have to be the same for learning to take place. I may teach a course in French with an aim of getting all my students to pass an examination at the end of the course. A student may not be interested in taking the examination but may wish to learn French in order to live in France. Differences in the remote ends do not effect possible agreement in immediate ends. Teachers may work at getting their students to share immediate ends, as Smith says:

> We none of us like to think we are manipulative, but perhaps all teaching contains elements of manipulation or even arts of seduction – trying to put students at their ease, to get through to them on a personal level and so on.

> (Smith, 2003, p. 489)

The indoctrination sense in which teachers may get someone to parrot lessons is not discussed here. This is a use of the term 'teaching' in which what is taught may be true or false, rational or irrational, probable or improbable, since it is not subject to any of the modes of criticism or constraint that apply to learning as defined above, in the sense of the learner coming to understand and be able to use knowledge. Parroting here can be used to manipulate rather than teach people, what Martin has called 'a kind of teaching-learning nihilism' (Martin, 1969, p. 63).

Rather than talk of teaching in general, which could include a considerable number of activities relating to the role of the teacher. Hirst's term 'a teaching activity' is useful to get at the primary meaning of 'teaching' in relation to learning, involving teachers and learners. A 'teaching activity' is:

> the activity of person A (the teacher), the intention of which is to bring about an activity (learning) by a person (B) (the pupil), the intention of which is to achieve some end-state (e.g., knowing, appreciating) whose object is X (e.g., belief, attitude skill).

> (Hirst, 1974, p. 109)

The teacher has to intend to teach something particular, because:

> it is only in a context where both what is to be learnt and who is learning it are clear, that we can begin to be clear about teaching B, X.
>
> (ibid.)

Hirst analyses the necessary features of a publicly observable kind, which all teaching activities must necessarily possess, and finds that they must fulfil two conditions. To meet the first condition, the specific activity must be indicative of X. By this he means must either implicitly or explicitly express or embody the X to be learnt, so that this X is clearly indicated to the pupil as what she is to learn:

> In this way the teacher makes plain in his activity what he intends to be learnt ... it must be available in some sense that the pupil's learning activity can be directed to this as its object'.
>
> (ibid., pp. 110–11)

To meet the second condition a specific teaching activity must necessarily be concerned with the teaching of X to a particular pupil B. So it must be:

> indicatively expressed so that it is possible for this particular pupil B to learn X ... A specific teaching activity must necessarily indicatively express the X to be learnt by B and be so related to the present state of B that he can learn X.
>
> (ibid., pp. 110–11)

It is fruitful to successful teaching to see it as essentially a triadic relationship. Viewing teaching in this way also constitutes good pedagogical practice, according to much research on learning (Donovan et al., 2000; Bransford et al., 2000; Watkins, 2001). In order to fulfil both of Hirst's conditions teachers need to think through a number of questions about how they will engage in any specific 'teaching activity'. Take the following example of a teacher who is planning to teach a Spanish lesson in an English secondary school following the national curriculum for languages in England. The teacher goes through certain steps to ensure that the two conditions are met. First she works out X, where X means the end state for the pupils (e.g., belief, attitude, skill). This end will determine what she will teach and what she wants the pupils to learn. In this particular case she wants the pupils to be able to articulate in Spanish a specific content and she formulates both her own teaching objective and the pupils' outcomes as specifically and precisely as possible. At this point she has decided that the pupils will learn to describe the things in their bedroom. They will revise the structure 'There is or there are' in Spanish and they will practice two specific structures with various items of vocabulary. At the end of the lesson they will be able to speak about their bedrooms and write a paragraph to a penfriend describing it. Before she formulates X she thinks about a variety of factors, among which are:

1. The pupils' prior knowledge, what happened last lesson and the one before that, and what they have already covered on the scheme of work, or from the textbook or syllabus. She makes a note of the dates of sports day and the oral examination, counts back how many lessons she will have with the class, and decides that she has enough time to use a whole lesson on X.
2. The context for the lesson – It takes place on Friday afternoon after the pupils have come back from games. She notes they will be tired and restless.
3. Pupil interest – How can she contextualise X so that the pupils can engage with the material? She decides to download pictures from a popular television programme of one of the characters' untidy room.
4. Pupil engagement – She looks up her class record in which she has noted information about the individual pupils. She has an individual profile for each pupil, with data about their prior attainment, work habits, and any factors advancing or impeding their learning. She knows how pupils are achieving in relation to others in the group. She has already built up this information from reports from previous teachers and from her own observations, by talking to pupils, seeing how they answer questions in class, the work in their exercise books and the way in which they work together in groups.
5. Working out the activities, tasks, exercises for pupils to do – She thinks through what activities to develop to get the pupils to learn X.

6. Working out how she will know whether the pupils have learnt X and how she will apply this information to further teaching activities – She decides to target several pupils for questions, choosing pupils who represent other pupils with a similar learning profile, so that she can gauge whether a range of different pupils have learnt X. Also she will set an exercise to do in class, take it in for marking and she will record the outcomes and act on the information she receives.

After the lesson is over she evaluates it, by thinking through how it went, in terms of her own teaching and her pupils' learning. She marks the books and realises that several pupils in the class have not understood the use of the verbal structure. She decides to go over it again in the following lesson.

In the example the 'thinking through' stages described above constituted the teacher reflecting on her practice both before, during and after an actual lesson. While teaching and managing the classroom she needed to be adjusting to the flow of the moment. Before and after the lesson she needed to engage in a process of anticipation and evaluation. Had she been unable to reflect on her practice she would have been unable to teach, because the criteria for teaching to happen could not have been fulfilled.

The example illustrates one way in which a teacher may engage in a reflective process and some of the processes of the teacher's thinking and the decisions and judgements she made in order to teach her pupils in this specific case. Can any characteristics be extrapolated from this account? First there is a specific content to the reflection, related to the definition of teaching. For teaching to occur certain decisions were taken, based on information and analysis. Second there were clear criteria for how to analyse the information, based on the end, which was the achievement of X. There are also criteria for what constitutes reflection capable of being well-grounded in practice. The criteria relate to whether the aspect of the practice, in this case the lesson taught, was well done or not, which in practice means determining whether the pupils learnt what they were taught. To answer these questions there are further criteria, such as whether the teaching and learning objectives were well formulated, in that they were relevant to the pupils. The question of relevance relates to the wider question about aims in the syllabus or scheme of work.

The Teacher in the Reflection

The planning and evaluation process described above relies on the teacher's knowledge and understanding of a number of factors, among which are the individual pupils; the syllabus or scheme of work; the Spanish language, and language teaching methodology. For successful teaching she also needs to understand factors such as how pupils' sense of well-being influences their motivation. This kind of understanding is not just a matter of understanding learning theory: it relies on teacher qualities in a deeper way than her grasp of technical, pedagogic and pedagogic content knowledge. She needs to be sensitive to pupils' reactions and able to adjust her actions to them in the moment. It is not enough to know what to do; we also need to know when to do it and when to refrain from doing it, which requires judgement (see Chapter 5). Some teacher qualities and dispositions aid the achievement of well-grounded reflection, although it is not possible to isolate these and produce a taxonomy as teaching is too complex to yield itself up to such a list. It is possible, however, to indicate some of the qualities and dispositions that might support it.

The teacher brings to her teaching relationships her own situatedness. The ability to develop as a teacher is built on a number of qualities and dispositions, such as the ability to 'think on one's feet'; open-mindedness; resilience to having one's fundamental assumptions challenged; willingness to welcome advice and support. Others are the ability to make connections between one's own experiences so as to be able to generate new learning and changed behaviour. Another could be the capacity to trust in one's own judgement while keeping an open mind. Undoubtedly a capacity for optimism is also called for, as many might agree, is courage. The list could become long, as it is clear that a number of qualities and dispositions are called into play. The ability to engage in well-grounded reflection cannot be divorced from the particularities of the teacher herself, the kind of person she is. Additionally, engagement with processes of reflection that are well-grounded helps to develop the qualities and dispositions needed to teach well. How far these may be capable of being developed by deliberate action is open to question.

A primary capacity for well-grounded reflection is the ability to see things from the learners' perspective, to show 'pedagogical thoughtfulness' (van Manen, 1991) and to make adjustments when necessary to any action, which may be the ongoing classroom situation. The same principles that apply to the pupils' learning also apply to how a teacher learns to teach. If we move one step backwards and think of the teacher as the learner, it is the mentor who stands in the dialogical relationship to the trainee teacher. This learning relationship is discussed in Chapter 6. In the earlier example in this chapter of the teacher who was unaware of how the reading age of a pupil had impacted on the pupil's behaviour, the teacher's own presuppositions about the causes of the pupil's bad behaviour had caused continuing difficulties. This teacher came to a more fruitful understanding of the problem through reflection, guided and aided by mentoring. Over time, this understanding contributed to a resolution of the experienced problem. Reaching the new understanding required the teacher to reassess his previous beliefs; to try a different way of working with this pupil, and to reflect on the success of his new approach. This suggests the need for a certain open-mindedness, as well as flexibility in adapting to new understandings.

Teachers need to make rich and connected understandings (Davis. 1998), drawing on a range of 'cognitive perspectives' (Peters, 1966). They need to be reflective about teaching, and by the same argument so do pupils. However, reflection is a means to an end, which is good teaching. Being a reflective teacher is not a sufficient condition for being a good teacher:

> Teaching involves more than reflection. We would think little of a teacher who was rich in the capacity to reflect (in whatever sense) but who was unable to establish appropriate relationships with pupils, or was disinclined to invite them to engage in any work.
>
> (McLaughlin, 1999)

There is a normative dimension to teaching, and we generally expect teachers to be exemplary figures (McLaughlin, 2004). Two major characteristics of good teachers implied in the account in this chapter are being flexible, or adaptable and exemplifying certain professional values. The two characteristics are inter-related. We want teachers to hold to certain values, but we also want them to exercise judgement in how their values apply to particular cases. So flexibility is required. The notion of flexibility and adaptability is also used in an educational discourse about responding to social change and to a certain extent this connection is a valid one. For pupils the need to respond to change has been enshrined in the aims of the National Curriculum, which claims among other things that education should

> enable pupils to respond positively to opportunities, challenges and responsibilities, to manage risk and to cope with change and adversity ... (and that) education must enable us to respond positively to the opportunities and challenges of the rapidly changing world in which we live and work. In particular, we need to be prepared to engage with economic, social and cultural change, including the continued globalisation of the economy and society, with new work and leisure patterns and with the rapid expansion of communication technologies.
>
> (DfEE & QCA, 1999a, pp. 11–12)

This reminds us of a particular pressure on teachers to fit their teaching into these NC aims, relating to what Giddens (1991) calls 'conditions of modernity', in which employees may need to lead 'portfolio lives', able to transfer their skills to new jobs, as technology changes the way jobs are done, and globalisation and the internet as well as other new technology gives rise to new and different jobs, new work. Since it is not possible to define in advance of the developing situation what these will be, the transferability of skills and self – promotion and 'marketability' become important. The NC statement tends to view flexibility in the narrow sense of having transferable skills and the willingness to do different kinds of work. My conception of the desirability of flexibility is a wider one. Having transferable skills and being adept at learning new skills does not necessarily lead to employment.

If a person is disappointed in employment, or lack of it, she will need inner resources to remain optimistic and happy, so the need to develop flexible work skills cannot replace the aims of education to enable pupils to lead a good life. Therefore, we are led back to the notion of teaching as a normative activity and to the idea of the importance of teacher qualities and dispositions.

Being dispositionally able to engage in well-grounded reflection relates to the discourse of social change in a further way. Taking Giddens' formulation that in our time we cannot appeal to predetermined social structures to create a framework for lifelong development: it is advantageous to be able to take responsibility for one's own development. Giddens defines 'the trajectory of the self' as

> the formation of a specific life-span in conditions of modernity, by means of which self-development, as reflexively organised, tends to become internally referential.
>
> (Giddens, 1991, p. 244)

Self-development is important in the general context of a person's life. In the context of teaching, a teacher able to engage in well-grounded reflection may be equipped to develop what van Manen (1991) has called thoughtful pedagogy.

The Scope and Practice of Reflection

The examples given in this chapter support two main reasons why teachers might need to undertake reflection on practice. First, for their own development, to increase their range of strategies, their knowledge and understanding about pedagogy and practice. More significantly, without well-grounded reflection, the opportunities to learn from practice are, at the very least, curtailed. If teachers cannot learn from their teaching, they will not be able to manage the learning of their pupils so that pupils do successfully learn. An analogy would be a speaker presenting a paper at a seminar and receiving comments from listeners. If the presenter was unable to consider any objections being raised, any flaws in her arguments, any missing stages or exemplification, she is unlikely to produce a better or possibly a good argument, other things being equal.

We value the quality of open-mindedness in someone who is dispositionally inclined to consider other view points and we value flexibility in adapting to new perspectives. However, we could also envisage the case of a seminar in which the audience were not 'up to speed' with the thinking of the paper presenter, and made inappropriate and irrelevant comments. Here the presenter might change nothing and her paper may be the better for that decision. Similarly there may be a rare case of the inspirational teacher, who may not go through any systematic reflection on her practice and yet may have happy and successful learners in her charge. For the majority of teachers not blessed with this inspirational charisma, the ability to reflect in a well-grounded manner on one's own practice can provide guidance for understanding, which can lead to better teaching. The extent to which each teacher reflects or needs to reflect on practice is related to the ends of the reflection. Too much reflection might be stultifying and here practical judgement is crucial (see Chapter 5).

So where and how is reflection useful and when is a non-reflective teacher to be discouraged? An example would be a teacher who teaches reading from an established scheme or syllabus but cannot adapt it to fit the individual pupils or context of a class, whereas the dialectic of teacher-learner requires constant adjustment to what is going on in the moment, as well as the ability to work to a plan. In teaching as in most situations the wise action is to know when to divert from the plan, or the syllabus (and why) and what to do once we are 'making it up as we go along'. The teacher who uses the reading scheme unreflectively is unlikely to help all the pupils in her classes to learn, so reflection helps to develop and maintain rationality of a non-technical kind.

The essential peripheral activities, without which 'teaching activities' cannot be successful, are also developed through reflection, for example writing and interpreting syllabuses and schemes of work; understanding policy and statutory requirements; choosing and organising resources. Also, experiencing more and more examples of such practice builds up a store of instances, and reflected-upon-experience builds up a store of digested experiences, which may become 'action capable of educating' (Scheffler, 1974, p. 227). This is how a repertoire of strategies on which a teacher can draw in the heat of the practical moment is built up. The development of a repertoire of strategies is an important aspect of gaining expertise.

As practitioners develop, the scope and content of what is reflected upon is also likely to develop (Reynolds 1965; H. Dreyfus & S. Dreyfus, 1986) and trainees come to 'take for granted' aspects of their practice which initially preoccupied them, and move on to be concerned about (reflect upon) wider matters:

> This 'taking-for-granted' on the one hand, and reflection on the other, offers a view of how reflection-on-action deepens in the course of a career.
>
> (Atherton, 2003)

It is therefore important to build in opportunities and guidance for the achievement of well-grounded reflection from the beginning of ITET courses. However, there is a danger of building in opportunities for merely ritualised reflection. Just having opportunities, such as procedures for evaluating lessons, cannot transfer to trainees the understandings needed to use the procedures in a personalised, relevant and appropriate manner, such that new understandings ensue. Reflection without a clear purpose or guidelines could be unhelpful in this process. Guidelines might indicate some of the processes that could build well-grounded reflection, such as some of the behaviour as identified by Roth (1989), which includes:

- questioning the basis of what is done, the why and how things are done, others do things
- seeking alternatives
- keeping an open mind
- comparing and contrasting
- seeking the theoretical basis and/or underlying rationale
- viewing from various perspectives
- asking 'what if . . .'?
- asking for others' ideas and viewpoints
- using prescriptive models only when adapted to the situation
- considering consequences

- hypothesising
- synthesising and testing
- seeking, identifying and resolving problems.

The characteristics outlined above for teacher behaviour are suggestive of teacher reflectiveness. We might think of these characteristics as indicative of dialogical virtues and the application of rationality of a kind rooted in experience and involving judgement.

Because reflection entails engagement with personal experience, different modes of reflection may appeal to different teachers, at different times, for varying purposes, and can take different forms, including the production of a personal narrative or a case study, or a reflective journal. Reflection can take place within various 'sites' such as the planning and evaluation of lessons, discussed above; or when teachers engage with research literature or their own practitioner research, discussed in Chapter 7, and it can develop through dialogue and discussion, which is discussed in Chapter 6. It makes sense therefore to think that different modes of reflection might be appropriate in varying circumstances.

Conclusion

Teaching is value laden and values are opaque and deep and do not yield to crude appropriation. Reflection on practice is needed to understand all that is involved in being a teacher; reflection is important to the development of practical knowledge. There are various sites for reflection and it is possible to see if reflection is well-grounded: not all reflection is necessarily good. Reflection on practice can be thought of as well-grounded, if it enables the practitioner to reach new and productive understandings. It should lead to a critical review of what has gone before, thereby allowing new action, in the light of its analysis. ITET should therefore incorporate an element of reflective practice, and for this to happen the provision of specific guidelines may be helpful. (The question of provision of guidelines is further discussed in more detail in Chapter 8). The engagement with well-grounded reflection does not necessarily need to follow systematic procedures, but may proceed through lateral thinking, metaphorical thinking, even daydreaming, which might happen to come up with a good solution to a dilemma or question posed. Any possible solution would have to be subsequently subjected to new reflection, rational procedures, to see if it really is a good one for the particular circumstances. This is analogous to Popper's view (1972) that new scientific hypotheses have to be subjected to rigorous testing, but there is no procedure that will guarantee getting to them in the first place.

Being a reflective teacher does not *ipso facto* make a good teacher. The ability to engage successfully in well-grounded reflection relies on certain qualities and dispositions of the teacher. Some teacher qualities are not captured by the definition of teacher reflection, for example, the capacity for optimism and courage. There are other related notions, such as the exercise of professional judgement, which has an evaluative dimension, is based on experience and builds, through habit, into expertise. It may include a substantial element of engaging with others, mentors, other teachers and a wider community of practice. Reflection on practice is needed to gain and maintain the knowledge, skills and understanding required to be a teacher. Without reflection of some kind it is not possible to engage in the practice of teaching, as defined in this chapter.

Note

1. Originally published in 1949 (Ryle, 1949).

Chapter 4

The Nature of Teacher Knowledge and Understanding

Reflection is important for the development of teacher expertise. What kind of knowledge and understanding is deployed in the practice of teaching? When partnerships between schools and HEIs were developing in the early 1980s, HMI was concerned about an apparent non-coherence between 'academic' theory covered on a university training course and the practical teaching experience (DES, 1981). Trainees also expressed some dissatisfaction with the role of educational theory in ITET courses at the time (Benton, 1990). Hirst found evidence for

> ... a growing recognition among both academic educational theorists and self-critical professionals that the foundations of their own approach to educational theory and practice may well have been widely misconceived.
>
> (Hirst, 1990, p. 148)

Establishing and developing partnerships between schools and HEIs (Benton, 1990; McIntyre, 1990; Heilbronn & Jones, 1997) spurred discussion about the relationship between theory and practice. The university and the school were to work together to develop trainees' knowledge and understanding and early on it was questioned whether partnership models might be conceptualising this knowledge and understanding as a split between the 'academic knowledge' of the university and the 'situational' knowledge of the school. Such a split does not explicate teacher knowledge and understanding.

> Knowledge of both kinds and use of both kinds of criteria in understanding practice are important for students' professional

development . . . It is clearly recognised that each of these two convenient categories itself contains very diverse forms of knowledge and criteria.

(Hirst, 1990, p. 148)

Practical capacity is never fully developed in the study of theory and the nature of both practical capacity and theory is complex. The relationship between practical capacity and theory needs explicating.

Theory and Practice

What is the relationship between 'theoretical' or 'propositional' knowledge and 'practical' or 'procedural' knowledge and understanding? And first, what is the relationship between 'technical' knowledge and 'theoretical' knowledge, both of which are propositional? It is important to understand the difference and the relationship between these two kinds of propositional knowledge because in many high skilled practices technical knowledge is essential to practice in an immediate way, whereas theoretical knowledge is not. This has implications for training as well as for practice.

To begin to explicate the differences in context of these two kinds of propositional knowledge we can think about the basic skill of riding a two-wheel cycle, in terms of being able to move forward on the cycle for as long as one wished, without falling off, which in practice means without the bike wobbling so much that it toppled over. The child who can do this demonstrates a skill or a set of skills. An adult teaching a child to ride a bicycle successfully, usually involving the adult knowing when to hold and push the bike and when to let go of it, has technical knowledge about the way in which two-wheel cycles balance when in motion, and about how such devices need a third foothold on the ground when not in motion. Of course we may have technical knowledge yet not be able to successfully implement it. We may push too hard before letting go, without taking into account the level of competence of the learner. So having technical knowledge does not necessarily imply successful action reliant on that knowledge. Also the technical knowledge may not necessarily be articulated. The adult may not know that their actions rely on their understanding of the basic mechanics of bicycle riding. They may just 'help' the child to ride the bicycle, using their own practical know-how to do so and may indicate this technical knowledge in a form such as 'you need to keep peddling or the bike will topple over', or 'put your foot down on the ground when you stop the bike'. The adult in this case has technical knowledge but this does not amount to knowing any particular theory or theories. As Polanyi (1969) has said it is difficult to articulate 'tacit' knowledge, which he thinks of as a form of personal knowledge, an active awareness that we rely on while we are involved in activity. It is difficult to articulate tacit knowledge because 'it is embodied in skills that are located inside practices, ways of doing things, knacks, sensitive touches, etc.' (van Manen, 1991, p. 124).

Stevenson and Lennie (1992), however, do theorise about the injuries that result from non-helmet wearing accidents suffered by children. They have analysed accident figures arising from various studies on cycle riding, isolated the wearing of helmets as a factor in injury and have issued advice on how to build strategies to increase bicycle helmet wearing among children. They have engaged on a theoretical level and not only a technical level with an aspect of bicycle riding. Consider now an adult riding a bicycle in a busy road and making constant adjustments to the flow of traffic and the other unique contingencies of the situation. In this case the rider exercises practical judgement about what to do when, as is discussed further in the following chapter.

Knowing How and Knowing That

The distinction between 'knowing-how' (KH) as practical knowledge which manifests itself in successful action such as bike riding, and 'knowing-that' (KT) as propositional knowledge such as found in a text book about bicycle mechanics, is useful at this point (Ryle, 1963). The relationship between KH and KT is complex as shown in the bike-riding example and also in the account of the making of the samurai sword in the Preface to this book. The sword maker, without a knowledge of modern scientific theory, has a great deal of KT in the form of applied technical knowledge, demonstrated in the successful making of a sword, which involves the KT being actualised in the demonstration of KH. Further, there are indications about how some KT may be acquired through experience, as is the case for the apprentice sword-maker shadowing his master.

There may be different ways in which KT is acquired. Some KT is acquired in clear and overt ways. In the ITET context, overt acquisition might be involved in knowledge of individual pupils' attainment records, knowledge of statutory requirements and research findings about how pupils learn. In practice, how an individual teacher believes what she has read and is told is also influenced by her own personal experience, including her own observations and discussions with other teachers. If, after reading some of the relevant documents and hearing about relevant research, she can articulate some general principles on which she has worked, incorporating some of this KT, it would make sense for her to say 'this is the theoretical basis on which I have planned my teaching', or 'the theoretical basis of what I do'. The advantage of talking in these terms, rather than talking about 'theory' per se, is that there is an acknowledgement of an essentially provisional and practice related nature of the theoretical element that is demonstrated in the practice. The KT is provisional because a critical perspective needs to be maintained about any theory or research findings, to subject them to further substantiation in the light of further practice or new KT. (This is further discussed in Chapter 7, where the need for teachers to be 'research literate' is argued). The teacher may have well-warranted beliefs underpinning what she does, which could be called her theory about planning, or language acquisition, for example. This does not mean that there is something called 'theory' as such (see also Carr, 2006, pp. 142–43). It is more a case of propositional knowledge providing procedural knowledge with 'the context in which such knowledge can flourish' (Winch & Gingell, 2004, p. 42).

There remains a question as to whether procedural knowledge may in all cases be reduced to propositional knowledge. If we take the case of the adult riding a bicycle in traffic and exercising practical judgement in order to ride safely, and if our object is to help riders to develop the judgement to enable them to avoid accidents, it is not important to answer this question. What matters is to find an answer to the question of how to develop the judgement to expertly demonstrate the KH of safe bicycle riding, as well as the relevant KT, such as understanding the rules of the road, factors relating to responsible bike ownership, maintenance and so on. Similarly the current discussion aims to find an appropriate ITET model, based on what teachers need to know, understand and be able to do. The starting point of the discussion is not epistemological but practical.

This chapter now moves into a consideration of the kind of knowledge and understanding teachers need to demonstrate to become and develop as teachers. It may be that this is 'Ryle's true legacy ... (which) is a sense of the difficulty but also the importance of determining the nature of "knowing how to" ' (Snowdon, 2003, p. 28).

Practical Knowledge – A Deweyan Perspective

In Chapter 3 Schön's attempt to conceptualise the nature of expert practical action was discussed, and his notion of 'reflection-in-action' found to be inadequate. We can now return to Dewey's account of practical knowledge, on which Schön drew, to illuminate the need for ways of working with new teachers, which chime with the way in which KH is developed and KT is actualised and we can make a link to the critique of standards in Chapter 2. This is because the attempt to capture the complexity of practical knowledge in standards discourse indicates a mistakenly objectifying stance towards KH, which significantly falsifies its nature. Such an attempt is an example of a technically rationalist enterprise, in the sense that Dewey analyses in his discussion of traditional empiricism, an outline of which follows.

There are some difficulties with Dewey's account, which it is well to deal with at this point. Dewey's use of the term 'knowledge' is at times ambiguous and the under-determination of his concept of knowledge raises difficulties for a complete understanding of his views on knowledge (Perkins, 1952, p. 573; Kulp, 1992; Tiles, 1992; Hickman, 1998, pp. 166–78). This is a problem if explicating his views of KT. It is not a problem for this present discussion when it is clear from the explanations that contextualise his use of the term 'knowledge' that he is referring to KH. He also uses the term 'knowing', uniquely for KH. However, under-definition of terms does not diminish the force of what he has to say about KH, which is to invite us to be sceptical of the idea that there can be some form of abstracted KT, which is not embodied in some form of enactment. Dewey's work in epistemology prompts us to look in the right direction to find the subtly grounded, experiential nature of KH.

Some critics have claimed that Dewey is a relativist with regard to KT (Kulp, 1992; Tiles, 1992) and it may seem as if endorsing Dewey's view of KH ties me into his views on KT, or in any case into a sceptical view with regard to KT. However, we may fortunately leave aside the thorny question as to whether all procedural knowledge may ultimately rely on propositional knowledge, as some have claimed, as a discussion, which is not relevant to establishing the nature of teacher knowledge and understanding.

Technical Rationality – Dewey's Critique

Previous chapters have suggested that technical rationality is inadequate to account for teacher knowledge and understanding. Dewey's notion of 'experimental empiricism' is a critique of technically rational modes of empirical inquiry, when these are applied to practice. Technical rationality emphasises implementation of means over choice of ends. Prediction is a key outcome in the application of technical rationality, exemplified in scientific research in which objectivity is sought through carefully controlled procedures, aimed at preventing interests, desires and values from influencing outcomes. On this paradigm such outcomes are sought in order to provide the basis of reliable information on which to build future action.

Dewey believes that this process does not fit practical activities but rather that the 'exaltation of pure intellect and its activity above practical affairs is fundamentally connected with the quest for a certainty' (Dewey, 1960, p. 6). Practical knowledge however is characterised by its *uncertainty*, because of its contingency:

> The distinctive characteristic of practical knowledge, one which is so inherent that it cannot be eliminated, is the uncertainty which attends it ... Judgement and belief regarding actions to be performed can never attain more than a precarious probability.

> (ibid.)

Technical rationality functions on the scientific model, which Toulmin (1990) has characterised as

> an abstract enterprise, whose progress could be defined and appraised without reference to the historical situation in which that progress was made.
>
> (p. 137)

Dewey's view is that technical rationality uses a purely empiricist notion of the possibility of objectivity in acting upon nature, akin to the Platonic idea that 'true beliefs' are arrived at by obeying mechanical procedures. Whereas, Dewey believes, scientists work as science practitioners.

> Perfect certainty is what man wants but it cannot be found by practical doing or making.
>
> (Dewey, 1960, p. 21)

It is important to understand that Dewey's account is based in the perspective of practice. The thrust of his argument is directed at showing that the traditional use of the term 'knowledge' commits 'the great intellectualist fallacy' (Dewey, 1960, p. 219) and his view is that if we draw our conception of knowledge

> from reflection upon actual conditions of science and life instead of from the prejudices of history ... we would understand that there is no split between theory and practice, between what is known in traditional epistemology as 'knowledge' and human activity/ practice.
>
> (ibid., p. 72)

In Dewey's exposition of the experimental nature of scientific inquiry he was acting against the notion that rationality consists in being constrained by rule and Dewey understood that the *methods* of scientific inquiry, rather than its positivist goals, could provide a *process model* for what constitutes knowledge and understanding. He therefore attempts to ground his theory of knowledge in practice. For this, he needs to discuss the contribution of science to the debate about knowledge. This involves him in reassessing practical activity, empirical inquiry, *a priori* reasoning and the scientific method. He begins:

> Practical activity suffers from a double discrediting because of the perpetuation of these two features of tradition. It is a mere external follower upon knowledge, having no part in its determination. Instead of evolving its own standards and ends in its own developing processes, it is supposed to conform to what is fixed in the antecedent structure of things. Herein we locate the source of that internal division which was said to characterise modern philosophic thought. It accepts the conclusions of scientific inquiry without remaking the conceptions of mind, knowledge and the character of the object of knowledge that are involved in the methods by which these conclusions are reached.
>
> (ibid., p. 71)

Dewey highlights the fact that in the absence of a robust account of KH there remains a danger of slipping into a default interpretation of 'knowledge' as KT and this liability often underlies technical rationality:

> We are so accustomed to the separation of knowledge from doing and making that we fail to recognise how it controls our conceptions of mind, of consciousness and of reflective inquiry.
>
> (ibid., p. 22)

Dewey leads on to an account of the nature of experimental empiricism as a form of reflective inquiry, based on the nature of practical experience and practice-based learning (ibid, p. 22). The nature of practical knowledge is that it cannot conform to the norms of technical rationality, which insists 'that security is measured by certainty of knowledge ... independent of what men do in practical activity' (ibid., pp. 28–29).

An experimental methodology is needed, Dewey believes, to liberate epistemology from a mistaken view of the nature of practical knowledge. Writing in 1934, in lectures on Heisenberg, Dewey points out that science 'in our own time ... has finally emancipated itself and arrived at a consciousness of the principles contained in its own method' (ibid., p. 71).

Dewey's Historical Analysis

To support his view Dewey undertook a 'radical dismantling of the epistemological tradition' (Toulmin, 1984, pp. ix–x). Starting with Plato's work, in which

> the depreciation of practice was given a philosophic, an ontological justification. Practical action, as distinct from self-revolving, rational self-activity, belongs in the realm of generation and decay, a realm inferior in value as in Being ...
>
> (Dewey, 1960, p. 18)

For Plato certainty about what is to count as knowledge must be stamped with 'the warrant of reason' (ibid., p. 27), and for Dewey this was the first step in the 'historic grounds of the elevation of knowledge above mankind and doing' (ibid., p. 4). He further explores his initial question as to why modern philosophy has 'contributed so little to bring about an integration between what we know about the world and the intelligent direction of what we do?' (ibid., p. 71).

> In spite of great changes in detail, the notion of a separation between knowledge and action, theory and practice, has been perpetuated, and ... the beliefs connected with action are taken to be uncertain and inferior in value compared with those inherently connected with objects of knowledge, so that the former are securely established only as they derived from the latter.
>
> (ibid., p. 29)

Having established that there was historically an 'epistemological gap', which relegated practice-based knowledge to second-class status and therefore to the realms of unreliability, Dewey goes on to establish his own episteme through a discussion of Spinoza, Hume and Kant, following this with a discussion of the rise of science and of the scientific method. A detailed analysis is made of Spinoza's attempt to construct a theory of knowledge, which synthesised scientific knowledge about nature, with his religious faith in the Absolute. This was a significant step in modern philosophy. Dewey states that

> there have been few attempts in modern philosophy as bold and as direct as this one, to effect a complete integration of scientific method with a good which is fixed and final, because based on a rock of absolute cognitive certainty. Few thinkers have been as willing to sacrifice details of the older tradition in order to save its substance as was Spinoza. The outcry in all quarters against him proved that, in the minds of his contemporaries and successors, he had made too many concessions to naturalistic science and necessary law.
>
> (ibid., p. 55)

Dewey delineates two significant aspects of Spinoza's work. The first is that

> Nature as the object of knowledge, is capable of being the source of constant good and a rule of life, and thus has all the properties and the functions which the Jewish-Christian tradition attributed to God.
>
> (ibid., p. 56)

The second is that

> Spinoza exemplifies with extraordinary completeness the nature of the problem of all modern philosophies which have not deserted the classic tradition, and yet have made the conclusions of modern science their own.
>
> (ibid.)

Spinoza is a key thinker for Dewey in the reintegration of the practical-lived experience as a constituent of knowledge, for he is a step on the way from absolutism, which is from grounding knowledge on *a priori* truths. Spinoza took account of the 'new science of nature' (ibid., p. 58).

> What makes Spinoza so admirably the exponent of this problem is that he adopted with ardour and without the reservations displayed

by most modern thinkers the essential elements in the Greek tradition of intellectualism and naturalism, the Hebrew-Christian idea of
the priority and primacy of the properties of ultimate Being which
concern the control of human affections and endeavour, and the
method and conclusions of the new natural science – as he saw
them.

(ibid.)

Dewey's critique of Spinoza leads him to react against the Kantian
assumption of an all-embracing ahistorical context in which every
species of discourse could be categorised. Dewey claims that a false
dichotomy between theory and practice is set up in the mirroring
metaphor of traditional theories of knowledge. 'This is as true of
idealism as of realism, of theories of synthetic activity as those of
passive receptivity' (ibid., p. 22).

In traditional theories of knowledge 'the theory of knowing is mod-
elled after what was supposed to take place in the act of vision' (ibid.,
p. 23). A false analogy is made, assuming the 'knower' to be in the
position of a 'spectator', making judgements about the world, or discovering facts about it, without acting upon it. In explicating Dewey's
analysis Rorty has correctly pointed out that 'the metaphors of vision,
correspondence, mapping, picturing and representation which apply
to small, routine assertions' do not necessarily apply, as traditional
epistemology assumes to 'large and debatable ones' (Rorty, 1982, p.
164). It is from this basic error that the idea arises that where there
are no objects to correspond to we have no hope of rationality but
only individual prejudice. Practical activity cannot conform to the
standards of certainty embodied in technical rationality. However,
there is the possibility of rationality of a different kind in KH, and to
explicate this Dewey points to a different view of scientific inquiry.

Experimental Empiricism

Dewey maintains that:

if we frame our conception of knowledge on the experimental
model, we find that it is a way of operating upon and with the

things of ordinary experience so that we can frame our ideas of them in terms of their *interactions* with one another, instead of in terms of the qualities they directly present.

(Dewey, 1960, p. 107)

In situations of complexity, such as are experienced in a classroom while teaching, a number of variables interact[1]. This interaction is experienced by an individual, for instance the teacher, in a particular and contingent manner.

We may say that *it is the working body which learns* in activity, some of which is mental, some of which is physical. The point is these activities are experienced holistically, by people in daily life, in social inter-relationships, and often through the leadership of good teachers, who track through these inevitably embodied experiences with the learners. In this sense, learning is written on the body, rather than ascribed to the Cartesian mind in the machine.

(Beckett, 1998)

In order to operate at all the teacher responds in certain ways, in some non-literal sense she manages to relate variables together in some way, to make sense of her situation, in order to act within it. In standards discourse we talk of teachers being able to 'manage the classroom' and 'respond appropriately to pupils' for example. Dewey's concepts of 'operational definition' and 'operational relationship' are helpful in suggesting how we might link the experience of operating fluently in complexity with standards discourse descriptors. In Dewey's account, operational definitions reside in the subject of experience, are rooted in experience, yet also build into concepts. Dewey gives what he calls 'a simple case', of the term 'length', tracing the origin of the concept back to empirical roots, in which two objects are compared with one another:

This type of operation, repeated under conditions themselves defined by specified operations, not merely fixes the relation of two things to each other called *their* length, but defines a generalised concept of length.

(Dewey, 1960, p. 128)

Other 'operations' evolve other definitions, such as 'mass' and 'time' and Dewey states that these concepts become 'operational definitions', 'by means of which a multitude of relations between bodies can be established' (ibid.). He sees the history of science as the history of a growing understanding that definitions needed to be made in terms of *relations* and not of antecedent things (ibid., p. 126). This represents a shift from essentialism, away from the notion that for conceptions to be valid 'there must be antecedent properties resident in objects' (ibid.). The key idea here is that 'theoretical certitude is assimilated to practical certainty', to what Dewey calls 'security, trustworthiness of instrumental operations' (ibid., p. 128). Again this is a pertinent notion applied to ITET (see Chapter 7 for its implications in practical terms).

Practical Knowledge and Two Models of Initial Teacher Education and Training

Two different ITET models emerge from the discussion so far. The first based on a competency/standards model and the second on ideas of reflection and reflective practice. The first model has been seen to be based on a technically rationalist view of practice, characterised by a belief that there is agreed and defined KT about *what* to teach, and *how* to teach it. The imposition of directives about what and how to teach, in the form of strategies, which appear to be research based, implies that the research is in some sense 'objective' and that the data on which it is based are universally applicable. However, the data to back up the research have been gathered from within an already defined vision of what data are needed. In the post-Kuhnian era it is a common postulate that science is not an infallible mode of inquiry and that it works on models that are accepted for as long as they 'do the job'. They are paradigms, valid until a new paradigm arises. As Burbules (1997) has argued, we know that both subject content knowledge and pedagogical content knowledge do embody substantive assumptions. For example, if we group by ability and give standardised tests, we will have a different learning outcome than if we adopt a mixed ability group work approach, where we ask for a group outcome and where we have controlled the composition of the groups.

ITET is concerned to develop and support new teachers, so that they can successfully function as teachers, within specific contexts. Both the standards-based model of ITET (SBM) and various versions of the reflective practitioner model (RPM) are currently promoted in ITET, the first as a statutory requirement and the second in various ITET courses. We have seen that the SBM lacks defensible normative bite and fails to account adequately for character, the effect of an individual teacher's distinctive array of dispositions and qualities and affective factors. The picture of the individual operating in a complex situation is inadequately theorised in the SBM. We have also seen that the RPM needs to have processes leading to well-grounded reflection. Dewey's concept of experimental empiricism is useful in attempting a reconciliation between the two models, because it addresses the experience of teachers dealing with complexity in situations with many variables. 'Experimental' engages with a rationality that is not technical in nature. This is important for tutors and mentors who may require some guidelines for articulating and directing their own expertise onto the particular situation of their trainee, in order to guide the trainee to well-grounded reflection on the trainee's own experience.

Different conceptions of ITET work with various sets of concepts, such as what is a good teacher, good behaviour management, good moral example and so on. The SBM attempts to describe these in replicable terms. The RPM does not promulgate general descriptive statements, although individual mentors and tutors do work to norms (see Chapter 6 on mentoring). If we accept that descriptors of good practice are important to articulation, promulgation and assessment, but cannot encompass all dimensions of teaching, and that individual teachers come to understanding as individuals in individual contexts, we can see that Dewey's formulation can be helpful in our quest for a reconciliatory ITET model. When Dewey explains how he conceptualises operational definitions and relations we have a tool for connecting the individual experiencing subject with the wider explanatory descriptors in the public domain. A further example might clarify. If we take the concept of weight and force for example, we know what the words mean, understand them when written and spoken and can define them all separately from one another in a commonsense way. A scientific definition of weight, or we might say an explanation of what weight actually is, states that weight stands for the force of attraction of two bodies (masses). To say that a person weighs 30 kilos means that the earth is pulling her with a force of 30 kilos. She will weigh less on the moon, which has a lower gravitational pull than the earth. From the experiencing subject's point of view we do not experience our weight in terms of the earth's gravitational pull. Standards discourse functions like early empiricist and rationalist traditions of which Dewey states:

> Only slowly ... did there dawn the full import of the scientific method. For a long time the definitions were supposed to be made not in terms of relations but through certain properties of antecedent things. The space, time and motion of physics were treated as inherent properties of Being, instead of as abstracted relations.
>
> (ibid., pp. 128–29)

It is not helpful to conceive of such terms as 'behaviour management' in isolation from the complex variables that go to make up any demonstration of this art. One needs to look at the relational context for the application of descriptors of good practice. To know how to act in a situation of complexity is to have a repository of strategies which have been established through experience and which are recognised as relevant to the present moment of the subject. So the concept of 'behaviour management' cannot be understood by reading a manual but previous experience in the use of learnt strategies and interventions can be helpful. In a situation of changing events what is important for a participant subject is

> the correlation among these changes or events. When these correlations are discovered, the possibility of control is in our hands ... (they are) in particular the thought of reality from a particular point of view, the most highly generalised view of nature as a system of interconnected changes.
>
> (ibid.)

When reflecting on her experience in the classroom a teacher may remember, in the sense of re-experience, what has happened, and relate her experiences to her theoretical understanding. This may influence what she does in the future, although she will not consciously think about what she does when doing it. (We have already seen in Chapter 3 the difficulties with this notion when we rejected Schön's concept of 'reflection-in-action'). A teacher behaving appropriately and expertly within a complex situation in the classroom can be said to be able to carry in her practical activities, the theoretical understandings she has developed, just as a musician might compose a symphony in the way that Mozart stated he did, by 'hearing' it all within the space of a few minutes. He took cognisance of the symphony in this way, even though he then spent many hours and days writing out in musical notation what he had experienced. Mozart used his applied technical knowledge in writing out his music so that other musicians could gain propositional knowledge of the music, so that they could play it. When these musicians play Mozart's music expertly they are no longer conscious of the KT involved.

A teacher in a classroom can be helped to understand what elements play a role in building the totality of the classroom situation and how they relate and inter-relate. Some KT involving aspects such as planning or child development can help to structure a trainee's learning. What will make it real for her, and become part of her repertoire for performance, will come about when she is able to act on the knowledge gained in theory, in her practical situation and successfully cope with the reality of planning, teaching and managing lessons for the particular pupils in her groups.

An expert professional like a teacher in the classroom can apply this KT without thinking about it consciously in the moment and can grasp the whole complex situation in which she is acting, even extending across time. The situation can be 'understood' in a moment, although if one were to spell it out it would take a long time to do so. One way in which an expert teacher can help to spell out much of the KT involved in teaching is through mentoring, which is discussed in Chapter 6. Another way in which a trainee can gain some of the KT involved is through teacher research, discussed in Chapter 7.

Application of These Deweyan Concepts

A defensible RPM requires some criteria for being able to say if reflection is well-grounded, and for being able to research and promote it. Dewey's exposition of experimental empiricism focuses on 'three outstanding characteristics' (Dewey, 1960, pp. 86–87), which can support a justifiable RPM.

1. Experimentation involves making definite changes in the environment or in our relation to it.
2. 'Experiment is not a random activity'.
3. The outcome is 'the construction of a new empirical situation in which objects are differently related to one another'.

The second condition that 'experiment is not a random activity' ensures a parameter for reflection, which in the case of an ITET RPM can be related to some prior descriptors of good practice, which would be interpreted and applied or modified within an individual situation by a particular trainee, possibly with the support of a mentor or tutor. The first and third conditions are important if reflection is to be well-grounded. It is significant that Dewey uses the term 'knowing' and not 'knowledge' for the cognitive gains in the process he has described above:

> knowing is itself a mode of practical action and is the way of interaction by which other natural interactions become subject to direction. Such is the significance of the experimental method as far as we have as yet traced its course.
>
> (ibid., p. 107)

The power of using empirical experimentalist methods to resolve questions arising from practical situations is not limited to the new understandings that are developed. Through the process of reflecting as discussed in Chapter 3, new methods relating to the inquiry in question may be developed, which in turn may give rise to new understandings which could not exist previously, such as when new tools are developed in a particular industry, because they are needed to perform some practical task for which existing tools were inadequate.

After their development, unforeseen uses, and outcomes may arise. A typical case of the development of a new tool might be that:

> something needed to be done to accomplish an end; various devices and methods of operation were tried. Experiences of success and failure gradually improved the means used. More economical and effective ways of acting were found – that is, operations which gave the desired kind of result with greater ease, less irrelevancy and less ambiguity, greater security. Each forward step was attended with making better tools. Often the invention of a tool suggested operations not in mind when it was invented and thus carried the perfecting of operations still further.
>
> (ibid., p. 124)

How does this plausible account relate to the practice of teaching? Specifically it implies that the meanings which are created in teaching only emerge in the practice. The teacher may enable the learner to gain a sense of the significance of a concept, or to develop a skill, but the precise way in which this outcome will be achieved cannot be regulated in advance of the situation in which it is created, although some facts about how to achieve a similar, desired outcome might be known. Take for example a typical French lesson in which the teacher is trying to get her pupils to know, understand and be able to use correctly, in context and from memory, structures related to the weather. She may decide in advance on a variety of techniques to achieve her objective. There is a body of empirical and theoretical work on language teaching, and a body of knowledge about the practical applications on which she can draw. When the teacher teaches the lesson she has planned, with a particular group of pupils, on a particular occasion, it will emerge and be received in a particular way.

If the teacher is able to reflect on what happened she is likely to do something differently next time she teaches the same lesson, (provided she believes that something different is required to achieve the outcome; knows what this is, and understands how to go about it). In a language lesson for example, pupils produced the French phrase for 'foggy day' when the stimulus required 'rainy day'. The teacher reflected first on the clarity of her visual stimulus, which she improved, with no better result. She next asked about her pupils' experiences of fog, and discovered these to be limited, but in the process of asking, a usually shy pupil offered an account of her experience of monsoon rain in India; gained class attention and a boost in self-esteem. The discussion was deepened by someone mentioning the recent Thailand tsunami. Spiritual values were expressed about respect for the earth and ethical questions were raised about aid and compassion to the victims.

The relevance of Dewey's tool-making analogy is the conclusion that Dewey draws from his example that there can be no *a priori* test or rule for the determination of the operations which define procedures developed in practice. In practical affairs procedures are always provisional: the way that things need to be done, or should be done can only be determined by doing, reflecting and redoing. 'The operations which govern ideas originate in what men naturally do and are tested and improved in the course of doing' (ibid.).

When doing something, new ways of doing it may emerge for future application. Dewey describes this process as the development of 'the operations of the art of scientific experimentation' (ibid.). It may seem paradoxical to put 'art' and 'science' together in the way he does, but the phrase is a good description of teaching and both of those concepts are made coherent with each other through the notion of experimentation. In practice though, it may not always be a case of *steadily* improving, gaining new understandings ('tools') and making more sophisticated or refined or appropriate interventions in a progressive way. The process may well go in fits and starts – hence the need to be alert to the ongoing situation. Past reflection also plays a part in providing insights for this ability.

In the ITET debate as earlier described the SBM starts from the assumption that objective knowledge about good teaching is both possible and desirable. The RPM starts from the notion of the import of experiential learning. This debate is part of a wider discussion. Standards discourse takes an objective stance, outside the perspective of the practitioner, and attempts to elaborate statements about verifiable good practice. Dewey is concerned with questions of value and experientially gained KH. His views on the integration of 'science', conceived as a kind of objectifying tool, and 'nature', defined as the physical world are relevant to the integration of a thin SBM, with broad brush strokes and headings, with a thick RPM, which gives an account of how reflection could and should be well-grounded. This can be illustrated by Dewey's argument for 'the unification of science'[2] by which he means bridging the gulf between:

> the widest gap in knowledge ... that which exists between humanistic and non-humanistic subjects. The breach will disappear, the gap be filled, and science be manifest as an operating unity in fact and not merely in idea when the conclusions of impersonal non-humanistic science are employed in guiding the course of distinctively human behaviour ... In this integration ... science itself (is) a value (since it is the expression and the fulfilment of a special human desire and interest).
>
> (Dewey, 1939, p. 66)

Interestingly the view expressed here predates the debate between the qualitative and quantitative researchers by around 50 years. Today mixed-mode research methods are widely accepted as appropriate to the social sciences, the humanities and education (see Chapter 7). Further support for this position comes from a number of philosophers who have developed 'post-positivist' views. Quine (1969), for example, developed a form of 'epistemological naturalism', which he argued was compatible with Wittgenstein's later work and Garrison (1999) has written about Dewey's 'naturalising epistemology'[3].

There *are* difficulties with Dewey's epistemology, in the sense of a lack of a clear view or interpretation of what he means by 'knowledge'. However, if we read Dewey as a thoroughgoing relativist we reveal contradictions in his thought, because practically everything he has written, including his propositions on education, democracy, society, rest on the notion of the 'warranted assertibility' of 'facts', or 'data', which can certainly bear the interpreted title 'knowledge'. Invoking Wittgenstein's view in the *Philosophical Investigations* that the limits of our language are the limits of our world, it is interesting to speculate that if Dewey had been writing in French he might have been less confusing, in the sense that there are two verbs for 'to know' in French. 'Connaître' means to know *someone* or *something* by acquaintance, that is, through experience. 'Savoir' has two meanings, the first to know *how*, as in 'to know how to play the piano' and the second to know *that*, as in 'I know that it is raining'. When a fluent French speaker stands in relation to a fact, a person, a place or a problematic situation for example, she already has a slightly larger repertoire of terms for the subject-object relationship, for the relationship between herself as subject, and that which is the object of her thought or experience. She draws on this language repertoire at a level, which could be defined as intuitive, since no thought is required to use the right structure at the appropriate time. *Connaître* is clearly rooted in the individual participant subject's experience, whereas to know something for which 'savoir' is used, is clearly to participate in the wider world, to know something which some others know too. Although the manner in which those others know what I know when I use the verb *savoir* cannot be exactly the same, I can be confident that there is enough common understanding to enable me to view our common knowledge as outside of myself and in the wider world. I use this case as an example of how the language we have acquired in a particular context can affect the way we 'see' the world. It is however important not to try to push the example too far, in the sense that

> grammar does not tell us how language must be constructed in order to fulfil its purpose, in order to have such-and-such an effect on human beings. It only describes and in no way explains the use of signs.
>
> (Wittgenstein, 1974: 496, p. 138)

The sociologists Berger and Luckmann's book *The Social Construction of Reality* is subtitled 'A Treatise in the Sociology of Knowledge' and they grapple with the difficulty of holding a social constructivist view of knowledge, which is not a relativist view of knowledge. Early in the book they write that 'consciousness is always intentional; it always intends or is directed towards objects' (Berger & Luckmann, 1967, p. 20), and that:

different objects present themselves to consciousness as constituents of different spheres of reality ... My consciousness is capable of moving through different spheres of reality. Put differently, I am conscious of the world as consisting of multiple realities ... Among the multiple realities there is one that presents itself as the reality par excellence. This is the reality of everyday life. Its privileged position entitles it to the designation of paramount reality.

(ibid., p. 21)

An example of this would be Dewey's treatment of the concept of length for example, or any other empirically reached piece of 'data' or 'fact' (Dewey, 1960, p. 128). In this case it seems that Tiles is correct when he wrote in 1992 that a sociologist could better understand what Dewey was writing than an analytic philosopher (Tiles, 1992, p. 2).

Conclusion

The present discussion on teacher expertise, knowledge and understanding has shown up two seemingly oppositional camps, a standards-based model versus a reflective practice model. These camps may be reconciled through two means. First standards should be conceived 'thinly', with broad brush strokes and headings and at the same time reflective practice should be conceived 'thickly', with guidelines for well-grounded reflection. Secondly, Dewey's concepts of experimental empiricism and operational relationships can show how the underlying epistemology of the two positions does not lead to an insoluble dilemma. These concepts have a synthesising power:

... the rationalist school was right in as far as it insisted that sensory qualities are significant for knowledge only when connected by means of ideas. But they were wrong in locating the connecting ideas in intellect apart from experience. *Connection is instituted through operations that define ideas, and operations are as much matters of experience as are sensory qualities.* When, on the other hand, it is seen that the object of knowledge is prospective and eventual, being the result of inferential or reflective operations which predispose what was antecedently existent, the subject-matters called respectively sensible and conceptual are seen to be complementary in effective direction of inquiry to an intelligible conclusion.

(Dewey, 1960, p. 126)

This chapter endorses Dewey's process-based view of KH acquisition, of 'knowing as a going concern' (ibid. p. 71). The next chapter introduces the further Deweyan concept of *intelligence* and relates it to the development of practical judgement.

Notes

1. Connell (1995) has pointed out that Dewey's understanding of experimental empiricism relates to the science of evolutionary biology, in so far as biology focuses on the relationship of organism and the environment, and works with interactive models of complex and dynamic systems.
2. Dewey's *Theory of Valuation: Foundation of the Unity of Science* was published in 1939 and may have been aimed largely at the logical positivists. Ayer's *Language Truth and Logic*, which had been published 3 years previously, appears in the bibliography (Ayer, 1952).
3. Discussions continue around what may be termed 'problematic aspects of Dewey's terminology and philosophy' (Siegel, 2001, p. 577). However this chapter is based on Dewey's use of the notion of practical knowledge (KH) and avoids problematic discussion of Dewey's possible views on KT.

Chapter 5

Experience as a Foundation of Practical Judgement

The previous chapter established the importance of skilful action, the application and fluent practice of the 'know-how' of a particular practice. That account needs further illumination through the idea of judgement. It is through the exercise of judgement that appropriate action can be skilfully directed in any particular, contingent moment. In the first section of this chapter the role of judgement in teaching is established and some significant features of judgement are identified. The second section builds on Chapter 4 to show how judgement develops in and through experience and reflection on experience, within communities of practice. Part of the story of this development lies in the enabling action of 'intelligence', in Dewey's conception of the term, in organising experience into requisite know-how. The conclusion draws implications for ITET.

The Role of Judgement in Teaching

Knowing how to respond appropriately in situations of complexity seems to involve a kind of practical sense that might be identified as Aristotelian *phronesis*. However, the meaning of *phronesis* is open to interpretation and different translations into English, which attempt 'to capture the full meaning of the term' (Noel, 1999, p. 273) can give rise to different conceptions of teaching and of education (ibid., p. 274), which are interconnected in Aristotle's works. Dunne points out that 'there is a complexity and multi-layeredness in the concept of phronesis which would make it an extremely uncomfortable fit in any ... schematisation' (Dunne, 1993, p. 245). Noel has identified some characteristics of phronesis as situational perception and discernment. This aspect chimes well with the conception of judgement promoted here, in the second section of the chapter. *Phronesis* and related concepts, such as *techne* and *praxis* do not translate exactly into our context and 'bring certain distortions with them' (Smith, 1999, p. 327). Accordingly, the term 'practical judgement' (Smith, 1999) rather than *phronesis* is used in the following account. Interestingly Hager (2000) extended the term to 'workplace practical judgement'.

Four conspicuous features of practical judgement seem important. The first is context specificity. Expert practitioners know what to do in specific situations[1]. Dunne has characterised this aspect of practical judgement as the idea of phronetic insight, which he develops from within 'an intuitive sense of the nature and texture of practical engagement' (Dunne, 1993, p. 8).

> Phronesis does not ascend to a level of abstraction or generality that leaves experience behind. It arises from experience and *returns into experience*. It is, we might say, the insightfulness – or using Aristotle's own metaphor, "the eye" – of a particular type of experience, and the insights it achieves are turned back into experience, which is in this way constantly reconstructed or enriched. And the more experience is reconstructed in this way, the more sensitive and insightful phronesis becomes – or rather, the more the experiencer becomes a *phronimos*.
>
> (ibid., p. 293)

The second characteristic of practical judgement is its responsiveness to individual circumstances, its flexibility. Discussing the distinction between *techne* and *phronesis* in Aristotle's writings, Dunne identifies this characteristic of *phronesis* as the notion through which Aristotle allowed into his conception of knowledge 'the greatest degree of flexibility, openness, and improvisation' (ibid., p. 245). Expert practitioners can respond flexibly to changing situations, so practical judgement differs from *techne*. As Dewey says,

> the distinctive characteristic of practical knowledge, one which is so inherent that it cannot be eliminated, is the uncertainty which attends it.
>
> (Dewey, 1960, p. 6)

We cannot know in advance what individual situations will throw up in the way of stimuli requiring response. Experts respond flexibly. Since there cannot be the definitive, right way to respond it follows that any expert response might not be the best one for the circumstance. Therefore, reflecting on practice, interrogating aims, purposes, outcomes of particular choices in particular teaching situations, can be a fruitful source of knowledge and understanding and support the development of practical judgement.

If equally productive actions are possible in particular situations it follows that there can be no universally applicable, infallible theory or pedagogical intervention, as sought by Reynolds (1998) for example, as a 'science of teaching' or as embodied in the various government strategies. (See Chapter 1. Also, further implications of teacher fallibility are discussed in Chapter 7.)

A third feature of practical judgement is its normative nature. Practical judgement has virtuous qualities, in the sense of demonstrating qualities of phronetic 'practical wisdom'. A good teacher could be said to be a wise person, someone who exercises an ethical sense of doing what is right, of acting for the good. An example would be a teacher who rejects a strategy for gaining order in the classroom, which would involve humiliating pupils, in favour of another, involving more effort based on developing trusting relationships. As Smith (2003) has stated the importance of relationships between students, and between them and their teacher cannot be over-emphasised. Teaching is 'thoroughly relational' (Noddings, 2003, p. 249) and many of the virtues are exercised in relation to others in a pedagogical space of trust (van Manen, 1991).

A fourth feature of judgement is its rootedness within an individual person, with a particular character, dispositions and qualities. When a teacher decides what is to be done in any situation, for example with a recalcitrant pupil, even if her decisions seem intuitive they carry with them her prior experience as well as her values. There is more than one available course of action and the individual teacher makes a choice of what she considers the right action in the circumstances. Her choice may be based on a number of different factors, involving practical and ethical choices. A teacher's character, her dispositions and capacities, underlie the exercise of practical judgement. Good teachers can be said to exercise sound practical judgement, which involves exercising virtues such as justice, tolerance and courage, and qualities such as patience and optimism. The theme of teacher qualities and dispositions is significant. We have already seen the role of integrity and trustworthiness, motivation, open-mindedness and the ability to learn from experience in Chapter 2. Chapter 3 drew on teacher perceptiveness, pedagogical thoughtfulness, open-mindedness, flexibility, adaptability and resilience. The following two chapters (6 and 7) draw on the place of solidarity with others, and the importance of courage and endurance. Chapter 6 discusses the nature of teacher example, and Chapter 8 discusses issues relating to the fundamental place of teacher qualities and dispositions in ITET.

Habit and Practice

Habit is important to the development of teachers' responses to any given situation, in that actions need to be spontaneous but also build on a repertoire of previously rehearsed responses, where possible and appropriate. Habit has a role to play in character development, as well as in the development of propositional knowledge (such as when chanting vocabulary of a foreign language or the capital cities of the world can support long-term memory retention). Habit may therefore play a role in the growth and development of judgement. Habit can of course function negatively: bad habits can hinder appropriate, 'good' responses. In rehearsed spontaneity one has a repertoire of possible strategies and actions on which to draw when faced with the complexity of the unknown teaching situation. One does not have limitless possibility for action, but is drawing on experience gained. This spontaneity is rehearsed through a reflective process, as discussed in Chapter 3, in which experienced situations have been examined in a particular way and the new understandings have been re-applied, building a store of possible actions and reactions with which to respond to similar situations in the future. Maintaining a habit of such reflection enables a larger stock of actions to become part of one's repertoire. This is akin to an actor who has a script that outlines relevant features of a situation in which her character will need to react, but who does not have specific stage directions or dialogue. The actor is rehearsed, because she has researched a number of specific features that will figure as operational relations in the scene she needs to improvise. These operational features might include her character's biographical details, emotional makeup, motivation and relations to the other characters. She will need to know these very well if she is to react appropriately and act her part well[2]. In a similar way, a teacher who regularly reflects on her practice in a well-grounded way, and has specific qualities to enable this process, builds up a repertoire of possible actions. She can then draw on these in an almost instinctual way, in order to respond 'in-action', fluently and effortlessly adjusting to the complexities of a given situation. In normal, fluent action she seems to be responding with some kind of intuition, akin to Polanyi's 'tacit knowing' (Polanyi, 1969).

Like a musician, or a sportsman, a teacher produces assured and spontaneously reactive-enactive responses after a great deal of practice. In order to practice the craft, like the musician or sportsman, a teacher may use the technique of breaking down into reproducible elements, the aspects of the situation that need to be mastered. Thus a cricketer may watch himself bowling on a video, and isolate one aspect of his performance, such as the angle of his arm as he lets go of the ball. He may practise this aspect many times and thereby build up a memory of how to do the action. We could say the practice is successful as it builds up a memory, which, although a mental function, includes mental, physical and psychological aspects (including emotional). The key contribution of motivation and drive is acknowledged by all expert performers, as is the need for much practice. By constantly repeating an action it becomes habitual. The repertoire can also develop through unreflective action. If I constantly throw a ball using an ineffective technique a habit builds that is difficult to break and learning to throw 'well' involves a certain amount of 'unlearning' or reorientation. Habit is not neutral and can be both positive and negative in conditioning a performance: we talk of 'bad' and 'good' habits.

The analogy with sports practice is only useful up to a certain point, however. Being a good sport, obeying the rules, being courteous are factors in good sportsmanship, but a teacher's responsibility of care for her pupils extends further, governed by her role. The sportsman has a responsibility to his opponent and his team and supporters to play by the rules and not to injure anyone by reckless behaviour but teaching has a more extended moral dimension of care. Drawing on Dewey's analysis of the habitual aspects of moral judgement, Hansen has drawn attention to 'the moral significance of habit' and pointed to the importance of the teacher reflecting on her habitual practice in the classroom. He asks:

> how does one reflect on habit? ... What is at stake are the dispositions and attitudes toward students and toward learning itself that teachers express through their everyday conduct.
>
> (Hansen, 1997, p. 168)

What appear to be intuitive reactions of approval or disapproval in certain situations are, in Dewey's words:

> the results of prior experience, including previous conscious thinking, that get taken up into direct habits, and express themselves in direct appraisals of value.
>
> (ibid., p. 169)[3]

A teacher who responds to a pupil's response with a snort of derision or a hasty dismissal conveys an evaluation of the worth of the pupil's participation and by extension of the worth of that pupil herself. The pupil senses how the teacher lives the relationship between them. If the behaviour is frequently repeated it seems reasonable to conclude that there may be repercussions on the pupil's sense of self-esteem, leading to lack of confidence, manifesting in a seeming lack of motivation and lower achievement. Teachers learn appropriate behaviour in professional relationships, just as children learn habits of politeness or ways of ensuring fairness from others, in social situations. We can fruitfully think of teachers learning, in relation to a number of communities of practice.

Communities of Practice

The community in which a practitioner learns and practices is influential in forming her conception of the practice, her practical judgement. Whether teaching is a practice in itself or a feature of other practices has been much debated (MacIntyre & Dunne, 2002; Carr, 2003; Dunne, 2003; Hogan, 2003; McLaughlin, 2003; Haynes, 2004), and it seems evident that MacIntyre's claim that teaching is not itself a practice, but 'a set of skills and habits put to the service of a variety of practices' (2002, p. 9), falls under scrutiny. MacIntyre's analysis revolves around using 'teaching' to refer to the act of teaching. In this book the term 'a teaching activity' or 'engaging in teaching activities' has been used when referring only to this aspect of teaching. However, teaching is more than the sum of many individual teaching activities and encompasses the whole enterprise of teaching (Haynes, 2004, p. 5), which is wider than the aggregated sum of a number of teaching activities. There are a number of ways in which a practice of teaching can be conceived and described and the particular way chosen at any time depends on the purpose one has for so choosing (ibid., p. 6).

Carr has pertinently commented on this issue that one reason why it is hard to get a clear view of the nature of teaching as a practice

> is because a certain tendency to construe teaching in the latter sense of social or professional role obscures our vision of the wider non-institutional human and moral significance of both teaching and education.
>
> (Carr, 2003, p. 255)

It seems clear that teaching, in the wider, non-institutional and morally significant sense, is clearly a practice. Indeed, an individual teacher is likely to engage with and in several practices (McLaughlin, 2003). The different subjects of the curriculum may have different traditions, with different underlying conceptions, which determine judgements about what is taught and how to teach. Teaching history is not like teaching design and technology in this respect. A vivid example may be teaching astrology or astronomy. There are different goods in various conceptions of teaching, so for example, a teacher of French may be a member of a subject association such as the Association of Language Learners, serve on an LEA language working party, take part in an internet chat group about Marcel Pagnol, each of which may embody different conceptions of the teaching of French in England. To these we may add her membership of a professional association, such as the National Union of Teachers, and a Teacher Development Agency sponsored work group on the National Literacy Strategy, each with a particular body of expertise and beliefs.

These different groupings to which the French teacher belongs may each represent a community of practice, which Wenger defines as social structures in reference to a mutual engagement in a common practice. Wenger notes the importance of communities of practice in creating a *communal memory* that 'allows individuals to do their work without needing to know everything' (Wenger, 1998, p. 46). He has usefully identified what he calls three domains of communities of practice, the *domain* of knowledge, the *community* of people within the practice and the *practice* that they are developing (Wenger, 1998). In the community domain, members build trust and personal relationships, and encourage their willingness to help and share ideas. Some members are referred to as experts, through the establishment of formal or informal roles. The way in which these roles based on the relationship of trust might facilitate or enable teacher professional workplace learning is discussed in Chapter 6. A community of practice develops propositional knowledge about the practice as well as procedural knowledge. Novices are able to learn from within the practice with the aid of experts.

> The continuous *participation, reification* and *negotiation of meaning* between the core and the peripheral groups, helps for the legitimisation of the community's roles and practices. These practices are being developed in order for the members to be effective in the community's domain, and they include all the information, codified knowledge, tools, language, style, and stories that the community members share.
>
> (Paprgyris & Poulymenakou, 2004)

Dewey's account of the development of tools in industry, discussed in the previous chapter, foregrounds Wenger's conception, which is useful in understanding how teachers may be embedded in a tradition or mode of working, relating to pedagogy such as a formal or informal learning, and also participate in a variety of communities of practice, such as a subject specialist group. These embedded contexts inform the development and exercise of practical judgement. It is also true that holding certain concepts makes certain experiences possible. If a particular practice is conceived in a particular way, which is passed on from expert to novice, a particular conception of the practice is imbibed. This means that the kind of ITET which trainee teachers pursue creates in some sense a 'self-fulfilling prophecy', since trainees' beliefs are affected by what they expect to discover. ITET should, as far as possible, leave doors open to alternative interpretations about what constitutes good teaching. (Implications are developed in subsequent chapters, mentoring in Chapter 6, teacher research in Chapter 7 and assessment in Chapter 8).

Phronesis Revisited

It is useful now to summarise some notable aspects of practical judgement as they have emerged in this chapter. Practical judgement manifests flexibility of response and is based on the practitioner's knowledge and understanding. This knowledge and understanding has developed within a particular set of embedded contexts; is experienced by a particular individual; is underpinned by that individual's values, dispositions and qualities and draws on propositional and procedural knowledge. Practical judgement seamlessly brings together 'human reasoning, will, and emotion: cognitive, conative and emotive capacities of humans are all typically involved in workplace judgements' (Hager, 2000, p. 289).

> *Phronesis* ... has developed an "eye" (Aristotle) or a "nose" (Wittgenstein) for what is salient in concrete situations. The *phronimos* does not, indeed, lack knowledge of universals ... The crucial thing about *phronesis*, however, is its attunement of the universal knowledge and the techniques to the particular occasion.
>
> (Dunne, 1993, p. 368)

Teachers need to develop and exercise practical judgement. The second part of the chapter considers how practical judgement develops through experience and builds on this consideration, in order to determine how ITET might encourage and facilitate its development.

The Development of Judgement through Experience

The notion of practical judgement is required to account for how practitioners operate fluently, in situations of complexity and unpredictability. Experience is personal to each individual. Consequently we are not neutral observers of our experience but bring to it conative, affective and evaluative factors. We are constantly interacting with what is being experienced. Our experience is '*of* as well as *in* nature' (Dewey, 1958, p. 10). We are situated within what we experience and 'feel' it in certain contingent ways, dependent on ourselves, which is not to say that there is no outside world capable of being experienced by other people.

Individual qualities, dispositions and values play a role in the development and exercise of judgement. Two different people might experience differently what appears to be the same situation according to their own memories and the feelings invoked by the situation. An example might be that of two sisters watching a toddler playing, who have two different 'takes' on what is happening. An elder sister looking at the baby has a positive view of the toddler playing, construes the toddler as 'confident', coloured by feelings coming from childhood memories of her own younger sister at a similar age and in similar circumstances. The younger sister's feelings are different, stemming from a childhood in which conflict with the older sister over toys and her unequal strength was prevalent. The younger sister's 'idea' of the toddler is different from her sister's and she construes the toddler as anxious and vulnerable. Clearly the two may behave differently to the toddler, since they are in a sense viewing a somewhat different small person. The implications for teaching are direct, in that how we view a pupil can have specific repercussions on the pupils' learning as well as more general repercussions for both the teacher and the pupil.

The way we experience things is in part determined by our memories, cognitions, affections, beliefs and values. There is no direct, unmediated experience. Significantly, since experiences are personal even if there were a body of standardised knowledge about good teacher behaviour, it could not be passed on in the form of a technical manual. Each teacher experiences her place of work or study through her own meaning-making. These personal experiences are the ground on which practical judgement builds and is connected to action.

How does practical judgement build up through experiences of teaching and learning about teaching? Rockwell, quoting work by Gibson, draws attention to the concept of 'affordances'. He describes driving a car as follows:

> What we experience is not shapes and colours, or even objects, but specific opportunities for driving action: the field of safe travel, the minimum stopping zone, the distance required to reach from the brake to the clutch. Each of these fields is called an affordance, because it affords an opportunity for a specific kind of action ... The network of affordances that defines our relationship to our world is constituted by opportunities to utilise 'knowing-how' skills and abilities.
>
> (Rockwell, 2001)

Rockwell extends Gibson's concept of 'affordances' to include not only skills and abilities but also goals and emotions. On this interpretation, to see something as 'an affordance' might in some cases be to see it as potentially useful for some purpose. This conception is not far-fetched. In experiencing, something is happening to and hence being experienced by, an individual, sentient human being: experiences do not take place in a void. In developing a sense of skilful adjustment to complexity, the whole person is involved, including motivation, aims and emotional elements[4]. For example, in a French lesson, a teacher became annoyed by a pupil's continual calling out while the class was doing a listening exercise. In the affordance of the moment she reacted seemingly intuitively; stopped her tape and scolded the pupil, using an acceptable register of annoyance that parents speaking French might address to their own child. She accompanied this with appropriately exaggerated gestures of annoyance. Although play-acting for the purposes of managing the situation, in reality she *was* annoyed, and the vocalisation was 'authentic'. Using 'authentic' language is a foundational, recommended pedagogic tool for teaching a foreign language. Unexpectedly, in an end-of-term oral test the pupil in question remembered very little of the taught language content of the term, but did remember and accurately repeat much of the utterance of annoyance to him. (This reinforces the importance of engaging with the pupils' own experience when teaching).

Teaching thrives on affordances, for example when a child asks a question out of personal curiosity and the teacher harnesses it to an explanation relating to a particular point. The teacher is dynamically engaged, seizes the unpredictable pedagogical moment. In this sense 'teaching contains elements of manipulation' (Smith, 2003. p. 489). Teacher educators can also train or educate new teachers into creating situations where affordances emerge, such as for example getting new teachers to ask open-ended questions, to draw on pupils' personal responses.

The concept of affordances is a useful one in the context of how practical judgement is developed in teaching. Rockwell gives an interesting example of someone driving a car.

> If we recall that no one ever drives a car unless she plans to go somewhere, and no one goes somewhere unless she has a reason, we see there is no reason to stop the structuring principle of affordances at the level of simple motions like walking and balancing. The act of driving is itself an affordance to getting somewhere, and so on ...
> If we extrapolate to the higher cognitive and/or experiential functions that are the subject matter of epistemology ... we end up with something very much like Dewey's concept of experience.
>
> (ibid.)

Having established that experience is personal and builds upon previous experience we can accept that knowing how to do something is related to the process of experiencing 'by being the reservoir of previous experiencings that "fund" the current engagement between the self and the world' (Daly, 2002). As these experiences build up, we develop knowledge of what works and what does not in certain situations. We also develop the concept of what would count for something to work. Judgement is the capacity to initiate a response which is 'fit for purpose', the right thing to do or to refrain from doing in the lived moment. Reflection-on-action is important to the development of judgement because it enables evaluation of experiences, which can change future actions. Experiences also 'fund' the development of habits, which may form a part of the repertoire of responses on which a professional can draw.

The examples and discussion so far leads us to understand that judgement develops from experience, which has been reflected upon, and that values, emotion and cognition are involved. The subject of any experience, the doer, thinker, or participator, acts and reacts, responds and initiates within the experience, bringing aspects of former experience, which condition, inform and help to direct her present experienced moment.

> If we see that knowing is not the act of an outside spectator but of a participator inside the natural and social scene then the true object of knowledge resides in the consequences of directed action.
>
> (Dewey, 1960, p. 196)

The last chapter suggested that the notion of *operational definitions* is helpful to conceptualising this individual participation in the construction of procedural knowledge (KH), which develops experientially, through the connections between cognitive and emotive factors, made by the subject of the experience. The two sisters in the earlier example had different experiences. It could be said that they connected the variables of the given physical and psychological situation in different ways. Their 'operational connections' were different and we could say that each sister constructed a different meaning, or (using Dewey's term again) that they had different 'ideas' about the toddler:

> the *consequences* of these operations establishes connectivity within concrete experience. *Connection is instituted through operations which define ideas.*
>
> (ibid., 126)

We might say with Lipton (1991) that 'to judge is to judge relationships, either by discovering relationships or by inventing them'
(p. 16). One feature of the discovery of relationships is that the individual makes specific connections, or in Dewey's term, establishes
some *operational relations.* So happening *x,* may be experienced in
relation to happening *y.* From these relationships an idea for future
action may be suggested, as in the example in the previous chapter about new understandings developing, or Dewey's example of
the development of tools in industry. Moreover, a rung in the ladder of habit may be built, thereby aiding reinforcement about what
is a pertinent course of action, in what may be perceived as similar
circumstances in the future. A significant factor here is that the connections are made by an individual in a specific situation. We will
look now at the notion of intelligence as a further step to understand
how connections made in experienced situations might lead to the
development of practical judgement.

'*Intelligence*' and Judgement

'Intelligence' has been widely debated as a concept in philosophy,
for example by Ryle (1949, 1974), Skemp (1979), Sternberg (1990)
and Collier (1994). The particular meaning of the term in what follows in this chapter is the Deweyan sense of 'intelligence', following
the discussion on experimental empiricism in the previous chapter.
Dewey's concept of 'intelligence' is pivotal to his conception of practical knowledge and understanding (Ratner, 1939; Boisvert, 1988;
Garrison, 1997; Stengel, 1998).

For Dewey, an individual uses 'intelligence' in her interaction with
the environment, through 'intelligent action'. In this sense 'intelligence' is a kind of dispositional concept for Dewey, as it is for Ryle.
Fluency in operational complexity could be called *intelligent action.*
The operation of practical judgement is, in this sense, founded on
intelligent action. We have established in Chapter 3 that well-grounded
reflection is important to developing know-how. Well-grounded
reflection involves a number of individual, contingent, personal
factors, such as motivation, motives, values, aims and purposes,
and emotional responses. Well-grounded reflection follows reliable

criteria and leads to new and productive understandings, capable of generating new action. It is the bedrock of the growth of practical judgement. Well-grounded reflection is a function of 'intelligence'.

> Intelligence . . . is associated with judgement; that is, with selection and arrangement of means to effect consequences . . . In the large sense of the term, intelligence is as practical as reason is theoretical.
>
> (Dewey, 1960, p. 245)

'Intelligence' underlies fluency of response, where a number of operational relations are perceived and a course of action is embarked upon. What, for Dewey, are the characteristics of 'intelligent action'? First, it is 'personal' in that it is necessarily heuristic and involves choices, for example about actions and methods followed. Secondly, it is 'reasonable': it is not random or capricious but relies on some kind of basis for validity, as outlined in the discussion on experimental empiricism in the previous chapter. Therefore, the outcomes of 'intelligent action' are reliable and trustworthy. For example, if I try to think through a dilemma in a rage I am liable to be swayed by emotion and unable to fulfil the second criterion for intelligent action. Any reactions may well not be 'intelligent'. If in this situation a friend helps me to calm down and 'see reason', I may follow rational processes more reliably. Although still engaged on my own personal problem I may employ 'intelligence' to elucidate ways forward. The two characteristics of the personal and the reasonable need to be fulfilled in order for 'intelligent action' to ensue. The application of 'intelligence' is akin to judgement here:

> Events are viewed in their connections . . . as the consequence of a cumulative integration of complex interactions.
>
> (Dewey, 1960, p. 247)

The interpreting subject, exercising 'intelligence' in the affordances of the moment, builds on a fund of previous experience. The exercise of 'intelligence' is key to the development of KH. Using the concept of 'intelligence' in this Deweyan sense is not limited to discussions about KH but is applicable to the wider dimensions of wisdom in judgement. Winch and Gingell, drawing on Ryle (1974) have stated, in a discussion about how individuals use propositional knowledge:

> It is not ... propositional knowledge which shows intelligence, but rather knowing how to organise such facts that you do command, so for instance, someone with few facts at their fingertips may deal with these more intelligently than someone who knows many such facts.
>
> (Winch & Gingell, 2004, p. 41)

Individuals exercise 'intelligent action' dispositionally when these 'intelligent' connections are made.

So far the discussion has assumed that intelligent action functions to develop judgement and underlie the exercise of judgement in a non-problematic way. We turn now to look at situations in which someone cannot act with 'intelligent', operational fluidity. Such situations are often the bedrock of further development of practical judgement.

Problematic Situations

What we do when things go wrong to keep working through difficult situations seems to me crucial to the exercise of practical judgement. The experience of blockage and setback is as much a formative experience as success in teaching and Dewey's 'logic of inquiry' can usefully add to our understanding of the growth of professional know-how in problematic situations. Dewey's description of 'the logic of inquiry' is now introduced, with three caveats for the reader. First, Dewey describes 'three phases of inquiry' and these should not be interpreted as logically separate steps, which would leave 'inquiry' open to criticisms such as those raised by McLaughlin (1999), which were discussed in Chapter 3. There it was argued that Dewey intended the phases of inquiry to be taken as a flow, in which the stages are not discretely separated. The second caveat concerns the term 'knowledge' in the citations used below. As in the previous chapter relating to Dewey's lack of distinctive terms for KT and KH 'knowledge' in what follows is interpreted as KH. Any problematic questions about interpretations of KT are left aside, as not of immediate concern to the discussion. The third concerns the application of the term 'inquiry', which is used only in the specific sense of referring to problematic situations, as explained below.

In examining the experiential nature of judgement Dewey describes the occurrence of a disabling problematic situation, which ends in an enabling understanding of what to do next, in new 'know-how'. This examination of troubling situations is useful:

> According to the pattern set by the practice of knowing, knowledge is the fruit of the undertakings that transform a problematic situation into a resolved one.
>
> (Dewey, 1960, pp. 242–43)[5]

Inquiry is a useful concept in the context of perplexity, when something is not working and needs reconsidering or adjustments need to be made to what one is doing. In the first phase of inquiry, someone experiences herself to be in a problematic situation, with a sense of being 'pulled up short' or 'hitting the buffers', aware that she is not able to operate as she normally does: the flow of her actions is interrupted, requiring 'something to be done'. In the second phase she recognises what has troubled the instinctual behaviour and caused her to be 'pulled up short'. Dewey's formula is that 'cognitive elements enter into the process as a response to precognitive maladjustment' (Dewey, 1991, pp. 108–22). In this phase she takes cognisance of what the problem is. There are many possible ways in which she could 'read' the situation. She will only be able to isolate a few of these possible interpretations, such is the nature of cognition within the fleeting and constantly changing moments of phenomena (Sartre, 1938; Heidegger, 1962). Her 'reading' or 'interpretation' of the experience of being 'pulled up short', is the basis on which she subsequently operates. How she determines 'what her problem is' becomes a basis for the last phase, in which she is able to extract ideas, suppositions, theories, and muse on these as hypothetical solutions to the 'blockage'. These readings, or interpretations of the situation can occur seemingly spontaneously while still actively engaged in the situation, in which case the adjustments are akin to biofeedback. This may be what Schön was trying to explicate with his notion of 'reflection-in-action'. The readings or interpretations of the situations can also be at one remove, such as when analysing a problematic situation while not actually in it. This is more akin to Schön's 'reflection-on-action' accepted as a useful term and discussed in Chapter 3.

Dewey's account might seem to imply that any expert physical activity, such as an acrobat on a wire constantly making adjustments as she walks, involves conscious thought about what to do next, but this is to misread Dewey. The acrobat on the wire is not going through any explicit cognitive, logical thinking. Dewey's view of 'inquiry' is largely an attempt to describe a flow of experience and a concurrent flow of cognisant moments, in which the subject is adjusting to experience 'instinctively', involving a biofeedback mechanism. So, although Dewey broke down the process into what looked like discrete stages, it is an error to view this breakdown as anything other than a conceptual device to aid comprehension, as in the paradox of Zeno. As we saw in Chapter 4 some critics have taken him to mean that there are literally discrete stages between moments of adjustment within action. This cannot be the case, since it does not correspond to how we act seemingly instinctively. We do not need to think about walking in order to walk and if we do think about where to put our feet we may stumble.

Conclusion

Teaching takes place within a complex environment. Teaching is a complex activity. Teaching is also a practical activity for which specific procedural knowledge (KH) is required. KH builds up through experience. Being able to learn from experience and change and improve is crucial to being a good teacher. Experience is necessarily an individual 'possession'. Aspects can be described and conceptualised but each individual teacher has to integrate her experiences in the classroom with her experiences of mediated pedagogy, including theoretical elements. Reflection, when it is well-grounded, and 'inquiry' when problematic situations are encountered in action, aid and support the development and exercise of professional knowledge and understanding. The ability to undertake some kind of well-grounded reflection enables the 'operational variables' to be meaningfully related so that they may generate a repertoire of useful teaching activities and responses. Flexibility in response to change and complexity are key characteristics of good teachers because of the non-routinisable dynamic of teaching X to Y. Teaching is not a formulaic activity.

As the novice teacher develops into an accomplished professional she develops more and more successful and fluent ways of dealing with operational complexity. Practical judgement develops from a buildup of habits, 'funded' through 'affordances' and is both driven by, and mediated through, values, aims and purposes. Practical judgement as manifested in teaching is made possible through 'intelligent action' in situations of operational complexity. Practical judgement is exercised by someone acting wisely, and involves more than mere 'effectiveness' in one particular area. It is based on personal qualities and dispositions, on the possession of procedural knowledge (KH) and propositional knowledge (KT). Standards-based practice (SBM) defines good teacher knowledge and understanding in a number of descriptive statements of varying import and range. Wise judgement seems to entail KT and KH on a wider and deeper level than is definable in the standards-based model. It involves the wisdom gained through experience, reflection and understanding. With such judgement, one's actions draw upon an internal, personal source of knowledge and understanding, based on cognitive, emotional and evaluative factors. Practical judgement enables someone to act competently, appropriately and wisely, but it is contingent. Practical judgement cannot deliver the perfect action, reaction or response. Fallibility is built into the individual nature of the exercise of practical judgement.

The next chapter considers how the development of practical judgement might be supported on school-based placements.

Notes

1. Hager (2000) has usefully characterised some of the salient features of practical judgement operating within specific situations.

2. The technique is well explained in the Director's Commentary to the film, *Gosford Park* (Altman, 2002).
3. Hansen quotes from Dewey's, *Theory of the Moral Life*, p. 125.
4. Although philosophers have long been sceptical about connectivist theory it is worth noting that some experimental psychologists maintain there to be a valid body of evidence for experience as the fundamental basis of 'knowing how'. Shusterman (1994), for example, on the conditioning of behaviour through 'habits and purposes' and Rockwell (2001). This evidence suggests that both sensations and thoughts, knowing-how and knowing-that, are constituted by processes that are essentially the same and essentially linguistic and propositional. It seems to offer evidence that experience is constituted by the kind of skilful coping, knowing-how, operating independently of the subject's ability to put any thoughts into words, comparable to intuition, the unconscious exercise of judgement, or an effortless adjusting to the moment.
5. Dewey may be suggesting that all knowledge creation results from the transformation of a problematic situation, but this is not directly relevant here.

Chapter 6

Mentoring

A key process that supports the development of practical judgement in learning to teach is mentoring, specifically through the mentee engaging in a grounded reflection on practice. Mentoring involves the practice of a particular kind of 'disinterested' dialogue, in the course of which the mentor exercises practical judgement and helps to develop it in the mentee. It follows that mentoring does not involve the mentor handing down judgements on the trainee's practice[1]. The mentoring process can help to initiate the trainee into teaching and to develop the trainee's knowledge and understanding, which the trainee can then articulate to a certain degree, as she develops a 'language of practice'. The ways in which this process works is in some sense continuous with the ways in which children learn the language of their communities and in the process develop as 'social selves'. The chapter will give examples of practical judgement in action, both that of the trainee and the mentor. The mentor has a certain understanding, which the mentee needs to develop, about the meanings of various aspects of the teaching, when put into practice, which could be described as a:

> sense of relative values or perspective: a sort of scale by which we can appreciate the relative worth and significance of things ... for when we come to practical life it is not merely knowing that two and two make four which counts, it is putting together this two with that other two; in other words, the ability to size things up at their right value.
>
> (Dewey, 1990, p. 337)

The mentoring dialogue develops shared understandings about the meanings of that practice, through a collaborative exchange.

School-based mentoring in ITET is largely a result of the rise of school-based training and has a wide literature to support its merits (for example Calderhead, 1991; Barrett et al., 1992; Earley & Kinder, 1994; DfES, 2002a). A large-scale literature review reported in Oliver and Aggleton (2002)[2]. raised issues from recent research on mentoring across a range of professional settings, including teaching, nursing, medicine and social work. Different models of mentoring and their potential relevance to the professional development of practitioners emerged. The review team posited four main types of existing literature:

> First, there are studies examining the application of mentoring in specific fields. Few of these contain a clear description of methodology and fewer still are comparative in design. Second, there are descriptive accounts of mentoring in practice. Here, the context of the work is usually described, as well as the approach to mentoring adopted. Third, there are a large number of accounts, written in a journalistic style, of what mentoring should, or might, be about: many of these have been written by trainers and management consultants. Fourth, there is a growing number of practical guides and manuals on how to set up a mentoring scheme and how to be a mentor.
>
> (Oliver & Aggleton, 2002, p. 32)

The reviewers found an 'uneven level of development of the literature on mentoring in the different professional fields under discussion'. Mentoring in education has a wide literature, which is under-theorised from a philosophical perspective.

Oliver and Aggleton trace three 'rather distinct models of mentoring' in teaching, using Maynard and Furlong's formulation of 'the apprenticeship model; the competency model, and the reflective practitioner model' (Maynard & Furlong, 1995, p. 17). Taking these models in turn the apprenticeship model, in which teacher apprentices work alongside and 'emulate' the behaviour of expert teachers, was current in England a century ago (Thomas, 1990; Gardner, 1996). This model may be adequate for a transmission model of education, in which rote learning forms a major part; the development of pupils' independent powers of reasoning is of little importance, or the primary emphasis is on the development of technical skills, but it cannot be appropriate to teaching. Two current routes to qualified teacher status (QTS) allow trainees to undertake their training wholly in the workplace, through a form of apprenticeship: the School Centred Initial Teacher Training Schemes (SCITTs) and the Graduate Training Scheme (GTS) and it is possible to gain QTS through these schemes with very little engagement with theoretical elements found on most HEI-based ITET courses. This model does not match the ITET partnership model in the account given in this chapter.

Maynard and Furlong's second mentoring model, the competency model, deserves some consideration because competencies were the forerunner of today's standards-based QTS assessment. We saw in Chapter 2 that standards fail to capture adequately all that is involved in being a good teacher. Nevertheless, as suggested in that chapter, the standards *attempt* to conceptualise good teaching as a complex, normative practice. This attempt is illustrated by the fact that the standards contain references to values, attitudes and dispositions. They function differently from competency statements and a mentor currently working within the parameters of teacher training in England and Wales does not have to work within a narrowly defined competency context. This is not to say that all mentors recognise the complexity of their practice. Some mentors do work reductively, treating the standards narrowly, using standards trackers as if taken from a technical manual. While this is a danger, there seems to be no evidence of anyone currently advocating a competency model *per se.*

Maynard and Furlong's third mentoring model, the reflective practice model, is promising as a basis for elaborating an account of the role and function of mentoring in the development of teacher knowledge and understanding. Mentoring takes place within the relationship between mentor and a mentee. The concept of the practitioner able to engage in well-grounded reflection needs to be joined with the concept of the dialogical relationship between mentor and mentee, which is the subject of the next section of the chapter.

Mentoring as a Relationship

Mentoring another person is essentially a dialogical experience. Like teaching and learning, one needs two people, one 'doing the mentoring' and one 'being mentored'. (Admittedly it is possible to utter the sentence 'I was my own mentor', but this would be an unusual use of the term). The dialogical nature of the mentor and mentee relationship mirrors to some extent the way in which each individual develops knowledge and understanding from infancy. There are differences between the general developmental context and that of mentoring, in that mentoring exists within a professional practice or set of practices, whereas the self develops from infancy within the social spheres of the infant's first relationships. However, mentoring is highly compatible with very general notions about how we develop as persons. We discover who we are in a fundamental and ontologically primal manner, through dialogical relations. We may discover who we are as teachers through similar dialogical relationships and so the processes underlying the development of self are also relevant to the development of the teacher-self.

Relationships and the Self

Turning first to the general developmental context, an infant engages in developing a concept of self, in interaction with others, from her earliest moment (Mead, 1934; Quarantelli & Cooper, 1966; Mischel, 1977). Babies develop a sense of the meanings of things in a particular, pre-verbal way. Meanings for a baby are pre-verbal, in that a person who is interacting with a baby responds to a baby's movements or sounds. In so responding the person engaged with the baby interprets the baby's gestures as communicative, and through the feedback given to the baby, reinforces or develops a meaning. So gestures, such as are made through eye contact, body movements, variety of voice response, become vehicles for meaning. The baby learns 'the meaning' of each gesture in the context in which the gesture is experienced. There are many physiological and biologically determined 'meanings', for example human beings in all cultures laugh and cry in similar circumstances. There are also many culturally determined 'meanings'. For example, a child eating certain foods with her fingers in one culture is seen as eating 'properly', whereas in another she is reprimanded for bad table manners. 'Meanings' of a great many gestures that are offered to a baby might be said to be social property, given that they are shared meanings. Through the build up of a communicative, interactive relationship the child is 'socialised' (Richards, 1974). The child could be said to be initiated into the practices of inter-personal communication within a particular social group, which is likely to be some kind of family group initially, widening out to other social contexts as the child grows. (See also Mead, 1934, pp. 76, 81; Quanterelli & Cooper, 1966, McCall, 1977.)

The communicative process develops through an interactivity of 'organism and environment' until the child has developed 'the social context of language' (Mead, 1934, pp. 46–47). This does not imply that a baby cannot develop any sense of what things mean without a dialogical interaction with another, but cases of 'wild children' and severely deprived children show us what it means to develop without language development opportunities (Graff, 1999).

Language develops within a social context, as a child learns how a 'language function' is used and begins to experiment with it in communication with others. Precisely how this occurs and how to conceptualise it is the subject of ongoing controversy in sociolinguistic and linguistic research (Carter & Sealey, 2000; Naigles, 2002). The role of language in the development of a child's sense of her social self is not, however, in dispute. As Elliot (1981) has shown, the young child who is learning language in interaction with others is also 'developing on all fronts, not just the linguistic one, and is trying to make sense of his social environment and the world of objects around him, as well as of his linguistic input'. The development of language relates to 'other cognitive and social kinds of knowledge, which changes during development' (pp. 37–38). We might even go so far as to say that 'there is little justification in assuming that language has independent existence for the young child', in isolation from development as a social being' (ibid., p. 37). Once the infant begins to speak, language takes a key role in the interaction of the developing self in relationship with others. For example a child learning to use the personal pronouns,

'I', 'me' and 'you' is learning about the relationships in the network of persons around her:

> Personal pronouns are not learnt as referential atomic names, but rather as a system for which mutuality of person recognition is a necessary condition.
>
> (Harré, 1977, p. 340)

When we observe an infant's developing understanding of the use of all the pronouns, *I*, *me* and *you*, as well as all the other personal pronouns, we witness a 'revelation of a theory of the social word as grammar' (Torode, 1976, p. 87. See also pp. 88–97).

Being initiated into the social world is to learn 'referential intersubjectivity' (Bruner, 1983, pp. 27, 122). Bruner describes how initially children do not understand the difference between their own mental activity and the separate thinking and being of others, but even very young infants have communicative intentions which they try to clarify through constant and repeated negotiations. I have observed this myself recently when a young child was given a toy and heard the phrase 'here you are'. The child asked for objects with an approximation of the phrase, and the adults repeated the 'game' many times. She then took her refined approximation of the phrase to another child and was rewarded with understanding and the required toy. Bruner says that such interactions are a form of negotiation and that over time they lead to the development of more complex communication and then to recognisable linguistic 'procedures'. Language learning consists not only of learning grammar, but 'of realising one's intentions in the appropriate use of that grammar' (Bruner, 1983, p. 38).

The Dialogical Self in Adults

The concept of the dialogical self in adults has been well explored and established in research in developmental psychology (Fogel et al., 2002). In philosophy the concept of the dialogical self appears in the work of Mead (1934) and the pragmatists, and also Buber (1958) and Levinas (1969). It can be said that the transactional self exists in 'webs of interlocution' (Taylor, 1989, p. 36). Goffman has shown that developmental social psychology supports the view that human beings from a very early age form 'webs' (Goffman, 1971). This notion has been analysed in detail from multiple perspectives[3].

The self develops through interaction with others and is inherently social, and in possessing a language one possesses a particular insight into the culture of that language, since language inherently carries and embodies culture. In this sense we could say that 'I define who I am by defining where I speak from' (Taylor, 1989, p. 35). As discussed in the previous chapter we could also say that I have become who I am, holding certain specific values and beliefs, through my participation in various communities of practice (Lave & Wenger, 1991). It is now generally recognised that language plays a key role in learning, in the sense that it is the medium in which the learning and teaching of almost all school subjects is carried out (DES, 1975). Also, language embodies and carries 'culture'. Language is not culturally neutral in this sense (Goodman, 1987; Wells, 2004).

As inherently social beings, interacting through language and gesture we enter the various communities of practice of our environs. The baby learns to talk through the interaction of another person who is alert to the construction of meaning with and for the baby. This is an example of what Vygotsky has termed the 'zone of proximal development' a 'zone' where someone is able to develop further with the help of someone else, than she could on her own:

> the distance between the actual developmental level as determined by independent problem solving and the level of potential development as determined through problem solving under adult guidance, or in collaboration with more capable peers.
>
> (Vygotsky, 1978, p. 86)

In summary then, the process of mentoring seems to be analogous in a general sense to the way we develop as persons. The analogy is not a total fit in that we discover who we are on a general plain in social situations, dialogically. In being tutored by a mentor we discover who we are as teachers. We are embedded in a professional practice. Nevertheless the fundamental dialogical processes, which work in mentoring, are ones with which we are familiar and comfortable. In a sense we are 'programmed' for learning through dialogical processes.

Mentoring As Co-Construction of the Meaning of Practice

It follows from the foregoing that a mentor may fulfil an important role for the new teacher's development of productive understandings. The process of working through one's understandings with another person is an important way of learning. It may be possible for some people to come to these kinds of understanding on their own. A new teacher may learn to teach through trial and error or through watching others, without any professional discussion of the meaning of what has been observed. However, the impact of interaction with a more experienced and skilled person, can help the new teacher to understand her experience and to develop her capacities as a teacher, and it mirrors the paradigmatic examples of learning noted above, in which relationships are fundamental. Indeed, an investigation into teacher education in all the countries in the present European Union, and in countries seeking to join the expanded Europe, found that for successful teacher development:

> the rhetoric of institutional partnership should not obscure the fact that we are essentially talking about a series of relationships whose strengths derive from the day-to-day exchanges of all the participants.
>
> (Stephenson, 2000, p. 24)

Boud et al. (1985) call the professional dialogue about practice 'a learning conversation' and point out that the mentoring relationship often begins with someone talking over his or her ideas with another person, using the other person as a 'sounding board'. They have usefully conceived the 'learning conversation' as:

> a form of dialogue about a learning experience in which the learner reflects on some event or activity in the past. Ultimately, it is intended that people will internalise such conversations so that

they are able to review learning experiences systematically for themselves, but at the beginning, the learning conversation is carried out
with the assistance of a teacher or tutor ... it is a dialogue on the
process of learning; the learner reflects on his or her learning with
the assistance of a teacher or tutor.

> (Boud et al., 1985, p. 92)

There are likely to be stages in the 'learning conversation', as the
mentor and mentee share the practice through their contextualised
dialogue, the quality or nature of this dialogue is likely to change. A
model might be that:

first there is the intervention point, the 'mirroring' or feedback
which needs to be specific, behavioural and non-interpretative.
Then the trainer has to deal with the emotional context of the
learning, building up a supportive relationship which helps the
learner through the period of trauma and disintegration of skills.
Finally, the teacher or trainer helps the learner to articulate the
new dimensions of quality. The learner needs to identify referents
with which he or she can identify – significant others, peers or professional groups; this can provide the learner with new standards
against which to measure performance.

> (Boud et al., 1985, p. 92)

It is to be hoped that trainees on teaching practice do go through a
learning process in which they are able to understand and put into
practice what might make their teaching better, and as Boud says
be able to 'articulate the new dimensions of quality'. It is important
too that new teachers integrate within their communities of practice,
so the final comment in the citation also seem reasonable, in the light
of the discussion in Chapter 5, although the language of standards
and performance jars. Crucially, the learning conversation needs to
be based on the mentee's experience. Good mentors find ways to
come to the learner from the learner's perspective because as we
have seen earlier, cognitive and affective factors influence learning.
Therefore in mentoring as in teaching mentors need to start from the
person's own experience, so that the mentee can begin to understand
the parameters and dimensions of the experience.

As we concluded at the end of Chapter 2 on the QTS standards, some *a priori* categories might be useful as approximate descriptors of good practice. The mentor could find such descriptors helpful in articulating expectations and defining areas for discussion and further exploration. These descriptors can be seen to function as a means of engagement in the learning conversation, not as final descriptors of what good practice is. What is important is that these descriptors do not have a fixed set of 'meanings'. In this sense they are not like the Kantian *a priori* categories, or the Chomskian view of language acquisition as relying on a hard wire programming for 'grammar' (Chomsky, 1965). Given the experiential nature of learning, it is prudent to understand that any descriptor of good teaching practice or of any particular practice is provisional, being socially constructed and imposed.

The process by which learning comes about in mentoring involves a collaborative elaboration of the meanings of the practice. Tips, rules and maxims may be useful in structuring the dialogue and providing points of reference, but they do not and cannot function as *a priori* categories of how good teaching is achieved. Techniques for achieving aspects of good teaching only support the development of practical judgement if put into context and if there is the possibility of reflecting on their application.

Strategies are often translated into 'rules' or into folk wisdom, such as 'don't smile before Christmas', meaning 'assert authority first and then establish a friendly relationship with the class'. While it is true that such strategies may work without much or any reflection or examination, they carry no guarantee of success. There may well be times when such strategies do not have the desired effect, or are difficult to apply. The teacher needs to be able to explore what 'went wrong', what factors intervened to prevent the smooth application of the advice. One way of doing this is for the mentor and the mentee to discuss what happened from their own perspectives, with a view to understanding the perspectives of the other participant. After this they might develop a joint understanding of what happened and why. From this point, strategies for more successful teacher behaviour may be discovered and later applied, to be later discussed. In this sense, a good mentoring relationship is not one of a master and an apprentice in the traditional sense of these terms, the one imparting technical knowledge and the other learning how to apply it. We have already considered in Chapter 3 why this version of 'technical rationality' (Schön, 1983) does not fit the development of teacher knowledge and understanding, which needs to be based on the mentee's experience and to arise from a co-construction of meaning, in the way conceptualised by Freire, as a critical analysis of a 'real or concrete context' which:

> involves the exercise of abstraction, through which, by means of representations of concrete reality, we seek knowledge of that reality. The instrument for this abstraction in our methodology is codification, or representation of the existential situations of the learners.
>
> (Freire, 1972, p. 31)

In this case the existential situation of the learners is their experience of their classroom practice and the codification is the development of interpretations of how particular principles may be applied to the actual situation of the mentee. Articulation develops out of experience, through reflection, which can be aided to a large extent by good mentoring processes and practices. It follows that the mentee's experiences need to form the basis of the process of interpreting meanings, articulating practice. Freire has well encapsulated this requirement as 'the context of authentic dialogue between learners and educators as equally knowing subjects' (ibid., p. 32). Mentors do however have a broader perspective than the mentee and have a role to play in mediating external conceptualisations, but the two parties are 'equally knowing', in the sense that they both bring to the dialogue their own experience of what they discuss, through and on which they build a mutual comprehension, which is itself a conceptualisation.

The mentor and mentee co-construct the meaning of the practice in the sense that whatever is agreed between them includes later corrections of previous understandings. In other words, the construction of meanings is an on-going process. Meanings are not finalised, merely refined. The deepest insights are gained by co-construction, although with the proviso of some place for the mentor's direction of the discussion. So for example, if a teacher has unsuccessfully implemented various strategies in relation to behaviour management, she may *not* raise relevant questions with her mentor, such as which pupils did not respond to a particular intervention in the desired way. The teacher may not see those pupils' responses and any ensuing difficulties as problematic, in which case the mentor who was able to analyse the situation, would need to raise it herself, in order for the thread of the conversation to develop. The conversation would need to develop into analysing what went wrong. The advice in the strategy would need to be critically examined. Early in such a dialogue the question might be posed 'Was the advice put fully into place?' From here the mentor can go off in a number of directions, guided by the responses of the mentee. Various conclusions may be reached and it is not possible to stipulate in advance of any such mentoring conversation what these might be.

Some possibilities in this case are that both parties may agree that the advice was good but was inappropriately applied. They may decide on trying again to implement the advice, with additional understandings about possible contingencies. Alternatively, the mentor and mentee may disagree about the failure or otherwise to implement the advice. In this case the mentor who wishes to pursue the orderly management of lessons using the specific advice would need to find a way to come at the issue again. The point is that merely demanding that any particular strategy be implemented as it stands, without the mentee understanding why, will not lead to the mentee gaining a deep understanding of managing lessons such that her practical knowledge, her phronetic insight, is developed. A further outcome might be that the dialogue might take a different direction and the strategy itself might be called into question as a result of reflecting on the shared experience of trying to implement it, in the particular situation in question.

Elaborating a Language of Practice

We have seen how in the mentoring process mentors articulate what could be called the language of practice. What is true for the way human beings develop in relationships and develop a worldview through language, can be extended into understanding how the language of a practice develops and functions. 'The language of a practice' refers to the articulation of the practice through descriptions and analysis of the practice in a way that enables it to be communicated and beget future meanings. However, these meanings cannot be fully articulated, for three main reasons. First, the nature of the experience on which reflection and conversation pivots is complex, a function of many variables, and it is almost impossible for it to be completely recalled in memory. Only partial remembrances will occur. Secondly, these remembrances may be coloured by the emotional state of either of the reflectors in the dialogue. The affective domain is a significant determinant of what and how we remember events as was exemplified by the two siblings in the previous chapter. Thirdly, there are occasions when moral constraints impose a limitation on articulation, where the 'white lie' is actually 'the tact' of teaching (van Manen, 1991). A mentor may 'wrap up' what she says to a particular trainee teacher. Where any perceived shortcomings in the mentee's behaviour or understandings may rely in some way on the mentee's underlying qualities, the mentor may decide that this practice should be articulated incompletely, and only in the service of better teaching. For example, the trainee may be experiencing serious difficulties because the pupils do not like her, despite her sincere efforts to gain their confidence. The mentor may choose to 'wrap up' what is said in a less than accurate articulation of what the mentor believes to be the case in order to spare the trainee's feelings.

So the 'teaching conversation' is not a disinterested dialogue as one would expect to occur in a purely academic seminar for example. It is a dialogue governed by measures fit for that particular purpose, which include balancing articulation and solidarity. On some occasions the mentor may decide not to be explicit in her evaluation about something that the mentee needs to develop or change in order to spare the mentee's feelings. At other times the mentor may decide to be explicit. Discriminating between occasions when it may be appropriate to be tactful and when it is expedient to tackle a particular issue is a matter for practical judgement.

It is part of practical wisdom to know how to secure real benefits effectively; those who have practical wisdom will not make the mistake of concealing the hurtful truth from the person who really needs to know it in the belief that they are benefiting him.

(Hursthouse, 2003)

It may also be a matter of judgement for a mentor when to use a standard protocol and when to put it aside. The mentor needs to exercise judgement on the extent and pertinence of the standard protocol in relation to a particular mentee in a particular circumstance. Take the case of a trainee who does not follow the standard rules for how things should be done in the classroom but who has a natural ability to enthuse the pupils and excellent subject knowledge, through which the pupils pick up much of value and importance relating to the subject taught. Some mentors, in my experience, are prone to stick rigidly to the standard protocol and to view the mentee as a 'cause for concern' because she does not fit the 'standard' picture. Other mentors are able both to tolerate the mentee's lack of 'orthodoxy', and to use the standard protocol sensitively to try to enable the mentee to develop aspects of practice which the standard protocol advocates and which the mentor understands to be valuable and trustworthy. In such cases there is mutual trust and respect between the mentee and the mentor and this relationship of trust, supplemented by guidelines and parameters of accepted 'good practice' can help to develop the mentee's practice further. What makes one mentor able to act 'outside the box' and set aside the protocol may be a function of their own practice. A number of factors come into play. It is likely that the mentor is a comfortable 'risk taker' in her own teaching, able to take constructive criticism and is supported in this teaching behaviour through a favourable school culture[4].

Divergent Views

Generally it is through the mentor and trainee's dialogue that a common interpretation of the practice is created. This interpretation is clearly not a definitive account of the meaning of the experiences shared and explored. The mentor and the mentee may disagree, and this disagreement may range across a continuum from minor disagreement about an aspect of practice, to serious and far-reaching conflict of views. There can in fact be no definitive version of the truth in the case of two people interpreting their own experiences. It is more 'the fusion of horizons that takes place in understanding' (Gadamer, 1975, p. 273). As in textual analysis so in analysis of situations. In hermeneutic understanding the truth is to be found in the reading rather than in the text. The notion of textual interpretation is taken as analogous here with interpretation of the teaching situation or events in a mentoring process. When we research into the historical context of a literary text, or provide biographical details about the author we may have a context for understanding the text, but a person reading or hearing a text brings her own cognitive and affective 'baggage' to make a meaning. Texts might be said to 'speak' to the readers' or listeners' current situations. This does not mean that all interpretation of text or speech is purely subjective: the text itself will place limits on how we can understand it. In mentoring, the mentor may bring explanations taken from a standard protocol, which may illuminate the mentee's understanding of her practice, as biographical details may illuminate the reading of a text. However, the mentee undertakes a synoptic process in integrating this 'information' with his or her own experience of the teaching. Since we do work from our own individual perspectives when discussing practical situations, in a sense we all have a certain bias. There are rational means for establishing common viewpoints, such as dialogue or appeal to evidence. ITET procedures usually specify which people should be approached and under which particular circumstances of differences and conflict.

It is the case that different views about teaching situations are not always resolvable. This is significant for teacher education and education in general because it suggests that diverse viewpoints are possible. A variety of views about what constitutes good teaching may also be valuable, and there is a genuine diversity to be found in teaching. There are however, the constraints of pupil achievement and, arguably more importantly, there are normative constraints to welcoming diverse viewpoints in teaching. For example, I would personally take issue with a teacher whose pupils learnt little and I would be prepared to argue from evidence that my 'view' was rationally grounded. I would also take issue with a teacher who pronounced racist views however 'genuine' the teacher's personal perspective on history and race.

McLaughlin (2004) has rightly pointed out that the philosophically significant burdens and dilemmas of common schooling require resolution at classroom level via a form of pedagogic *phronesis* on the part of teachers, previously discussed as the phronetic insight aspect of practical judgement. Teachers exemplify good practice through their subject knowledge and their enthusiasm in representing their subject. They also act as an example in their conduct (ibid.). Therefore it is important to recognise and challenge inappropriate exemplification of good practice in normative and subject matters. However, what counts as inappropriate exemplification may be a matter of some debate. Contexts vary, different communities of practice may practise very differently to each other.

With the above reservations in mind it is reasonable to conclude that there cannot be one definitive view of good practice, since each teacher must re-create afresh in her own classroom the teaching for the particular pupils in front of her. While there are generic skills and tried and tested curriculum content and methods, each new lesson is a unique undertaking. Just as each class will contain to some extent a diverse community of learners, similarly each cohort of trainee teachers will contain a varied group of trainees. In ITET it is important to take account of the different ways in which teacher trainees may experience their ITET learning. Teacher educators need to understand the individuality of each learning situation for each trainee and to build in mentoring opportunities at all possible course stages. The fact that different views are held makes us interrogate our own conceptions. In reality there *are* constraints on promoting a plurality of views about good practice to our trainees, who may be obliged to teach a particular curriculum by government or by their schools; may experience pressure to teach to a particular prevailing orthodoxy, or pressure from within a school to teach for high examination results, to the detriment of the progress of non-high achievers. Any of these constraints may force a particular view of what good teaching is and disable a tolerant view of diverse perspectives.

The Mentoring Process

Articulation

With the above account in place it is now useful to look at an example of how mentoring might work in practice. A typical mode of mentoring in initial teacher education involves a gradual initiation of the trainee into the practices of teaching through the development of collaborative practice. This initiation builds primarily and fundamentally on the mentor and mentee's shared experience of particular examples of teaching, exchanging this information, and developing a common experience of what constitutes good practice. This is akin to Hirst's comments that:

> In common language we created practical discourse that in its concepts, propositions, rules and principles encapsulates our practical experience of our world ... practical principles are the outcome of successful practice, generalisations are valid only insofar as they capture what successful practice entails. The more complex the practice and the more it is connected with differences in human attributes and differences in contexts, then the less such generalisations can possibly hope to capture what the practice entails.
>
> (Hirst, 1996, p. 171)

The language of practice develops in the practice, with the proviso that a basic lexis is helpful, through some descriptors of good practice, such as might be encompassed in a set of standards judiciously used. So while Chapter 2 has warned against using a set of standards as the *only* determinant of good practice, as Hirst has stated:

> the pursuits and achievement of practices serving non-cognitive goals cannot begin to be captured in merely theoretical terms, but although theoretical reasoning cannot itself provide the basis for generating rational practice that is not to say it cannot provide crucially important knowledge and understanding of ourselves and our physical and social context. Such knowledge sets out the boundaries, the framework within which rational practices can be developed.
>
> (ibid.)

As we saw in Chapter 2 there is some point in having descriptors of good teaching as a basic form of articulation to underpin the process of constructive professional dialogue on practice. Elliott and Calderdale (1995) pointed out in a review of the articled teachers scheme the danger in not having such an underpinning.

> ... since these mentors did not have extensive experience in professional development they had not formulated an appropriate language to talk about alternative ways of viewing classroom contexts ... They may have been hampered in bringing about changes ... because of the lack of an appropriate framework in which to do so.
>
> (p. 51)

Classroom Observation

The on-going mentor and mentee dialogue on practice is typically heavily based on classroom observation, both by and of the mentee, particularly in the early stages of the training, when the trainee usually begins by observing various teachers' lessons, followed by reflection on that experience with the mentor. It has been established that lesson observation, where it is accompanied by informed discussion with a trusted and skilled colleague is a highly valued form of professional development for most teachers and that the most successful schools in training can develop a culture

> in which the critical observation of teachers and lessons together with dialogue and constructive feedback becomes part of the fabric of day-to-day practice. Observation practices informed by research perspectives and by evidence of what works can be incorporated into the teaching and learning strategy of a school. This in turn acts to create a milieu in which professional insight and judgement concerning good teaching is refined by experimentation and corroboration in the context of collaborative evaluation.
>
> (DfES, 2002a, pp. 11, 15)

The key to the power of classroom observation as a developmental tool is the notion of the professional dialogue on practice, which accompanies it and in which it is situated. Classroom observation both of and by the trainee needs to be part of a wider conception of the development of teacher knowledge and understanding. Trainees often begin work with their mentor by discussing lessons, which the trainee has seen taught, often by that mentor, followed by discussion. Given the complexities of the classroom it is impossible to observe 'everything'. There is a body of pedagogic knowledge and pedagogic content knowledge and as we have seen previously, practical knowledge of how the theory relates to classroom practice is gained experientially, through doing and reflecting.

Watching a classroom is a form of 'doing', which can be deconstructed afterwards and just as one needs to decide what to teach in a lesson, it is also helpful for trainees to know what they might look for in a lesson observation. If an observer has little understanding in advance of what she is looking for, she is most likely not to be able to see it, although she may well see some things of interest. This is analogous to a person with little understanding of car engines watching a roadside mechanic repair her car. Without prior knowledge of the function of the parts being manipulated it is difficult for her to understand what she sees. Her friend, however, has a basic knowledge of car mechanics, and after observation of the procedure of the repair is later able to make a similar repair. The novice teacher too is helped by a prior understanding of the cogs and wheels of the lesson, so it is helpful for a specific focus for the observation to be chosen in advance, such as how the teacher manages the resources, or the behaviour in the classroom. Having the experience to understand what it is useful to choose as a focus, and how to record notes of what happens in the classroom, require a wider perspective than most novice teachers possess. The mentor can fruitfully frame the coming observation for the trainee, by setting in advance the parameters of what is to be noticed and noted.

Recording

Practical wisdom needs to make use of technical rationality in the sense of asking 'what is the technically effective way of doing this particular task?' This section discusses why mentors need to consider how they record what they see, based on the principle that mentors who watch trainees teach have a responsibility to feed back accurately and helpfully what has been observed, in the context of the parameters that were set in advance. This follows from earlier comments about the necessity for new understandings to arise from a shared experience, in which both parties respect the perspective of the other. The mentor needs to be able to tell the trainee what the mentor has seen and heard in the classroom for the trainee to understand the mentor's 'take' on the lesson. The mentor and mentee can discuss what has been observed on the basis of recorded observations and impressions. This presupposes good recording techniques, which can enable the trainee to see that what is said about the practice is based on actual observation of what has happened, and not on prejudice or presuppositions. While it is true that some people have good recall without any form of note-taking, the success of any subsequent reflection on a lesson observation depends to some extent on the details recorded. When mentors observe trainees using a recording and feedback mechanism, which enables trainees to learn from their recording and the subsequent discussions, they also teach trainees how to use such formats themselves, when *they* observe experienced teachers and later reflect with those teachers on what has happened in the lesson. The questions and observations arising from both kinds of lesson observations, of and by the trainee, become a fertile source of dialogue about the practices being considered, those chosen for the focus and any wider questions raised. In this way the trainee teacher builds up a repository of shared experiences of analysis of practice, which develops an understanding of the practice.

Good Mentors – Qualities and Dispositions

Trustworthiness

Since mentoring is a relational practice, in order for the mentoring relationship to develop into productive dialogue a teacher needs to believe in the reliability and solidarity of the mentor, trust in her professional expertise and judgement and that she is telling the truth

(Earley & Kinder, 1994; DfES, 2002c), in other words that the dialogical virtues are in place. Trust underpins productive mentoring relationships. It is sometimes argued that trust rests on an optimistic view of human nature, whereas, it is claimed, most people tend to act out of self-interest. In exercising faith in 'a benevolent human nature', the 'pessimistic' argument goes, we cease to act rationally. The 'optimists' claim something like Hume's faith that sympathy makes human beings 'mirrors' of each other, and this gives them 'a remarkable desire of company, which associates them together, without any advantages they can ever propose to reap from their union' (Hume, 1911, vol. 11, p. 87). Rather than follow Hume's line of reasoning from the existence of an individual person's feelings of sympathy or empathy with others, it seems important to note that we are inherently social beings and therefore cannot exist without trust. In the example given earlier of a child interacting with a mother from its first moments, the child 'believes', listens, reacts and interacts in all trust and openness to the other. It is not that trust is necessary to create a social contract, but rather that social life pervades individual life, which is constructed in 'webs of circumlocution' as earlier seen (Taylor, 1989, p. 36). Kant's conception is closer to this notion. He makes trust fundamental to the relationships of respect between the members of 'the kingdom of ends', the ideal moral community, although this conception is different from trust enwebbed as earlier described, because he placed the categorical imperative within a system of transcendental idealism. It is more accurate to say that trust is 'the bedrock underlying all imaginable forms of human life' (White, 1996, p. 52). White cites Baier (1986); Bok (1978) and Luhmann (1979) for a philosophical treatment of the commonsense observation on the pervasiveness of trust in human life, and she argues for the particular role that trust must play in a democratic society, in public life and in personal relations. Mentoring covers all these categories as the mentee needs to trust the mentor as an individual support, and also trust in her professional judgement about teaching[5].

What does it mean to say one individual trusts another? There are some basic components of trust. If I trust someone I can feel confident that they will take care of something I value, even if they do not value it themselves, and that they will not harm me. This implies that they have respect for me, and to have this respect they need to have a certain humility with regard to their own perspective and views. White, analysing several texts on trust, points out that 'what seems common to all the different phenomena falling under the concept is that trust is a form of belief. It is a matter of believing that you can rely on X' (White, 1996, p. 54). She further rightly points out that what makes a case of trust more than a matter of simply believing that X will be the case, and that the person trusted will perform the beneficial action, is the element of risk involved:

> One believes despite the uncertainty. Related to the degree of uncertainty involved, there is a continuum of consciousness of the trust relationship.

> (ibid.)

Hargreaves (2003) further reminds us that good teaching is itself essentially a risk taking activity:

> In teaching risk requires a special kind of trust in processes as well as people. This *professional trust* is not a matter of passive blind faith in others, but involves active commitments to shared work, openness and reciprocal learning.

> (p. 19)

An implication of this as Bailey (2002) has pointed out is that when we trust someone we make ourselves vulnerable:

> But we do so in the confidence that the trusted will not exploit this vulnerability, and generally in the confidence that the trusted will actively take care of what we make vulnerable. This vulnerability and care can concern something tangible, such as when I trust my friend with my bike, or something less tangible, such as when I trust a stranger to be honest when I ask him the time.

> (p. 1)

Trust also involves commitment to the person or public ideal that is the object of the trust. This commitment may vary in degree. Mentoring is a professional relationship, embedded in the community of practices within the school, the profession, professional ethics, the community of pupils and parents. The mentee may trust in the professional integrity of the mentor to a lesser or greater degree. It is not clear how the degree of trust in the mentor, and commitment to the mentor's viewpoint might influence the success or otherwise of the mentee's development as a teacher. Such a subtle connection would be hard to establish.

The need for trust in the relationship between mentor and trainee to some extent mirrors that needed between pupil and teacher, if a pupil is to feel comfortable and thereby motivated to learn. It is not enough or even necessary for teachers to like their pupils. What is required is 'a respect for them as persons' (Peters, 1966, p. 58). Peters has written cogently and convincingly on this topic (op. cit. pp. 57–62). The extensive literature on motivation strongly suggests, in addition, that learning is best achieved when the learner is intrinsically motivated (Springer Science, 1992; Cordova & Lepper, 1996; Noels et al., 1999; Ryan & Deci, 2000a, 2000b), which again points to the importance of affective factors in learning. Trust in the teacher is important. Pupils have said they learn best from teachers they like and who respect them (Haager et al., 1993; Beishuizen et al., 2001; Trent & Slade, 2001; Wentzel, 2002). As Noddings has saliently pointed out:

> Teaching is thoroughly relational and many of its goods are relational: the feeling of safety in a thoughtful teacher's classroom, a growing intellectual enthusiasm in both teacher and student, the challenge and satisfaction shared by both in engaging with new material.
>
> (Noddings, 2003, pp. 249–50)

In this sense being a new teacher experiencing mentoring is akin to being a pupil learning with a teacher and, as with the pupils' sense of well-being, the school ethos plays a role in enabling good trusting relationships to develop (see White, 1996, pp. 60–63). It is likely that good mentor-mentee relationships flourish in a school where 'social trust' is strong.

Practical Judgement

The 'good' mentor that is emerging from the account in this chapter represents an example of practical wisdom. She is also a good teacher, able to apply her experience and knowledge in a timely, relevant and pertinent way to help the mentee's developing understanding. Recalling the account in Chapter 5 of practical judgement, the best mentors exercise judgement: they are able to operate in conditions of complexity; they have practical knowledge, practical 'wisdom'; they exhibit trustworthiness. A group of experienced mentors of trainees and NQTs reflected on the qualities, dispositions and practical skills they thought they needed for their mentoring role. Among other factors, they emphasised the qualities of open-mindedness, receptivity to new ideas, commitment to supporting the development of others and 'the ability to use a range of helping strategies, including providing constructive feedback and engaging in positive dialogue with the NQT' (TTA, 2001, p. 6). Trustworthiness is bound up with sympathetic regard for the mentee and assumption of responsibility for the mentee's well-being. In addition, the mentor needs to balance solidarity with the mentee with duty of care for the pupils' well-being and learning, so practical judgement is at the basis of good mentoring. We can see that a number of qualities can be isolated, for the purpose of description, but that in practice these interrelate in a complex and individual manner. As a mentor reported:

> You have to set up a relationship with NQTs in which they feel that they can tell you what difficulties they're experiencing, but you must back that up with your own observation and you have to develop a relationship in which you are able to give praise but also constructive criticism. But you also have to be prepared, to go into the relationship with each NQT knowing that it's possible that this NQT will fail ... So it's a delicate relationship.
>
> (Heilbronn et al., 2002, p. 382)

This highlights the need for mentors to feel solidarity with their mentees and the challenges they face. As the ITET experience develops trainees who are successfully engaged with their practice are beginning to develop understanding of the relationship between their pupils' ability to learn and their pupils' well-being. At the same time new teachers have their own learning needs. Having the support of a mentor with whom they are able to discuss issues arising from their teaching practice, and from their own personal situation within the practice, can be a decisive factor for some trainees' success in getting through their teaching practice. What Hawkins and Shohet (1989) have pointed out in relation to supervision in social work can apply equally to mentoring in teaching:

> In choosing to help, where our role is to pay attention to someone else's needs, we are entering into a relationship which is different from the normal and everyday. There are times when it seems barely worthwhile ... At times like these supervision can be very important ... It can give us the chance to seek for new options, to discover the learning that often arises from the most difficult of situations and to get support.
>
> (pp. 3–4)

Good mentors are dispositionally sensitive and sympathetic to their mentee's situations and their well-being. A mentor has said that she had

> to make an enormous conceptual leap, because we forget what it's like to be a new teacher, and most of us, certainly at my age, didn't have any kind of induction or support.
>
> (Heilbronn et al., 2002, p. 381)

Without a stance of solidarity and insight into the trainee's situation, it is debatable how far a mentor could enable a mentee to gain the necessary new understandings for development of the mentee's own practical judgement. This sense of solidarity means that good mentors are more inclined to think of the long-term professional practice of the mentee and are not tied to the final assessment as an end in itself (Wright & Bottery, 1997, p. 244). A good mentor is not likely to be narrowly focused on the mentee's qualifications for her career trajectory, but rather to look at the mentee's practice in terms of her effect on pupils in the widest sense and her own development as a professional practitioner. Good mentors are dispositionally inclined towards promoting the well-being of their mentees and the pupils.

Good mentors are also likely to come from schools where they are supported by the school culture (see Chapter 5) and where there are clear arrangements for the recruitment, training and support of mentors, careful consideration of the basis upon which mentors and mentees are matched, and ground rules for the mentoring relationship, including those relating to confidentiality.

(Oliver & Aggleton, 2002, p. 32)

The whole school community influences the practice of all of its members. How far the mentor could exercise some of the virtues required by the mentoring practice might be influenced by the limitations or facilitation of the school's procedures, practices and general ethos (see Chapters 2 and 5).

On the view of the dialogical virtues developed here, it follows that in exercising these virtues on behalf of the mentee the mentor is also engaged in her own flourishing. If, as is here suggested, knowledge and understanding of practical matters comes about through engagement with experiences, on which some kind of well-grounded reflection has taken place, it follows that by engaging virtuously with the mentee, the mentor is in a situation in which her own experience and understanding is extended. Virtuous engagement with the mentee involves the mentor in a trustworthy relationship with the mentee. The relationship is characterised by shared responsibility with the mentee for the mentee's success and well-being as a beginning teacher. The uniqueness of the individual engagement with the particular mentee, concerning a particular experience or set of interpreted experiences, raises the possibility of new insights and development for the mentor. We could say that the mentor has opened herself to such development and created the conditions for its possibility.

In purely practical terms, the mentor is likely to develop her mentoring expertise. As Kelly and Beck (1995) have said:

In trying to diagnose the practice of others you have to relate what you observe to your own experience and behaviour and thereby try to make sense of them before discussing alternatives.

(p. 257)

The mentor needs to be genuinely engaged with sharing her practice in the mentoring dialogue, in order to relate her expertise to the current situation of the mentee. In so doing the mentor is likely to be challenged to improve her own practice. A successful induction tutor said how much she valued her work with new teachers:

> In the vast majority of cases, they're young people who are enthusiastic, enjoy their work, and you know I find it very refreshing and I learn from them. I think this is the thing that's perhaps surprising, an experienced teacher can go and watch an NQT and still pick up some tricks.
>
> (Heilbronn et al., 2002, p. 381)

However, the nature of the commitment involved in mentoring, by both parties, means that some less felicitous situations can arise, as we have previously discussed.

This discussion is tied in with the fundamentally normative nature of teaching. To some extent there is scope for legitimate plurality in normative matters, both in conceptions of teaching and in methods of teaching. However mentors have a duty of care, which means being trustworthy. Also, if the mentor's own practice is bad, it would be difficult for her to help her trainee to develop her teaching, contribute to the pupils' learning, or to the wider professional obligations. A good mentor will also be a good teacher, drawing on her own practice to exemplify and model what good practice is. It is possible that a person A could teach a person B to do something which A cannot do herself. An example might be that A cannot type, but can teach people to type and can pass on the knowledge of how to teach others to type. This might be possible if A has read a manual, familiarised herself with the appropriate keyboard, and with the manual's training methodology, such as building up touch typing skills in a technically rational manner, using a series of specifically designed exercises. The teacher could conceivably explain this, place the novice's hands on the keys, show the novice the exercises and take the student through the exercises. This is different from teaching someone to play the piano, where initially such exercises might be used, but where feeling and interpretation arise as soon as 'music' is played. Typing text is not like playing music, so an apprenticeship model for passing on the technical skill of typing is possible.

Mentoring someone in the practice of teaching is evidently more like teaching someone to play the piano than to type.

In any situation requiring judgement between various possible actions, entailing different but possibly equally significant outcomes, merely technical knowledge will not suffice. This has implications for the choice of mentor for a new teacher, in that mentors need to be able to exercise good judgement about appropriate responses in various educational situations. Some ITET courses require 'recent and relevant' experience for mentors, and this seems appropriate as judgement is largely based on experience. What constitutes 'recent' and 'relevant' would need clarification of course in individual cases. The dispositional and normative dimensions are not covered by these two categories of experience, however.

Assessment Issues

Mentors have a dual role in the case of ITET and induction of NQTs, to support and develop trainees and also to contribute to the assessment of their practical teaching for the award of QTS. It might be argued that the roles of assessor and supportive mentor *necessarily* conflict with one another. However, this is not the case. First it is important that in mentoring a trainee or new teacher the processes by which decisions are made are seen to be fair, open to the mentee and open to critical scrutiny. To maintain the relationship of trust in which the professional dialogue flourishes, any assessment practices have to be transparently fair. By definition, an element of assessment enters into the professional dialogue, on an informal level, because the good mentor does need to maintain a sympathetically critical role. A typical case would be a weekly mentoring session in which areas for development are mutually agreed in advance of the session. Lessons are planned around a focus relating to the area for development, and possibly other learning opportunities are set up, such as relevant readings or meetings. The focus is decided collaboratively around the trainee's perceived learning needs at the time. What these needs are is a function of the particular circumstances of the trainee's development at the time, the classes taught, the curriculum, the ITET timetable and so on. In the next mentor session the trainee and mentor can discuss the trainee's learning around the focus that was chosen, using information such as the reports of lesson observations, accounts of meetings, trainee's and mentor's reflections on these. The trainee is aware from the outset of the dual role of the mentor and experiences this dual role throughout the mentoring process. The dual role may give rise to difficulties but the two roles do not necessarily conflict.

In practice, trainees and mentors may disagree about progress towards norms. In this case the teacher would usually call on a moderating mentor or tutor, either within the school, the LEA or HEI. Disagreement may occur in various ways, for example, the mentor relationship may be a good one, the mentee may be developing and learning according to the mentor's perceptions, yet the mentee may not be meeting the assessment criteria involved in gaining accreditation as a teacher or to pass induction. The mentor may have difficulty in reconciling the demands of the assessment with her role of support for the mentee. A study of the Licensed Teacher scheme did find that:

> ... mentors in this study generally did not adopt approaches involving open challenge of novices' images of teaching, but a number of reasons may be postulated. It may be that the intensity or the nature of the relationship established between the mentor and articled teacher impeded such strategies. Neither the mentor nor the articled teacher may wish to place the relationship at risk.
>
> (Elliott & Calderdale, 1995, p. 51)

This illustrates that the mentors in the scheme may have been inexperienced, since the articled teacher scheme was an early example of school-based accreditation relying on mentoring.

The two roles of support and assessment are not necessarily in conflict but more than this for good mentors the two roles are harmonious, for the following reasons. A good mentor has the well being of her trainee in mind, over and above the trainee's gaining the award of QTS or passing the induction standards. Therefore the good mentor exhibits solidarity in her support of the trainee. A good mentor has good practical judgement. She is able to judge whether the trainee has the potential for a career in teaching as the mentor conceives this in her current circumstances. The judgement is based on the mentor's understanding of a number of factors, crucially, the realities of teaching in those current circumstances; the trainee herself and the well-being of future pupils.

Conclusion

A good mentor can help a trainee to develop practical judgement through a dialogical process of mentoring, based on the shared experience of practical examples of teaching. Good mentors are exemplary figures, trustworthy, empathetic people and experienced, skilled teachers, able to maintain good relationships. As with all learners, the wider school context affects the mentor's ability to do the job well. Good mentoring embodies collegiate values of openness to change, the readiness to challenge prevailing assumptions as well as an understanding and application of protocols and norms, and the mentor cannot successfully work in isolation from a community of practice which itself values these principles.

Mentoring engages the mentor and mentee in elaborating a language of practice. In the current context, the QTS standards provide some descriptors with which to engage the dialogue. Teaching is a complex activity and the interpretation of the teacher's practice in the end relies on a hermeneutic understanding of that practice. However, a vocabulary of descriptors of good practice can prove useful in a discussion about practice. In the second part of the book implications of the account of the development of practical judgement for teacher knowledge and understanding are discussed. Chapter 7 deals with the role of educational research in promoting the practical judgement of teachers. Chapter 8 considers the assessment of practical teaching, in terms of matching the complexities of teaching and providing robust evidence of good practice. Assessment therefore needs to enable new teachers to account for the development of their practical judgement in matters relating to teaching in its widest sense.

Notes

1. In this respect there is a similarity with counselling, although the analogy does not fit closely, as mentoring here relates to the trainee's workplace 'self' in the role of the teacher, rather than someone undertaking counselling of a more existential nature.
2. The review covered the ERIC, BIDS, EMBASE and MEDLINE database and handsearches in the libraries of the Institute of Personnel and Development, the Institute of Education (University of London), the Royal College of Nursing, the British Medical Association and the National Institute for Social Work. Searches were restricted to studies published in the UK during the last 10 years
3. Discourse analysis in linguistics is a particularly relevant theoretical framework for the detailed analysis of underlying patterns of relationships carried through the discourse of participants in conversations and dialogues. The methods developed to undertake such analyses attempt to record and then unravel the web of relationships and the meanings conveyed by the interactive talk. A standard textbook on discourse analysis defines the method as (a) concerned with language use beyond the boundaries of a sentence/utterance; (b) concerned with the interrelationships between language and society; and (c) as concerned with the interactive or dialogic properties of everyday communication (Stubbs, 1983, p. 1). Discourse analysis can, in certain circumstances yield useful insights into social contexts. However, the term 'discourse analysis' is used with varying meanings. In one relevant version, discourse analysis 'foregrounds language use as social action, language use as situated performance, language use as tied to social relations and identities, power, inequality and social struggle, language use as essentially a matter of "practices" rather than just "structures"' (Slembrouck, 2004, p. 1).
4. See Awbrey and Awbrey (1995).
5. O'Neill (2002) has explored the theme of trust in public life and Bottery (2004) of mistrust which can pervade a social culture in which managerialism predominates and there is considerable literature on the concept of trust (see Hardin, 1993; Holton,

1994; Jones, 1996; Tschannenn-Moran & Hoy, 2000). Bottery questions whether teachers can trust each other in such a culture and whether they can trust governments to do what is best for education. He claims that in education government policies seem to indicate that teachers are not trusted to act on their professional 'wisdom'

Part 2

Implications for Teacher Training and Education

Chapter 7

Educational Research

This chapter argues that teachers need to be engaged with research for two reasons. First, as previous chapters have shown, teachers need to reflect on their activities, evaluate what they have been doing and how it might be done differently. Looking at various alternatives through an experimental empirical method is part of the exercise of practical judgement in teaching. From the model that has been developed in previous chapters it is clear that teachers routinely use research skills, when engaging in curriculum development and in preparing and evaluating lessons and resources[1]. For example, lesson evaluation as discussed in Chapter 3, requires formulating a question, such as whether the pupils learnt what was intended. There needs to be some kind of data collection, such as evidence of achievement from tasks done in class or observations of pupil responses. The posited question needs to be assessed against the data collected and the findings applied to planning new activities. These steps represent a recognisable research-based methodology. The possession of these research skills is essential for successful teaching.

Secondly, teachers need to be research literate since, without some understanding of the principles and practices of educational research they will be unable to evaluate theories, policies and strategies presented, in relation to the aims of their own teaching. In addition, some teachers may benefit from doing their own action research, as a means to understanding and improving their practice. Practitioner research is also discussed in this chapter.

Before discussing the two main reasons why teachers might benefit from research literacy and activity, we need to be clear about the nature of educational research and issues around quantitative and qualitative research, which have a particular application to ITET.

There is discussion around the validity or non-validity of qualitative research and this debate links with the previous discussion about technical rationality and its misapplication to ITET.

Definitions and Issues in Educational Research

The sense of the teacher as researcher described above would not fit most definitions of research, which emphasise the need for a 'systematic and sustained enquiry' (Stenhouse, 1980, p. 14) carried out to answer a specific type of question, 'by people well versed in some form of thinking' (Peters & White, 1969, p. 2), suggesting rigour in application of that 'form of thinking'. It is important to discuss the idea of 'validity' in relation to educational research. Attempting a comprehensive definition of educational research Best suggests that something counts as research:

> to the degree that it seeks to establish the truth (or 'truths') about something; is undertaken in a systematic (not haphazard) way; is rigorous and is not casual; is undertaken by someone whose intention it is to seek or establish truth(s) in a systematic and rigorous manner (i.e., someone who has adopted the perspective of a researcher); makes findings open to public tests of truth; and makes its methodology transparent.
>
> (Best, 2002, pp. 4–5)

Much educational research employs qualitative methods and does not fit the paradigm of academic, empirical research. Empirical research using quantitative methods has well-established means to validate its findings, although what such research might be thought to demonstrate is not unproblematic. Epistemological scepticism about the possibility of truth claims, discussed in Chapters 4 and 5, fuels a current debate between proponents of quantitative and qualitative research (Guba & Lincoln, 1989; Constas, 1998; Bridges, 2003; Humes & Bryce, 2003), and as Hammersley (2005) points out:

> Only knowledge claims which are judged, by most researchers in a field, to be above a high threshold of likely truth can be treated as

established knowledge. This is the cutting edge of scientific research as a knowledge production process.

(p. 9)

Educational research frequently uses qualitative methods to reach conclusions and cannot meet the criteria for scientific research suggested above. Dewey's principle of warranted assertibility for the establishment of the truth claims of propositional knowledge can here be invoked to counter a sceptical response to research results that do not use purely quantitative methods (see Chapter 4). Purely quantitative methods are not appropriate to complex situations:

> ... when the operations in which physical science is used are such as to transform distinctively human values in behalf of a human interest, those who participate in these consequences have a knowledge of the things of ordinary perception, sense and enjoyment as genuine and fuller and deeper than that of the scientist in his laboratory. Were we to define science not in the usual technical way, but as a knowledge that accrues when methods are employed which deal competently with problems that present themselves, the physician, engineer, artist, craftsman can lay claim to scientific knowing.
>
> (Dewey, 1960, p. 199)

Here Dewey refers back to his definition of experimental empiricism (Chapter 4) and suggests using 'competent' methods of inquiry which follow rational procedures and are in this sense 'scientific'. Best's definition of research can be applied to qualitative educational research, using a Deweyan faith in 'warranted assertibility', reached through 'experimentally empirical' methods, to substantiate KT truth claims. It makes sense to talk of trust in facts as warranted assertibility, rather than to use the discourse of truth and objectivity.

An implication of this claim is that we have a certain responsibility to choose among the best options available to us to construct the warranted assertibility of our knowledge. When we interrogate evidence, trusting others such as through a peer review process, or in personal relations when we ask for advice from friends, we are engaged with and collaborating with others. The discourse of the 'warranted assertibility' of truth claims is one of participation in communities of practice rather than that of individual 'autonomy' (see also Urban, 2005). There are limitations on our choice of what to believe and how to construct our knowledge, as the preceding chapters have discussed. Some 'facts' we take on trust and pass on unquestioned. We generally tend to value the imparting of a critical faculty in older children and young people, while trying to balance a healthy regard for some facts. What those facts should be is a matter of debate in a world rich in sources of information; for example in England, there is debate about what should go into a canon of 'good' work to be studied, or what facts should be learnt (the kings and queens of England, the capital cities of the world?) There is also debate about what constitutes fact. Barrow (1984) has usefully analysed some of these difficulties in detail in his introduction to curriculum theory (pp. 86–93).

Warranted assertibility as a guide to 'truth' does not imply scepticism about the possibility of truth claims. In this context it is important to state that either educational research is concerned with establishing the validity of its findings, 'or it collapses into incoherence' (Bridges, 2003, p. 67). Bridges usefully analyses various accounts of 'truth' as they relate to paradigms of educational research (2003, pp. 67–88) in his counter arguments to 'the seduction of many sections of the educational research community by the sirens of postmodernism' (ibid., p. 16)[2]. Hammersley has also usefully applied Wittgenstein's discussion in *On Certainty* to state that the exhaustive application of the argument of epistemological scepticism 'would force us to doubt things that there is no good reason to doubt, including some which the very act of doubting relies on' (2005, p. 9). (See also Pring, 2000b.)

Defining Quality Criteria

Given that qualitative methods may seem to be more problematic than quantitative ones, with regard to truth claims, it is hardly surprising that there is no one definition of quality criteria for educational research, as a survey by the National Educational Research Forum (NERF) revealed. In responding to this survey the British Educational Research Association (BERA) concluded that there is

a multitude of quality criteria for the design, conduct and reporting of educational research, based on concepts of "fitness for the
purpose", originality, rigour, transparency and accessibility.

(BERA, 2001, p. 15)

The various parties engaged in producing, peer-reviewing, disseminating and using research need security about the quality of the
research under discussion, but

> there is no generally agreed set of quality criteria. This is not for
> the want of searching. For example, over the years our association
> has attempted ways of defining quality, but cannot claim to have
> achieved a consensus ... Different groups within the broad church
> of educational research have widely different perspectives.

(ibid.)

Should this lack of generally agreed evaluative criteria be viewed as a
fundamental weakness of educational research, as some critics have
argued (Hargreaves, 1996, Tooley & Darby, 1998)? In my opinion
it should not. We should judge educational research by its 'fitness
for purpose' (Hillage & Pearson, 1998), with the proviso that we
do need to elaborate evaluation criteria to determine good research
from bad, meaning research whose findings can be trusted. So it is
not acceptable to state that

> there is diversity in educational research and that, in this context,
> quality means that, within its own terms, any particular research
> study or project should be of good quality with respect to those
> terms.

(NERF, 2000)

We need also to advocate evaluation criteria for research, which is
good in general terms and also allows particularities in application.
Such instruments exist, arguably the most influential being Guba
and Lincoln's *Fourth Generation Evaluation* (1989), discussed further
in Chapter 8 (on assessment). It has been claimed that Guba and
Lincoln's research evaluation criteria may lead to a sceptical view
of knowledge claims when it comes to evaluating the outcomes of

qualitative research (see Pring, 2000a, 2000b). However, this is to misrepresent their intentions here, which are the design of robust evaluation criteria that can be used to make warranted truth claims for knowledge created by the findings of any particular piece of qualitative research. They state that

> through a hermeneutic dialectic process a new construction will emerge that is ... more informed and sophisticated.
>
> (Guba & Lincoln, 1989, p. 17)

When we take into account the most 'sophisticated' interpretations, using the most evidence available, we have a 'good' evidence base. A 'more sophisticated' construction is 'better', and provides stronger warrant as a truth claim.

If we now link Dewey's concept of experimental empiricism and his related account of truth as warranted assertibility, with Guba and Lincoln's quality criteria (which are discussed in more detail in the following chapter), we have a set of evaluation criteria for individual pieces of qualitative research and we are not tied to a sceptical view of the possibility of propositional knowledge (KT). It is possible for different pieces of research involving qualitative methods to elaborate evaluation criteria in different terms and the variety of evaluation criteria does not, to my mind, pose a problem for the security of trust we might have in any one piece of educational research. There can be a variety of research designs, methodologies, conduct of research and writing up of reports. The key to validation lies in the formulation of the original research aims, objectives and design, through which assessment criteria will be built in.

The fact that there may be several different evaluation criteria for different pieces of research is not in itself a problem. An analogy would be an examination syllabus on which a curriculum has been designed with the aim of enabling students to pass the particular examination in question. Teachers routinely investigate different examination syllabuses because they have different assessment or evaluation criteria. For example, in the General Certificate of Education Advanced Level examinations (A Levels) teachers often look at the possible examination syllabuses published by the various examination

boards, choose one, discover what the assessment criteria are for each
of the parts of the examination and design a curriculum around these.
If a teacher were to enter students for a different examination board's
A Level syllabus, the curriculum she designs might be different. So a
modern foreign languages syllabus for one examination board might
grant more marks than another syllabus to listening skills than those
accorded to writing skills and accordingly be perceived as an 'easier'
A Level to achieve, by some teachers. Such a discrepancy between
evaluation criteria of different syllabuses does not pose a problem to
the individual students and teachers, as the actual assessment criteria
relating to them would be known to them in advance of and during
their study period. The teacher choosing the first syllabus is likely to
concentrate more curriculum time and resources on listening than
the teacher who chooses the second board. The teacher designs her
teaching curriculum, her scheme of work, on the aim of gaining as
many marks as possible in the final examination so as to pass the
examination with good grades. This does not preclude the existence
of wider aims, such as 'students will learn to understand short and
longer passages of both colloquial and formal register in the foreign language when spoken at normal speed, by a native speaker of
that language'. (The teacher may well have in mind these wider aims
as an additional, if not deciding factor when choosing an examination syllabus). Similarly, any piece of educational research will have
defined its aims, objectives and design, its possibilities of achieving
the outcome of new 'knowledge' about the researched subject. This
is what Hillage and Pearson meant by assessing educational research
'in its own terms'. There is certainly a responsibility for researchers
within this variety of possible practices however, to observe some of
the 'research virtues' identified by Pring such as 'a disposition find
out and tell the truth as it is, and not as one would like it to be'
(Pring, 2001, p. 421). In Chapter 6 we also saw this virtue operating
in relation to mentoring.

Quantitative and Qualitative Research Paradigms

The earlier chapters established an argument for a hermeneutic understanding of knowledge construction, within a dialogical

situation, rooted in a particular, complex, normative context. The chapter on reflection argued for rigour and some systematic ground rules to establish the warrant of assertibility. Accordingly the apparent clash between proponents of the quantitative and the qualitative research paradigms might be seen as a false dichotomy. As Pring has pointed out, there is a common

> failure to recognise the complexity of inquiry and of the nature of that which is being inquired into, which causes the blurring of the distinctions within the so-called paradigms and results in the sharp dichotomy between them.
>
> (Pring, 2000b, p. 48)

We have established earlier that practical knowledge is constructed through reflection in and on experience. Someone engaged in practice-based research needs to reflect on, and in a sense, interpret phenomena in which she herself participates. She chooses what, where and how to develop the research. Research aims and objectives are built on interpretations-become-understandings, affective and evaluative factors, and these drive any piece of research from start to finish. They determine choice of methodology, details of research instruments and procedures, and data interpretation. They cannot be completely isolated from the research context. So the research designer has a great deal of power to influence the research outcome. In the positivist paradigm the neutral research designer is by definition outside the researched context.

Taking account of the complexity of the teaching situation, the use of judgement involved in operating in situations of complexity, as we discussed earlier, a researcher operating from outside the researched context cannot by definition understand all the implications and ramifications of that context. Teachers themselves often undertake research, usually small-scale practitioner or action research. With regard to methodology and validation, teacher researchers need to understand the particularities, the extent and the limitations of the methods they use in their inquiries. They also need to have robust and rigorous means to develop their methodology, and to reach and report on their conclusions. Teachers need to have well grounded reflective processes and orientation towards their practice and this has implications for ITET programmes.

Practitioner Research – From Action Research

Do teachers need to *do* educational research, and if so in what capacity and for what purposes? Is it 'not enough that teachers' work should be studied, they need to study it themselves' (Stenhouse, 1975, p. 144)? 'Action research' and 'practitioner research' are widespread terms and both cover a variety of approaches taken by teachers undertaking research of their own practice, or in the practice base[3]. Generally this involves a basic action research cycle, consisting of a review, planning, action and observation, followed by an evaluation phase, leading to production of new knowledge (see Carr & Kemmis, 1989, pp. 162–63).

Elliott has stated that:

> Action-research might be defined as the study of a social situation with a view to improving the quality of action within it. It aims to feed practical judgement in concrete situations, and the validity of the theories' or hypotheses it generates depends not so much on "scientific" tests of truth, as on their usefulness in helping people to act more intelligently and skilfully. In action-research "theories" are not validated independently and then applied to practice. They are validated through practice.
>
> (Elliott, 1991, p. 69)

The validation lies in the findings being re-applied and then evaluated. For example, a piece of action research made by a secondary physical education teacher on a Masters of Teaching degree investigated whether teaching her students how to analyse video recordings of their performance in javelin throwing, using specifically designed criteria, would develop the students' understanding of their performance, and if so, whether this would lead to improved performance. In practice she was able to reach her goal, which was specific to her particular group of students. This is not to say that the research could not be repeated and some general principles developed, capable of wider application.

We can isolate five main characteristics of action research from this account. First, action research is specific in the sense that it relates to a particular question, in a particular context. Secondly, action research is related to values: the PE teacher in the example given above *chose* to focus on developing her students' understanding of their practice, thus indicating her belief that with better understanding of their practice students could learn to improve. Her choice implies a value judgement about the students' practice, and a commitment to them as sports performers. In this sense Elliott is right when he says that educational action research is a moral endeavour because it seeks to realise values in practice (Whiteheads, 1999). Thirdly, successful action research leads to new understandings about possible teaching interventions. Fourthly, criteria for *successful* action research need to be elaborated, in the same way as criteria for well-grounded reflection were described in Chapter 3. Some action research may not be successful because it may not lead to useful developments, capable of generating better teaching. Lastly, it is an advantage that the teacher in the example was able to generate new insights through her own actions and reflections. She was able to exercise a certain autonomy in her pedagogy and did not rely on an unexamined orthodoxy for her authority to teach using a given method. The fostering of autonomy through action research is the fifth main characteristic.

KH and KT in Relation to Action Research

Currently, there are many varieties of action research, referred to also as 'teacher research' or 'practitioner research' (Dick, 2003; Newman, 2003; Ewbank, 2004; DSEA, 2005; EmTech, 2005). We find

> ... sharp differences between variants of action research in the way they theorise the relationship between research and social (or educational) change: some see it as a technical (or instrumental) connection, some see it as a version of what Aristotle, and Schwab (1969) after him, described as practical reasoning, and others see it in terms of critical social science.
>
> (Kemmis, 1993)

Whatever version of action research is followed there is a key difference between its primary aim, which is to improve practice, and the
aim of research as normally understood, which is the production of
new propositional knowledge (KT). This does not mean that the findings or conclusion of a piece of action research are only valuable to
the researcher who does it, and cannot be useful to others. As Pring
points out:

> although such a practical conclusion focuses on the particular,
> thereby not justifying generalisation, no one situation is unique
> in every respect and therefore the action research in one classroom
> or school can *illuminate* or be suggestive of practice elsewhere.
>
> (Pring, 2000b, p. 131)

With these considerations in mind, educational research in the form
of action research is a useful, but not necessary means to developing
and improving practice. This is not an empirical claim but is based
on a particular epistemological stance.

> The unique feature of the questions that prompt teacher research is
> that they emanate from neither theory nor practice alone but from
> critical reflection of the two.
>
> (Cochran-Smith & Lytle, 1993, p. 15)

This is very close to Dewey's view that:

> Ends in their capacity of values can be validly determined only on
> the basis of the tensions, obstructions, and positive potentialities
> that are found, by controlled observation, to exist in the actual
> situation.
>
> (Dewey, 1991, p. 497)

In the light of the foregoing, Stenhouse's view is illuminating that
teachers could gain from systematically inquiring into aspects of their
teaching, as a basis for further development, and that they also need
to acquire requisite research skills (Stenhouse, 1983, p. 163). It is
apparent that teachers need to be reflective in some sense to be
teachers, so as to do their daily planning and teaching and that
the nature of teaching itself fundamentally presupposes reflection
(see Chapter 3). In a more contentious and second sense of teachers

as reflective practitioners the question remains as to whether teachers *should* engage in educational research on their own practice.

Clearly, being a teacher researcher is not fundamental to being a teacher. A teacher may never undertake any form of practitioner inquiry and still be a good teacher. Being a teacher researcher is not a good in itself, independent of the outcome of the research and of its application in practice to particular cases. In fact, the quality of teaching might even be undermined in some cases by a teacher doing research. While the findings of a piece of action or practitioner research might eventually be applied, and might improve on a habitual procedure or curriculum application, it is possible that in the process of gaining the information the teacher may have been neglecting some other aspects of good teaching, in order to gain the data she needed. In theory someone might claim that there could be 'good action research' while 'bad' teaching went on. So doing research is not a good in itself, nor do all teachers need to engage on research. It is rather a case of teacher research being a possible means of enriching the practical knowledge and understanding of those teachers who engage in it.

Reflection, Inquiry and Research

Chapters 4 and 5 suggested the power and relevance of Deweyan inquiry to an understanding of how practical knowledge is built. Inquiry is also relevant to the teacher as researcher and is close to Lewin, Stenhouse and Elliott's formulations of action research, in the way in which Dewey grounds inquiry on the 'intellectual organisation ... of experience' (Dewey, 1991, p. 85). Dewey's epistemology forms a link with the objectives of teacher research, in his elaboration of the method of critical inquiry to identify and resolve problems arising in and through the teaching experience[4]. Teachers researching their own practice under the criteria of what constitutes good research may come to new understandings about teaching. It follows then that practitioner research should form some part of an initial teacher education course. It is to be hoped that initial teacher trainees may develop skills of systematic reflection as outlined in Chapter 3. The regular habit of reflecting in and on action, as part of building professional knowledge, lays down ways of working on which practitioner research can be subsequently built. Trainees do not need to engage in a specific research project but do need to engage regularly with the kind of action research cycle of reflective thinking. Embarking on an actual research project would be more appropriate for a later stage, possibly the following year of teaching, if the teacher is ready.

One of the limitations of action research or practitioner research to the growth of professional knowledge is the isolation of the individual action researcher. The next section looks in more detail at the wider research community.

The Teacher As Researcher

Research Communities

In Chapter 6 the development of the social self within communities of practice was considered (Lave & Wenger, 1991). It follows from that discussion that individual teachers might gain as reflective professionals through extending their role as research users and doers beyond their immediate context. As also noted in Chapter 6, variability of contexts leads to variability of developmental opportunities for teachers. Some schools are more intense research contexts than others; they may have staff on advanced degree courses doing school-based research; school management teams gathering data on various aspects of school policy, usually as a tool for school improvement, and partnerships with LEA or HEI to develop policies. There may also be different communities of teacher researchers, each community sharing a set of principles, amounting to judgements on the research practices. Teachers may also be members of other communities of practice, such as subject associations, which are not necessarily research communities.

In a bid to involve teachers in promoting and developing teaching as a research and evidence-based profession what was then the Teacher Training Agency (TTA) set up the Teacher Research Panel in 1999. From the outset, the key objectives for the panel were related to raising achievement. In itself this is not contentious, although we have already made the argument that 'achievement' in this context is firmly related to the standards and high stakes assessment agenda, and so the scope of the panel was limited to initiatives which the TTA wished to fund or to investigate. The panel's objectives were to encourage research relating to achievement that would be relevant to teachers, and to enable teachers to contribute to a national debate on educational research and evidence-based practice, in order to raise standards. The panel's creation was firmly embedded in a standards agenda, in that practical outcomes of pieces of research were prioritised. Since these outcomes were dictated largely by the prevailing educational prescriptions and statutory guidelines it was suggested at the time whether practitioner research actually meant 'practical solutions', rather than challenging investigations, and what the implications of this might be (Heilbronn, 2000). However, the teachers on the panel benefited from peer exchange of information and expertise and from participation and comment on research initiatives and professional development activities. Teachers on the panel commented on a variety of research proposals; participated in a research conference, and contributed to the paper presented at BERA, identifying features of research reports and dissemination strategies, which make research accessible to teachers (Cordingley, 2000).

National networks such as the National Educational Research Forum (NERF, 2003) have a role in examining the policy and practices of educational research and in elaborating recommendations to the various parties engaged with educational research, such as researchers, users, practitioners or policymakers, but are not of immediate relevance to practitioners or initial teacher educators, who need to participate actively in research communities, if both empirical research and pieces of practitioner research are to have value beyond their immediate surroundings. In the case of practitioner research it is important that findings can be disseminated and submitted to active interrogation, so that misconceptions may be challenged and understandings developed and shared, although bearing in mind that the particular piece of practitioner research might relate to a particular and individual context.

The active reflection upon practice with a view to its improvement needs to be a public activity ... conducted in such a way that others can scrutinise and, if necessary, question the practice of which it is part. Others become part of the reflective process – the identification and definition of the problem, the values which are implicit within the practice, the way of implementing and gathering evidence about the practice, the interpretation of the evidence.

(Pring, 2000b, p. 132)

In the earlier case of the PE teacher, she disseminated her findings in locally organised Inset. Her suggested methods were developed and tried out in other schools and her findings were validated by other practitioners.

In Stenhouse's conception of action research, external researchers need to work with teachers and take the critical and disseminating role (Stenhouse, 1975, p. 162). The current partnership model of teacher education is an opportunity for joint research projects, for teachers to tap into the resources and expertise in HEI and for researchers in HEI to support research in and on the practice base. Journals that publish peer-reviewed articles arising from practitioner research are useful in disseminating such investigations and enabling scrutiny and discussion of such research[5].

Many examples exist of teachers undertaking practitioner research in tandem with outside bodies, such as LEAs and HEIs and there are various courses leading to professional qualifications with a requirement to undertake such research. In one example Essex LEA makes a good case for the role of the LEA in supporting school research, citing the LEA's ability to:

make strategic connections, facilitate research partnerships and networks, make links with other agencies and provide challenge and critique.

(Handscombe, 2005, p. 14)

An HEI based network, *The Collaborative Action Research Network* (CARN) states that:

The quality of our work in the professions depends upon our willingness to ask questions of ourselves and others, and to explore challenging ideas and practices, including the values that underpin them.

(CARN, 2005)

and describes its work as:

committed to supporting and improving the quality of professional practice, through systematic, critical, creative inquiry into the goals, processes and contexts of professional work.

(ibid.)

The three examples cited all aim to develop teachers as researchers through training and expert support and advice and to support the exchange of critique by creating a practitioners' research network or forum. Such initiatives are valuable when we consider the discussion in Chapter 6 on the dialogical nature of the development of professional knowledge and understanding. Being part of a well functioning network of informed researchers and practitioners can help teachers to undertake and evaluate their own research; disseminate the results and become informed interrogators of the research presented to them, under certain conditions.

Social Justice and Teacher Research

A strong social justice argument runs through much literature on teacher research (Corey, 1953) and some versions of action research make a strong link with the idea of social justice:

Action research is simply a form of self-reflective enquiry undertaken by participants in social situations in order to improve the rationality and justice of their own practices, their understanding of these practices and the situations in which the practices are carried out.

(Carr & Kemmis, 1989, p. 162)

Carr and Kemmis (1989) argue for a Habermasian, liberationist vision of the power of the teacher as researcher, based on their definition of professionalism, which it is useful to recap in itself (pp. 8–9). The authors isolate three characteristics of professionalism. First, the methods and procedures employed by members of a profession are based on a body of theoretical knowledge and research, as in medicine, law or engineering. Secondly, they have an ethical dimension, a commitment to the well-being of their clients. Thirdly, they are able to make 'both individual and collective autonomous judgements, free from external, non-professional controls and constraints' (ibid. p. 8). As Carr and Kemmis have pointed out, teacher autonomy is limited:

> For although teachers can and do make autonomous judgements about their everyday classroom practices, the broad organisational context within which these practices occur is something over which they have little control.
>
> (ibid., p. 9)

They argue that if teaching is to become a 'genuinely more professional activity it needs a firm grounding in educational theory and research' (ibid. p. 10). Further, both individual and professional autonomy should be extended and conceived as collective as well as individual[6]. This has strong roots in Stenhouse who also wanted the student, the teacher and the school to experience 'emancipation', which he defined as:

> intellectual, moral and spiritual autonomy which we recognise when we eschew paternalism and the role of authority and hold ourselves obliged to appeal to judgement.
>
> (Stenhouse, 1983, p. 163)

There is a sense in which teachers who gain research literacy and an ability to engage in well grounded reflection may become more independent minded teachers, able to evaluate the theoretical knowledge underpinning the educational policies they are asked to implement. Research literate teachers are likely to seek to understand the KT underlining the various educational strategies and are not likely to view teaching as the application of technical rationality.

Becoming 'Critical'

Being 'critical', in the sense of rationally examining research for its rigour and validity, is a necessary condition for this kind of development, as Hammersley states:

> starting from the assumption that the sole immediate goal of inquiry is the production of knowledge, criticism in that context should be primarily concerned with whether this goal has been achieved; and secondarily, with whether it has been pursued effectively . . . criticism is a means not an end: it is a means to the collective discovery of truths, or at least to the elimination of errors. This distinguishes it from much criticism in other spheres.
>
> (Hammersley, 2005, p. 7)

Earlier chapters have established the philosophical claims that teaching is a practice or set of practices and that practical wisdom, or *phronesis* is required to teach well. Procedural knowledge is gained experientially so one might argue that teachers who are not engaged critically, in the sense of reflectively, with their own practice are actually practising 'badly'. The skills of reflecting on one's own practice systematically can be extended to include reflection on wider educational issues, including developing the skills of evaluating good educational research and distinguishing it from bad research. There is a need for teacher educators to help teachers to develop these skills.

The next section looks at the currently promoted use of educational research as a tool to build up a knowledge base for teachers. We need to examine the origin and current practice of the idea of teaching as an evidence-informed practice.

Evidence-Informed Practice: Teachers As Users of Research

Both doing research and reading research require an understanding about what research is; how particular theories underpin what is researched; how research is carried out, and as far as qualitative research is concerned, the relationship of aims and values to the interpretative process of elaborating research findings. It is important for teachers to become research literate, in the sense of being able to question and evaluate educational research, in order to become more informed practitioners, so as to improve teaching practice and also to develop an informed, independent stance when presented with policies and strategies promoted as research evidenced.

Earlier we saw that there need be no problem in assessing individual pieces of research in isolation from other pieces, if one has a set of criteria for robustness of conclusions. Teachers as users of research, rather than doers of research certainly need to be trained to understand good research from bad, in order to gauge the reliability of findings for their own practice. As Winch has pointed out, teachers need to develop 'critical rationality as a practical disposition and skill' (Winch, 2006, p. 45)[7], and the nature of critical rationality is a 'settled disposition and set of abilities to subject authorities to evaluation' (ibid.). Therefore, any course of teacher education ought, in my view, to include some work on becoming research literate in this sense. Increasingly, teaching is being conceptualised as evidence-informed, with policy and funding decisions in tow.

Currently teaching is promoted 'as a research and evidence-informed profession as a means of improving teaching and learning and raising standards' (TDA, 2005a), an instrumentalist view of professional status. The TDA states that it aims to work with ITE providers:

> on building a professional knowledge base for ITT by identifying and disseminating effective practices and relevant research (nationally and internationally); commissioning research and development; identifying and harnessing the services and information available through the internet.
>
> (ibid.)

Earlier we established that educational research is a varied field, and that much depends on what research question is identified, from what perspective, for what purpose, and by whom. We have also established that teachers as practitioner researchers can investigate areas of practice in context, although admittedly quality does not always result, as good research relies on achievement of some pre-defined quality criteria. Research can be supported by partnerships, with HEI, LEAs or independent consultants. However, the time to do it, and to learn how to do it, then to disseminate and build on it, needs to be funded. The TTA did fund some teacher research scholarships from 1996 to 2002. The projects funded related to defined priority areas and these areas were defined largely by the parameters we have already examined in Chapters 1 and 2, the standards and effectiveness movement, the national curriculum and the strategies. The point here is that there is a danger that the evidence base for education that is being created is biased towards research which asks the politically acceptable questions or the questions which fit into current models of educational aims and purposes. So we are back with our series of questions, namely, whose evidence base, built for what purpose, and how?

To answer these questions we should look at the recent genesis of the idea of teaching as an evidence-informed profession and the questions about what a knowledge base for the teaching profession is and 'how would we get one?' (Hiebert et al., 2002). In the English context Hargreaves's 1996 address to the TTA was a formative event. He criticised educational research on several counts, for being 'non-cumulative' unlike medical research, which builds on previous evidence; of poor relevance to improving classroom practice; often partisan, taking place in a context of methodological controversies, which only interest academics and lastly for the poor quality of much research (pp. 2–3). Ofsted's commissioned report (Tooley & Darby, 1998) backed this criticism. The analogy between education and medicine may be unhelpful however. As we have seen earlier in this book, classrooms are complex places. 'In education the "treatments" consist of symbolic interaction, with all the scope for multiple interpretations and responses which that implies' (Hammersley, 1997, p. 141).

Hammersley further points out that what are regarded as the most important kinds of learning, relating to high-level, transferable skills or personal understanding are extraordinarily difficult to measure with any degree of validity and reliability (ibid., p. 142), and that unlike scientific research, we cannot set up blind control in any tests we do on our own practice, since we are engaged in the practice we are investigating. We therefore necessarily come up against problems in producing the kind of knowledge that Hargreaves demands.

> Teaching and learning embody practical knowledge not technical knowledge. Also, unlike medicine, teachers mainly deal with batches of pupils, rather than single clients, so that much medical research avoids many of the problems that face educational researchers, in particular those deriving from the peculiarities of the social world.
>
> (ibid., p. 148)

Where it does not, Hammersley suggests we find the same lack of cumulative evidence that Hargreaves bemoans in education (ibid., p. 150), and he cites a *BMA Journal* article, 'The Scandal of Poor Medical Research' (1994), referencing many papers published in medical journals with severe methodological weakness. They are of poor quality, he states, '*precisely* because they are carried out by *practising* doctors who are expected to engage in research, but are often inadequately prepared for or committed to it' (ibid., p. 150).

In promoting teaching as an evidenced informed profession the TDA on behalf of the DCSF wishes to develop a knowledge base where research builds on previous research, which practitioners can access. There are practical obstacles to teachers developing habits of regularly using research to inform their practice. Teachers need time, opportunity, know-how and motivation to inform themselves on even digested research findings, so resources need to be made available to support study time and support services (Hemsley-Brown & Sharpe, 2003; Bradley et al., 2005). The hope that teachers will access and use a research defined 'knowledge base' to inform their practice initially seems to be non-contentious. Another of Hargreaves's discussions is pertinent here, that of the idea of 'the knowledge society' and particularly 'the knowledge-creating school' (Hargreaves, 1998). There is much to welcome in the general conclusions about professional development for teachers, particularly his hope of 'turning teaching into a job with far more opportunities for teachers to be creative in ways that mirror the style of successful practitioners in other professions' (ibid., p. 13).

If this implies allowing more autonomy for teachers in choice of curriculum and methods than currently, the view is commendable. However, it is the notion of 'knowledge' that needs examining. What is 'the knowledge-creating school'? On one level it seems absurd to say that schools do not create knowledge, as one would suppose that at least some of the pupils must learn something at some time. The term in the sense used by Hargreaves is based on 'knowledge-creating organisations in other areas' (p. 27). The knowledge creating school:

- investigates the state of its intellectual capital
- manages the process of creating new professional knowledge
- validates the professional knowledge created
- disseminates the created professional knowledge (p. 27).

Intellectual capital is analogised as follows:

imagine a moderately large secondary school with 45 teachers and put the following questions to them. How many years of professional experience are there among the teaching staff of your school? How much of this professional knowledge is shared by all the teachers, shared by some of the teachers, locked in the heads of individual teachers?.

(ibid., p. 27)

The argument then moves to question how this intellectual capital can be shared and in a sense 'invested' to draw dividends. The evidence base then begins to appear to be something like a bank on which we can draw for professional knowledge. Hargreaves fleshes out his account with his concept of the validation of professional practice by first introducing the notion of '*best practice*', with reference to the electronics industry. He tells us that successful electronics firms do not require external validation of their '*created knowledge*' in the form of '*literature*' because the products created are subject to '*three obvious validation tests*', first, scientific principles, secondly that the products work and thirdly that they sell (p. 32 and pp. 49–50). By 'validating literature' he probably has in mind academic, peer reviewed theoretical or research-based publications.

These criteria do not transfer easily to educational contexts, such as schools. Schools are not economic enterprises in the same way as electronic firms and the concept of knowledge as economic capital does not transfer either. We know what it means to say that an electronic device works or does not work, but we need to have agreed, explicit and stated aims for the educational practice under consideration if we are to say whether *it* works or not. If our aims are outcomes based, and the outcomes are not achieved, we might *well* be able to say whether a practice has worked or not. If they are more general and liberal aims we could not say at a specific moment of time whether the practice has worked or not, because by definition we would be looking at longer-term processes. Are we commenting on whether someone's education helped him or her to live a 'good life', or are we determining an A Level examination grade? The first endeavour cannot be quantified, the second can.

In education, Hargreaves says, applied knowledge is validated when it is turned into a practice, which demonstrably and repeatedly works and can be used or adapted by different practitioners in a range of contexts. 'A practice that works only in very restricted circumstances or is not transferable to other teachers cannot be regarded as useful knowledge' (p. 32). So there is here an implied 'outcomes' definition of education since the 'working' of the practice has been divorced from the aims of education. It is important to bear this in mind when we come to consider the issue of promoting evidence-informed research as the favoured means of gaining 'knowledge' about teaching and learning, because it indicates that the knowledge gained may be related to one particular discourse about teaching.

Turning now to Hargreaves's central point about the validation of what he calls 'professional knowledge' in education he makes a distinction between *a good idea*, which may be worthwhile but has not been subject to any kind of test, *a good practice*, which implies some kind of validation that is sound and *best practice*, which implies a good practice that is demonstrably better than others (pp. 32–33). It seems apparent that a standards agenda underlies the argument in the next section's discussion of what 'better' refers to. Most people, he says, confuse a *'good practice'*, for which there is often no evidence of effectiveness, with *'best practice'*. His argument is that teachers in schools work for the most part on their own in a state of professional isolation, using the trial and error method, to discover through personal experience, what works for them. Knowledge validation is reduced to 'what works for me' but the criteria by which a practice is judged to work remain obscure. They may know what *'good practice'* is, but not necessarily what *'best practice'* is, which is one validated by research evidence and, he says, 'this is patently *not* a way in which standards can be raised' (p. 33).

The distinction between a good practice and best practice may be useful, but Hargreaves has not previously established any link between 'raising educational standards' and 'validating a professional practice'. We also need to ask what it is we are validating, is it 'knowledge' or professional practice, and whose professional practice? Again we come back to problems with underdetermined terms.

Some of Hargreaves's suggestions are sound. Many practitioners wish to engage in research and work in partnership with HEI personnel, providing they are given time and resources. However, we should question the underlying aims of the endeavour. An accumulation of research evidence may suggest that something works to improve a practice, but we also need to retain the right to ask, works for whom, and in what circumstances? Does the current drive for evidence-informed practice allow us to do this? We could argue that overall it is a good direction to go in because it recognises the interface between practice and theory, and the particularities of practical knowledge and understanding, but too narrow a conception of what this defined 'evidence' can do for us might be dangerous, by focusing us on outcomes divorced from aims. Just because we have evidence for something working does not mean it is a good thing, and what 'works' means here is inevitably contentious. We need to ask 'works' for what, and in the service of what? Morphine works to alter our moods. It is a bad drug for anyone destructively hooked on heroin and a good drug for pain control for the terminally ill.

A major plank in the evidence-base is the systematic research review. The next section looks at its genesis and issues relating to its use.

Systematic Reviews

This chapter has argued that teachers should be supported in engaging with research, both as literate consumers of research and experienced practitioners. We have seen that to engage in research teachers need support from experienced researchers and time and resources. As consumers of research how are teachers to benefit from research evidence? Policy currently favours the 'systematic' review to synthesise research evidence and to make it thereby user-friendly for practitioners and policymakers (Davies, 1999; Davies, 2000; Evans, 2000; Hammersley, 2001).

> The current interest in policy and research circles in systematic reviews and evidence-informed education is part of a general move in the UK and elsewhere towards basing policy and professional practice on sound evidence of effectiveness. In the health sector, for instance, it has become clear that much of what health care professionals do is not derived from reliable evidence, and that sometimes what professionals believe in with all the best intentions may not only be ineffective but sometimes actually harmful. This has led to systems being set up to ensure that professionals and policy-makers have constantly updated access to the findings of good quality research.
>
> (EPPI, 2005)

In medicine, syntheses of evidence on the effectiveness of healthcare interventions for practitioners and policymakers are published in the *Cochrane Collaboration*. The more recent Campbell Collaboration has a similar function in the fields of social policy and interventions. The Cochrane Collaboration developed 'a framework for conducting and verifying systematic reviews and meta-analyses of random controlled trials of medical interventions' (ibid.). This model was adapted later for social science by the Evidence for Policy and Practice Information and Co-ordinating Centre (EPPI-Centre)[8], established in 1993:

> to address the need for a systematic approach to the organisation and review of evidence-based work on social interventions. The work and publications of the centre engage health and education policy makers, practitioners and service users in discussions about how researchers can make their work more relevant and how to use research findings.
>
> (ibid.)

The EPPI-Centre is influential in promoting 'evidence informed practice' in education, through its Research Evidence in Education Library (REEL) commissioned by the DCSF.

> The Centre's vision is to be a centralised resource for people wishing to undertake systematic reviews of research in education and those wishing to use reviews to inform policy and practice.
>
> (ibid.)

To this end systematic reviews of educational research and access to databases for systematic reviewers are published on the REEL Website. Systematic reviews 'involve identifying research reports and reviewing them in an explicit and standard way so as to produce new and accessible syntheses of the evidence' (ibid.).

Systematic reviewing is seen as an important plank in the construction of teaching as an evidence-informed practice with implications for teacher training. The TDA wants systematic reviews:

> to identify existing and relevant research and evidence in initial teacher training (ITT), and to form a key strand of the Training and Development Agency's (TDA) ongoing ITT research strategy ... These research reviews are seen as part of the process of identifying current effective practices, and highlighting gaps in professional knowledge that is relevant to the training of teachers.
>
> (TDA, 2005a)

There are, however, issues about the reliability and validity of systematic reviews taking into account the assumptions about research, and about the task of reviewing, which are built into the concept of systematic review (Davies, 2000; Evans, 2000; Hammersley, 2001). A systematic review is a meta-analysis of research evidence, a research synthesis and not a narrative account of the traditional literature review, which is seen as highly subjective in its approach. The systematic review follows protocols that aim to render it objective.

> The intended result is a research synthesis that can be replicated by others, can create consensus among scholars, and can focus debate in a constructive fashion.
>
> (Cooper, 1998, p. xi, quoted in Hammersley, 2001, pp. 543–544)

Hammersley (2001, p. 544) identifies four distinctive features of systematic reviews before usefully examining the implications of these features. First, after framing the research question, relevance criteria must be specified. The study must be fully comprehensive, which means all the available literature matching the relevance criteria must be searched as exhaustively as possible. Next and equally as important, evaluation of the literature selected as relevant must be based on:

> an explicit hierarchy of types of research design, categorised according to the likely validity of the results they produce. In short, the criteria for inclusion and exclusion of studies must be operationalisable.
>
> (ibid.)

The aim is to make the reviewing process replicable, so the literature search procedure has to be described in sufficient detail for the reader, in theory to be able to regenerate an identical set of materials, which implies that the reviewer must rely only minimally on her own judgement. Quoting Slavin (1986, p. 7), Hammersley explains that:

> while no set of procedural or statistical canons can make the review process immune to the reviewer's biases it is believed that the use of explicit procedures will usually make the reliability of the conclusions high, and that explicitness allows the reviewing process to be assessed by readers.
>
> (Hammersley, 2001, p. 544)

Thirdly, systematic reviews do not simply discuss the contributions of individual studies but combine the findings produced by the various studies reviewed. It is believed that more robust conclusions can subsequently be drawn, relying on support from more cases than any of the individual studies included in the review could provide. Finally, because of the link between systematic reviews and evidence-informed practice, systematic reviews are frequently seen as concerned with providing research-based answers to specific questions about what works, or what works best, in relation to some practical problem.

They are treated as a bridge between research, on the one hand, and policy-making or practice, on the other. While narrative reviews are also widely believed to serve this bridging function, these often address large and complex areas involving multiple issues – frequently being designed to provide a map of research in the relevant field. They do not usually focus exclusively on specific hypotheses about the effects of particular policies or practices.

(ibid.)

Systematic reviews assume the superiority of quantitative methodologies over qualitative ones for evaluating the worth of research.

What are treated as of highest value are studies involving explicit and replicable procedures which provide for physical or statistical control and/or statistical generalisation. So, experiments, quasi-experiments, randomised controlled trials, and statistical analyses of system inputs and outcomes are at the top of what we might call its credibility hierarchy.

(ibid., p. 545)

Systematic reviewing also applies a narrowly positivist model to the task of producing reviews, according to Hammersley (ibid.) as not only must the reviewer judge the quality of particular studies in terms of positivist criteria, the reviewing process itself must match similar criteria.

In particular, as already noted, it must employ *explicit procedures* in selecting and evaluating studies: relevance criteria must be identified, and all studies meeting those criteria are to be included in the review and evaluated in terms of whether their designs meet the specified validity threshold.

(ibid.)

These criteria fit a narrow interpretation of the scientific method, rather than a version of the natural sciences, as described in Dewey's exposition of experimental empiricism. Hammersley is right therefore that we should view the knowledge created by systematic reviews of education research with a certain caution. Hammersley argues that the systematic review is no replacement for older kinds of literature review, and that it is founded on ideas about research and the task of reviewing that are questionable. He does not suggest that systematic reviews are of no value, but, wisely in my opinion, objects to the way in which they are currently being privileged in terms of the allocation of resources.

We need to heed Hammersley's warning that the pressure for such reviews could have undesirable consequences on the production of other kinds of research (ibid., pp. 549–550).

> The evidence-based practice movement tends to assume that research can specify not only what *has* been done but also whether it was *good* or *bad* and what *should* be done; yet it is clear that this necessarily involves value judgements which research cannot validate on its own.
>
> (ibid., p. 549)

Hammersley also warns that

> the relationship between research and policy-making has implications not just for the *kind* of research which will be privileged, but also for the whole mode of organisation within which research operates. Advocacy of systematic reviews, and of evidence-based practice, are closely associated with moves towards increased central control over educational research.
>
> (ibid.)[9]

Educational research, it is suggested, risks becoming subject to the kind of control outlined in Chapter 1, which charted a pattern of growing control over education in general and ITET in particular during the past 25 years. The problematic relationship between the nature of kinds of educational research and the evidence-informed practice movement has also been more fully explored by Thrupp (2001), Hammersley (2002) and Young et al. (2002). Hammersley notes the parallel between the notion of explicitness, which is central to systematic reviewing, and the current influential demands for transparent accountability from within government circles:

The idea is that systematic reviews can allow lay people to judge for themselves which policies and practices work. Systematic reviews purport to make research findings 'transparent', so as to enable users to judge what works without any mediation by professionals, including researchers. In these terms, perhaps the most serious charge to be laid against the systematic review movement is that it extends the myth of the audit society to research.

(ibid., p. 551)

As is to be expected the TDA, promoting systematic reviews, does not see them as problematic in the construction of knowledge, and the TDA Website outlines key features of systematic reviews, with no discussion of any issues around the review process itself. It is taken as axiomatic and unexamined that systematic reviews of the kind undertaken by the EPPI-Centre, produce 'knowledge capable of informing practice' (see TDA 2005a). The TDA's priorities come largely from the school effectiveness agenda (Thrupp, 2001, p. 7), and in recent years school effectiveness research (SER) has become increasingly criticised for being a socially and politically decontextualised body of literature, which provides support for inequitable educational reforms. It has been suggested that the TDA does not respond to these criticisms, primarily because it does not share the same epistemological commitments as its critics.

Nevertheless it is argued that the concerns of critics should be taken seriously by SER proponents because they speak powerfully to a number of key problem areas within the SER field. Three such areas are ... the overclaiming of SER; the continued under-theorising of SER, and the inability of SER to control the political use of its findings.

(Thrupp, 2001, p. 7)

Accepting the arguments raised in this section we can see that the relationship between evidence and policymaking or practice is complex, affected by relationships, ideologies and professional preferences as much as by evidence. It cannot be invoked for all contexts and practices (Ginsburg & Gorostiaga, 2001; Crewe & Young, 2002; Simons, 2003). The implications for the teacher as researcher are that with the proviso of robust, rigorous procedures and practices, her piece of practitioner research may be as useful to her practice as research she takes 'off the shelf'. Of course, she may benefit from knowing what previous research has found, and ought to do some investigation, possibly using a systematic review, but she needs the skills to interrogate research, and to understand the potential partiality of its perspectives.

Systematic reviews cannot adequately deal with a synthesis of the aims and objectives underlying the research synthesised and so cannot embody the sophistication of practice. The aim of such reviews is to create KT about education, which can be applied to future educational policies and practice. This endeavour fails for two reasons. First, because of the defects in its methodological assumptions as analysed in this section of the chapter. Secondly, as we have seen in Chapters 4–6, the relationship between KH and KT is complex. When teachers apply theoretical knowledge in their practice it is always in a particular context, mediated through their own KH. Systematic reviews rely on technical rationality, ungrounded in practical judgement.

Conclusion

This chapter has been concerned to establish that teachers ought to be encouraged and supported to research their own practice with a view to creating new understandings or confirming previously held views, because they are uniquely able to understand the precise conditions in which the research takes place. Knowledge about what works and does not work in education needs to be broadly textured because there are so many contexts and criteria in play. Teachers need to know how to evaluate good research and have the time to interrogate findings from accumulated evidence. The practitioner researcher needs certain qualities, dispositions and motivation and in addition needs to be given time and resources to engage in any research project. The processes of well-grounded reflection are a good basis for developing research skills and time needs to be available in ITET programmes to allow for the development of such skills.

Notes

1. See Barrow (1986).
2. See also the discussion on pp. 171–176 (Bridges, 2003).
3. The term 'action research' is commonly credited to Kurt Lewin (1946) although Corey (1953) earlier produced an account of teachers as 'scientific' researchers of their own practice, in order to evaluate their decisions and actions, modify and reformulate their plans and initiate a cycle of improvement and development. (See Whitehead, 1999.)
4. See, for example, George Demetrion's relation of Deweyan inquiry to his work in adult literacy (Demetrion, 2006).
5. See, for example, Pachler, 2005 The impetus to produce this journal 'Reflecting Education' arose from the repeatedly high quality of the submissions to Masters courses at the Institute of Education, mainly involving practitioner research.
6. See Winch, 2006, for a fuller discussion.
7. See the illuminating discussion, Winch, 2006, pp. 32–71.
8. The EPPI-Centre is part of the Social Science Research Unit (SSRU), Institute of Education, University of London. The EPPI-Centre is the home of the Methods for Research Synthesis Programme of the ESRC National Centre for Research Methods and is a partner of Cochrane, and co-director of Campbell.
9. See also Thrupp, 2001; Hammersley, 2002.

Chapter 8

Assessment

So far it seems clear that the ability to teach well, applying practical judgement with all the manifest complexity entailed, is experientially gained and that a number of specific conditions to developing practical judgement are relevant to its nurture and sustenance. What kind of assessment of trainee teachers for the status of qualified teachers is best? What mode of assessment can best prepare trainees for entry into the community of practice of the profession and best account for the trainee's growing development of practical judgement and possession of the requisite theoretical knowledge and understanding? From the earlier discussion of the knowledge and understanding that teachers need to demonstrate in order to gain the award of QTS, it is apparent that teachers need to have relevant propositional and procedural knowledge; practical abilities, in the form of specific skills; general capacities and dispositions and also the ability to reflect on practice and be in some degree research literate.

In terms of the required propositional knowledge, theoretical knowledge and understanding, we can delineate five broad areas, which interrelate in the actual practice of teaching. These are:

1. Pedagogical content knowledge of subjects taught, such as history or geography.
2. Knowledge about methodologies in the subject taught.
3. Some educational theory, for example relating to educational aims and objectives, the subject area, curriculum analysis and planning.
4. Knowledge of certain educational policies such as the national curriculum and relevant strategies.
5. Knowledge of the statutory frameworks for teaching, such as current legislation regarding the 'children's' agenda' and health and safety.

It is now possible to specify some general characteristics of required teacher knowledge and understanding at QTS level. These are, it seems to me:

1. Propositional knowledge (KT) as outlined above.
2. Practical abilities, in the form of specific skills.
3. General capacities and dispositions, such as openness, flexibility, the ability to work hard or to maintain good relationships with others.
4. Pedagogical articulation, involving the ability to effectively reflect on practice and to be, in some degree, research literate.

Practical judgement is foundational: the bedrock of successful teaching ability. It enables the kind of discernment required to attend to all the manifold claims on competence and experience. Practical judgement interacting with general capacities enables successful reflection and hence comprehension and articulation, which is what makes it a foundational characteristic. Teacher educators have an interest in supporting new teachers in their growth and development. It is open to question, however, how far character, in the form of general capacities can be developed, so teacher educators have arguably less influence under characteristic 3, relating to capacities and dispositions. Tuition in the subject area and in educational issues and policies can help trainees to gain the appropriate propositional knowledge for characteristic 1. Development of practical abilities in relation to teaching (characteristic 2) is bound up with the ability to engage with well-grounded reflective practices. Fluent and expert teaching involves the exercise of practical judgement, which entails an initiation into and continual development within the various practices of teaching. We saw in Chapter 6 that it is beneficial for most teachers to engage in a particular kind of mentored dialogue on practice, in order to articulate the practice, and to develop well-grounded reflection, capable of reaching new and productive understandings. To become an appropriately articulate and critically literate practitioner (characteristic 4) in the sense established in the previous chapter, new teachers need to use discernment and an alertness of mind. The four characteristics are thus inter-related and underpin practical judgement, as we have seen in the account in this book.

Teacher educators need both a teaching programme and an assessment mechanism that are capable of encompassing all four characteristics of teacher knowledge and understanding. Standards, using descriptors of good practice as analysed in Chapter 2, are a helpful instrument on which to build a teaching programme and form an assessment mechanism for characteristic 1, relating to propositional knowledge. They also have an important role to play in the teaching programme and assessment of practical skills, with the caveat that these skills are not 'performed' in a vacuum. As we have seen previously, in deciding how well a teacher exercises a particular skill or set of skills, such as 'managing resources', a wider canvas of attitudes and values comes constantly into play. An assessor needs to know why certain resources were chosen over certain others in any particular circumstance. Examining such choices often reveals wider aspects of teacherly behaviour, such as the virtue of care for individual pupils' ability to access certain resources, or the lack of such care. We have seen that standards alone are inadequate to encompass those characteristics relating to general capacities, dispositions and pedagogical articulation. In order to foster these, teacher educators and assessors use their own practical judgement in developing that of their trainees. Therefore, QTS assessment would be more accurately able to account for 'good teacherliness' if it made more place for practical judgement not narrowly focused on the ends of standards assessment.

Before considering how standards-based QTS assessment might be enriched, some general assessment principles and practices need discussion, since guidelines for good ITET assessment practice can be built on such general principles. ITET assessment guidelines need to be capable of developing all four of the identified teacher characteristics and of fostering the foundational characteristic of practical judgement.

General Assessment Issues

Significantly for teacher education, general educational assessment has undergone a major review over the past 20 years (Gipps, 1994; Goldstein & Lewis, 1996; Mabry, 1997; Stobart & Gipps, 1997; Filer, 2000). It is now widely established in the literature that 'any assessment rests upon particular assumptions, exists within complex social structures and is informed by social and political preferences' (Goldstein & Lewis, 1996, p. 7). Broadfoot (1996), reviewing research on assessment practice, points to 'a long standing division between sociological and psychological theories', which have

> arguably led to a tendency to divorce the intra-personal factors affecting learning from those which reside in the social context. Common sense, however, suggests that the two must be closely related.
>
> (p. 27)

Influential factors cited are the learner's specific socio-cultural milieu, the school context and the individual classroom and school environment:

> It is through the discourse of assessment in its various forms, oral, written and non-verbal, and its various modes, which include cognitive feedback, behaviour management and encouragement, that individuals learn, are able to build up a sense of their identity as learners and thus, ultimately ... (their) motivation ... and hence achievement.
>
> (Broadfoot, 1996, pp. 27–28)

Given the earlier account in this book of the role played by affective factors in the development of teacher knowledge and understanding it is clear that some students are discouraged by getting low grades or critical comments and some are challenged to do better next time. Just as in ITET we considered the desirability of a mentor's sense of solidarity with the mentee, in teaching in general a teacher also needs such a sense when reporting the results of any assessment task to a pupil or student. Evidently, wise judgement leads to thoughtful teachers adapting their feedback to students for this reason, where this is possible. Assessment can be a factor in how students view their progress and effect their subsequent motivation. In this sense, assessment functions as a 'message system' (Bernstein, 1977) and like language, discussed in Chapter 4, is a 'conduit' and a constituent of knowledge and understanding. However, it is worth saying that summative assessment, such as in public examinations, may not be amenable to this treatment, since systemically there is almost no role for this kind of feedback.

In ITET we want teachers to develop their knowledge and understanding so as to develop their practical judgement. It follows that where we need to assess the teacher in order to enable her to pass through a particular stage of professional development, we need appropriate assessment practices and procedures. We have seen that the standards for the award of QTS on their own cannot account for all the dimensions of practical judgement operating in practice. It follows that standards assessment in ITET on its own cannot get at all the dimensions we need to examine in order to evaluate the nature and extent of the trainee's progress towards gaining her expert's capacity of practical judgement. Further, having *only* standards assessment in place can influence trainees' approach to learning to teach, as we have seen earlier. Where knowledge and understanding is experientially gained, such as in learning to teach, it might be defined as 'that reflective activity which enables the learner to draw upon previous experience to understand and evaluate the present, so as to shape future action and formulate new knowledge' (Abbott, 1994, quoted in Watkins & Carnell, 2002, p. 1).

Learning as a 'dynamic, flexible' process, (Henning-Stout, 1994, p. 59) needs some kind of assessment that is more responsive to individual learning circumstances than is currently the case. Watkins (2000) characterises current policy as performance orientated:

The performance idea that the important things about teaching are the observables does not fit with current understandings of pedagogy which highlight the complexity of orchestrating the classroom context, the multiple nature of teacher knowledge and the connected nature of teacher understanding.

(Watkins, 2000, p. 35)[1]

There is a 'relationship between the processes we assess and the processes we use to carry out assessment' (Henning-Stout, 1994, p. 59) and in order to establish a more appropriate form of ITET assessment it is useful to outline some broad dimensions of how assessment can 'lead' learning.

Self Direction

The kind of assessment tasks that are set can help learners to engage affectively as well as cognitively with the material. To illustrate this point, the good reflective practices examined in Chapter 3 allowed trainees to think through particular areas arising from shared understandings about particular instances of practice, based on negotiated focuses for discussion. We saw there that the way in which the mentor undertakes the role of elaborating the meanings of the practice in a critical yet supportive manner, can strongly influence the way in which the trainee learns. The mode and content of the assessment may encourage a depth of engagement with the learning or assessment task, which may influence the ability to retain and apply learning 'richly', across and within different contexts. In modern foreign languages, for example, a standard task involves setting a list of vocabulary to be learnt, abstracted from a particular text, which is subsequently tested. The aim of the task is to get students to retain specified vocabulary in order to add to a usable lexis. A different task would be to teach students how to use dictionaries and ask them to decode a text. There are times when the first task is appropriate and has its place in learning a foreign language. However, the second task encourages the student to engage more deeply with the vocabulary in question. Students are more likely to remember vocabulary they decode for themselves, and vocabulary that is contextualised within a text. Here 'contextualise' carries its literal meaning. The student here experiences the vocabulary as language in use. The application to ITET is that trainees who focus on the standards and attempt to tick them off throughout the practice are less likely to progress towards a deep understanding of the kind of connections they need to make between all the elements of the standards, than trainees who manage to reflect in a well-grounded way on specific instances of teaching that they have experienced.

Assessment may help students to understand if they are making progress, meaning if they are learning what is being taught, 'if such a process is built into the assessment procedures and supported by explication and example' (Broadfoot, 1996, pp. 28–29). To learn to evaluate their own learning learners need to understand what the assessment criteria are by which their progress is judged. Teachers are currently encouraged to make such principles clear to students and to 'teach' or give support for students to engage in peer review or self-review procedures at regular intervals, on specific review criteria. Pupils and students are encouraged to understand how they are progressing by relating what they have done to what they might do to improve. This requires an understanding of the assessment criteria. In ITET we know (through reports of tutors' visits to schools) that modes of engagement with the QTS standards are varied in different placement schools and that this influences the way in which trainees conceive their practice. (See Chapter 6 on mentoring and Chapter 3 on reflection.) This reinforces the earlier point that training focused narrowly on standards is likely to encourage a somewhat passive approach to self-directed and well-grounded reflection.

For the reasons considered above, what has been established about formative assessment for general education ought to underline ITET assessment.

Formative Assessment and the QTS Standards

The role of formative assessment generally in enabling or hindering learning has been widely accepted under the term 'assessment for learning' (AfL) (Black & Wiliam, 1998; Assessment Reform Group, 1999; Black et al., 2002; Black & Harrison, 2003). In this model, assessment is viewed not as an end product to test knowledge and understanding, but part of the process of acquiring it (QCA, 2005). The advocated, general model of good assessment practices involves teacher and learner sharing an understanding of the assessment criteria used. Good assessment, helpful to professional, practice-based learning, ought on this model to be integrated with the process of learning and on the whole, current ITET practices do enable the sharing of assessment criteria, since the standards are promulgated as the basis of QTS. How far the current assessment criteria are adequate for their job in assessing teachers for QTS is open to debate. As discussed in Chapters 1 and 2 these criteria are mainly couched in performance-related language, whose inherent limitations we have accepted.

Can elements of the 'assessment for learning' model compensate for shortcomings in standards-based ITET assessment, which gives little guidance in assessing the development of the practical judgement foundational to good teaching? Standards do provide some descriptors of good teaching performance and are capable of contributing to some elements of satisfactory assessment procedures. Used as assessment criteria the standards *are* by definition shared with learners, since trainees know at the outset that they must meet these standards at the end of their training. Also most trainees working towards QTS experience an element of process-based 'negotiated' learning, in that mentors and trainees regularly set and review some kind of developmental targets, as described in Chapter 6. However, there are many ways in which this 'negotiation' may be interpreted in schools and by mentors (Heilbronn et al., 2002). At one end of a continuum are some HEI-led courses, which engage trainees in a substantial element of reflective thinking (Benton, 1990; Everton, 1992; Totterdell & Lambert, 1993; Elliot & Calderdale, 1995; Moore & Ash, 2002). At the other end are some work-based schemes wholly wedded to target setting based on the standards, usually on those particular standards, which impact the most on classroom practice. Time factors dominate the mode of training and development both for trainee and mentor and sometimes standards can come to dominate meetings, at the expense of broader development of teaching capacities.

A major drawback with only having standards assessment in ITET is the extent to which it can 'lead' learning. We have seen in the earlier example of French vocabulary learning how assessment can engage a student in degrees of learning, from shallow to deep, and we are familiar with the use of questioning techniques ranging from closed to open-ended questions. The kind of question posed is a significant determinant of the answer given. Oral examiners for modern foreign languages are trained to structure their interviews with students to enable students to give the fullest answers possible, so as not to close down the possibility of the student gaining high marks. In the oral examination the students draw on their own knowledge of the language to interact with the question asked in a personal way. Similarly, too structured an expectation of what teachers will learn may prevent teachers from experimenting with ways of teaching, through which they may both learn to extend their teaching repertoire and also draw on their own individual qualities and dispositions. A more appropriate model of ITET, one not totally focused on standards-based assessment, could better enable the dialogue between mentor and trainee to forefront critical evaluation of teaching, as a step to the growth of professional knowledge and practical judgement. Since such knowledge and understanding grows out of experience, mediated through well-grounded reflection, experimentation within reason is a good thing, providing the trainee is able to interrogate her teaching in a well-grounded manner.

Such questioning in dialogue needs to be part of the practice of all the participants in an ITET partnership. In practice, the standards and time restraints limit how much reflection can develop through the 'critical friend' dialogue. An example of when such a critical dialogue might occur is on those occasions when trainee needs match school developmental priorities, such as when the trainee is learning about assessment and the school is coincidentally developing a new assessment policy and throwing fundamental questions into the public arena. The school staff may then be 'allowed' to take the time to question what is habitually done themselves, in a more fundamental way than is generally permitted by time and other restraints. In so doing, the mentors and other school staff would be engaging with joint, well-grounded reflection on the principles and purposes of the school-based element of the training.

Taking the QTS standards as a basis for reflection and dialogue alone hinders a deep and broad conception of teacher education. This is not limited to the English context as a review of teacher education in several European countries found that sometimes there was a

> worryingly fundamental ... lack of joint reflection about the principles and purposes of the training, both from the more directly involved actors, and from the institutions they represented and this was seen as fundamental to any improvement at all. Such reflection

had it occurred would have allowed not only the understanding of these principles but also the commitment to continuous improvement, thus increasing the potential of different but complimentary contributions for the improvement of the quality of training.

(Stephenson, 2000, p. 24)

One way in which we could broaden the application of well-grounded reflection in the English context is to supplement standards assessment with modes of learning that create tasks, which can be both opportunities for reflection and for assessment.

Alternative Assessment Tasks

Teacher Narrative

Having accepted the crucial role of well-grounded reflection in teaching, one vehicle that can aid reflection is the use of teacher narrative, meaning teacher constructed narratives about their experiences, which can be used in the professional dialogue on teaching. Narratives may provide 'teacher educators and prospective teachers with new possibilities and means of hearing the details of professionals' ways of knowing' (Beattie, 2000, p. 3). What are the characteristics of narrative that might make it useful as a tool in professional learning? First, it is based on the development of the whole person who is becoming a teacher. The construction of professional knowledge is understood as a relational and interactive process where the trainee is in a sense 'the pages she is writing'. The practice and the trainee are interconnected. In fact, '(the) educational process is one of continual reorganising, reconstructing, transforming experience' (Dewey, 1966, p. 50).

Beattie has identified some characteristics of narrative inquiry in teacher education (Beattie, 2000, pp. 3–4). First it may help tutors and peers to understand different, individual contexts within which teachers operate and against which 'standards' and 'performance' are judged. We have seen in Chapter 2 that variability of context is a factor in teacher assessment. For example, managing a classroom of fifteen pupils in a leafy suburb may well have more differences than similarities to the management of a large class in a disadvantaged, urban area (Ash et al., 2004).

Secondly, narrative can validate an individual's experiences of schooling, their personal biographies and family histories and experiences of growing up in different cultural environments. This perspective shared with a mentor or with peers advances growth in knowledge and understanding about the particular context under discussion. It may do so both because it offers another perspective through which to view the practice and because the teacher's whole persona, her selfhood is enwebbed in her cultural experiences, as discussed in the previous chapter. Understanding one's own practice can only come through integration of the personal and the social. Learning and development can be impeded, if not arrested, in cases where a mentee feels that her perspective is not respected, or feels reluctant to share an insight from another cultural perspective, or in a dominant cultural setting lacks confidence to maintain the validity of her own insights and perspectives. This relates back to the notions of trust and respect discussed in Chapter 6. Such blockage of an individual's perspective can lead to 'ritualistic reflection' (Moore et al., 2002) where the trainee becomes a strategic learner, compliant with the mentor's perspectives in order to get through the training course, but does not engage with wider issues that may emerge.

We have already seen that teacher qualities and dispositions fall outside standards discourse. Therefore Beattie's further characterisation of the use of narrative in teacher education is appropriate. It can act as a vehicle for acknowledging

> ... the complexities and the realities of becoming a teacher; the realistic and often stressful, conflicting demands of juggling too many roles, such as that of parent, wage-earner and student of teaching. The details of these realities and the ways in which they are experienced by individual persons ... show the creative and uniquely personal ways in which individuals deal with the dilemmas and challenges in their lives ... and use them as constructs (rather than obstacles) in the creation of a broader design.
>
> (Beattie, 2000, pp. 3–4)

The ability of narrative to open up new horizons is not in doubt, certainly not by most readers of *War and Peace,* or *Oliver Twist,* which was influential in changing perceptions of child labour. I can personally vouch for the use of teacher narrative as a vehicle to developing teacher knowledge and understanding. The first seminar of a module of a Masters of Teaching course began with participants sharing a narrative about a teaching experience of a 'critical incident' and identifying issues and comments for discussion. These issues developed into several discussions. When coupled with reading about the use of narrative in education, informed, scholarly discussion followed. I experienced myself that

> when it is understood that personal, familial, social, cultural and organisational stories are temporal arrangements of the way things are, and that these taken-for-granted stories can be re-scripted, there is the potential for change and transformation in personal lives, classroom situations and social and organisational settings.
>
> (Beattie, 2000, p. 4)

Narrative is interpretative and indicative. Sympathetically interrogated narrative can be a useful reflective tool (Burns & Pachler, 2004). What is at stake here is not objective truth, but how the trainee feels and thinks about the experiences of teaching, mediated through and by an analytic framework, using categories shared in mentoring sessions, or tutor sessions with an HEI. The teacher narrative contains material to be used for helping the trainee to new understandings. Therefore, the mentor or tutor needs to be able to discern what is relevant to the matter in hand, namely the training curriculum and the knowledge and understanding the trainee needs to develop. The mentor or tutor as expert can therefore guide the trainee, through an interpretative process.

The following sections look at ways in which the kinds of insights gained from the narrative mode might be taken forward into evidence for the development of teacher knowledge and understanding. Two suggestions for improvement in the assessment of trainees for the award of QTS are suggested, the use of the reflective teaching statement and the professional development portfolio (PDP). Both of these instruments exist in a variety of formats and a range of courses and institutions. What are the strengths and possible drawbacks of these instruments for assessing the knowledge and understanding of teachers for the award of QTS and beyond?

The Reflective Teaching Statement

When mentoring and peer review are successful, the new teacher is generally able to reflect on what is happening in her practice by discussing, analysing and synthesising aspects of her experience. Such articulation can help to integrate the initial teaching 'curriculum' of the standards with the experience of the trainee, within nested contexts. Useful prompt questions for producing a statement are:

- What do you view as the aims of education?
- How does your view on aims relate to your role in the teaching situations you have encountered?
- How do the teaching methods you typically use reflect your interpretation of your role as a teacher?

The questions have proved good starting points for reflection, as teachers are not generally asked to reflect on the aims of education in the current, standards-driven courses. When the questions are sympathetically and collaboratively discussed, the teacher becomes an active participant in constructing her own learning curriculum, based on her values and experiences, rather than waiting for the mentor to define what should be tackled at any particular time. This can help to impart a sense of agency, whereas belief that the standards must control the learning agenda tends to encourage a deficit view of the training curriculum, by focusing on work that still needs to be done against the standards. Further, in drafting the teaching statement values are explicit. The statement can be added to at various relevant points of development to include similar reflection on specific areas, such as reflections on pupil/student motivation and how to influence it; relationships with pupils/students as groups and individually and relationship with the wider school community. Here the descriptors of practice embodied in the standards may be useful prompts for reflection whereas at present they often function to take the initiative for formulating areas for development away from the trainee.

Whatever is added to the statement, whether it is a 'slim' or a more encompassing version, it is appropriate to revisit it at key points in the training programme. It is certainly important to write it at least twice, once near the beginning of the teaching practice, when sufficient experience has built up to enable informed judgement, and once near the end of the course. Re-visiting the statement is itself a developmental activity. In cases of successful reflection, possibly enabled by good mentoring and peer dialogue, the second statement may be informed by the transformations and developments brought about by early teaching. It may articulate how the teacher has developed since writing the first statement. It may include a narrative, possibly of a critical incident or a dilemma, and be illustrated with examples such as how the teaching methods used might reflect development, or how they have been modified in response to changes in pupils or other teaching experiences. The statement could also be reviewed at key points later in teaching, and referenced in a publicly accountable manner, for example, by offering annotated 'further readings', which help locate theories or practices in a wider discourse.

Formative assessment is necessary to learning and involves a sharing of meanings between participants in learning, a view widely held and applied in education through the AfL materials. At key points learners are enabled to reflect on their progress towards specific, articulated goals, using shared assessment criteria and resulting in strategies for further development towards defined goals. Guba and Lincoln (1989) call this kind of assessment process an 'assessment intervention process' (p. 237). This process is foundational in some courses of initial teacher education, and it is to be noted that there is currently no designated vehicle under the standards assessment regulations to support such a process. Drawing together the 'thick' version of reflection discussed in Chapter 3 we could talk about 'reflection for learning' as crucial to teacher development. The two mechanisms to support reflection for learning, 'teacher narrative' and the 'reflective teaching statement' can be constituents of a professional development portfolio.

The Professional Development Portfolio (PDP)

The use of portfolios in ITET and in professional development for teachers is a recent development (Lyons, 1998; Wenzlaff, 1998; Klenowski, 2002) and an 'official' conception of portfolios for professional development has begun to emerge in the English context. Research on the induction of newly qualified teachers cited in Chapter 6 recommended that a professional development portfolio was preferable to the Career Entry Profile, which was then a requirement for trainees to take from initial teacher education into induction. Teacher development is now seen as a continuous rather than a staged process (DfES, 2002a, pp. 148, section 12.16). Following policy and public consultation on a 'Continuous Professional Development' policy, the then TTA issued new guidelines on the use of professional development portfolios in the transition from ITE to induction and beyond (TDA, 2005b).

> The career entry and development profile (CEDP) is designed to help trainees and NQTs think about their professional development at key points towards the end of ITT and during induction. The profile process supports the continued reflection on teaching and professional development that has been established during initial teaching training, structured around three transition points: at the end of ITT and at the start and end of induction.
>
> (TDA, 2005b)

Since trainees are required to follow a reflective process at the *end* of their ITET and throughout their NQT period, it is sensible to enable trainees to use their professional development portfolios *from the outset* of their training and to incorporate them into final assessment for QTS.

Conceptualising portfolio use as an integral part of ITET assessment is important: 'the portfolio is in its infancy and has the power and potential to transform' (Klenowski, 2002, p. 9). There are several advantages to portfolio use in ITET. The creation and maintenance of a teaching portfolio:

- involves the teacher in a personal construction of meaning and therefore facilitates 'deep' learning and the development of practical judgement;
- provides a focus for professional dialogue on practice with a mentor or tutor;
- enables a record of teacher development as statements are revised and compared over time;
- provides evidence for areas which standards cannot capture such as values, dispositions and qualities.

Additionally the portfolio can also contain elements to support assessment of practical teaching, such as lesson observations; statements from colleagues and the teacher about activities such as pastoral work, team planning, curriculum development and research; student evaluations; review statements; videotape of teaching or other artefacts. While they may well contain the kind of evidence currently sought in the standards, the evidence could enable a deeper, more robust judgement to be made about the teacher.

Empirical studies on the use of portfolios in ITET point to 'the power of the portfolio' (Goff et al., 2000) as an evaluation tool, which 'carries a wealth of professional information' (Andreko, 1998)[2].

> Early research on the effects of these assessments suggests that they may be more valid measures of teacher knowledge and skill and that they may help teachers improve their practice. The stimulus to teacher learning appears to occur through task structures that require teachers to learn new content and teaching strategies as part of their demonstration of performance and through the processes of required reflection about the relationships between learning and teaching.
>
> (Darling-Hammond, 2001, p. 11)

At present in ITET assessment, the weight of assessment practices for QTS rests on standards. Goldstein and Lewis (1996) use the term 'multidimensional description' to contrast with the term 'single summary'. Transposing their notion from the field of statistics into that of teacher assessment we can say that standards assessment needs to be supplemented with something more multidimensional. This need can be fulfilled by the PDP, judiciously used. In moving to supplement standards assessment with portfolio assessment certain disadvantages may arise and these are discussed in the next section. But it is true to say that

> there are no 'solutions' which can simultaneously satisfy competing requirements: assessment procedures are almost always compromises between barely reconcilable aims, whether these be authenticity vs. standardisation or single summaries versus multidimensional description.
>
> (Goldstein & Lewis, 1996, p. 7)

In the case of the assessment for QTS, which is a teaching qualification validating fitness for entrance to a complex set of practices, the multidimensional solution is preferable to the summary.

One of the difficulties with the portfolio as an assessment mechanism is the question of validation.

Validity and Reliability of Portfolio Assessment

How feasible is the use of the portfolio in ITET assessment and how are issues of validity and reliability to be addressed? The validity of any assessment depends on whether the evidence gathered to support the assessment decision does evaluate what it is intended to evaluate, so it is important to be clear about the aims of the assessment in question.

Validity is a 'tricky' concept and in some sense 'all assessments reflect the value biases of the individuals formulating the assessment questions' (Henning-Stout, 1994, p. 62). The reasons for creating and using professional development portfolios (PDP) and for including them in assessment for QTS, are traceable to underlying aims. Mentoring is dialogical and developing practical judgement is experiential, personal, complex and contextual. The PDP can help to promote structured, dialogically reflected articulations of practice, providing publicly verifiable accounts of the teacher knowledge and understanding needed for rationally grounded present action and future development. This is the aim underlying the production of the portfolio and the artefacts, narratives and teaching statements collected. Since 'validity is usually defined as the extent to which an assessment procedure measures what it is intended to measure' (Henning-Stout, 1994, p. 62) a 'fit for purpose' assessment of the portfolios is achievable.

In this sense validity is 'process rather than a definitive state. The process of validating stretches across an assessment-intervention effort' (ibid.). So with a complex practice like teaching, a variety of different types of 'data' towards assessment need to be gathered and the process of collection needs to be monitored for each individual trainee, through negotiation and readjustment of the aims of collection of any particular piece. This is the case for assessment against standards as also for other modes of assessment. So in assessing a complex practice such as teaching, there needs to be some foundational set of 'data' laid down for consistency and coherence of assessment.

Reliability addresses whether repeated assessments provide a consistent result given the same initial circumstances. The individual nature of the portfolio might impinge on its reliability as an assessment mechanism in two ways. First, the evidence of development in knowledge and understanding might be open to self-censorship by the trainee's felt need to manage the impressions conveyed. The trainee may embark on ritualistic reflection and not identify points for development honestly. Secondly, the professional development portfolio being individually constructed may be difficult to grade. This section discusses how these concepts might be applied to portfolio assessment[3].

Guba and Lincoln propose the term 'credibility' in place of 'validity' for this type of 'assessment-intervention'. Credibility relies on repeated checking with those concerned with the assessment intervention process, in this case the mentor and the mentee, at the key times decided in the ITET programme. In partnership schemes there is certainly a role for the HEI tutor to play here.

Guba and Lincoln suggest a number of strategies to enhance the credibility of an assessment intervention effort, such as portfolio assessment. First there needs to be substantial involvement of those engaged in the assessment process, largely through immersion 'in and understanding of the context's culture' (Guba & Lincoln, 1989, p. 237). This is where the skills and experience of a mentor can play a crucial role, particularly if there is also a calendar of regular discussions related to the production of portfolio 'items'.

There then needs to be review and discussion of findings with a professional who is not involved with the setting or the individuals. In school-based practice the trainee would work with a tutor from the HEI or other outside agency, with the aim of clarifying views on the information gathered from the school base. It can be robustly argued that the issue of reliability in assessing a portfolio is no different from that in the current assessment against QTS for which an 'audit trail' of evidence is required. The professional development portfolio can provide such a trail; the content audited does not affect the process of the auditing.

The formulation 'reliability' may be misleading. Quantitative data might yield reliable evidence, but it may be better to use the term 'dependability' (Guba and Lincoln, 1989) for the 'assessment-intervention process' involved in producing a portfolio. Guba and Lincoln suggest that dependability can be enhanced through various means (ibid., pp. 237–39). One mechanism is oversight by tutors other than those directly involved in mentoring. Another is substantial discussion and review of findings with a professional peer who is not involved with the settings or the individuals. This would require a moderating university or school tutor other than the trainee's personal tutor and mentor. An interesting idea is for the 'service providers' (in this case likely to be the mentors) to record at key points their 'a priori constructions', in order to check whether their views of the trainee match with those of the trainee. Any discrepancy could be picked up and discussed by a moderator, either at key review points or at the end of the assessment. The mentor statements made at regular intervals could contribute to satisfying the dependability criteria.

It might be argued that moderation as part of a final assessment process, which includes a professional development portfolio and review statements of all parties, is not required on HEI-based courses because negotiations already take place between university and school tutors, when difficult decisions are made about trainees' passing or failing teaching practice. Further, in difficult cases an external examiner can be called in. On the employment-based routes to QTS an external assessor performs this role. In practice, however, negotiations do sort out many of the issues, but their *ad hoc* nature militates against reliability or dependability of outcome. External examiners are not moderators. Their remit is quality assurance and as such they remain 'outside' the decisions between school and university. External assessors on employment-based routes may overturn the decision of a school but here no negotiation or discussion takes place and the school is not informed of the assessor's decision until after the assessment visit is over. In both cases there is no moderation of the evidence before the final assessment by 'disinterested' parties. Therefore the mechanism suggested above could satisfy the dependability criteria more successfully than at present.

It might still be argued that consistency remains an issue in marking the portfolio, due to its individualised nature and the exercise of judgement involved in assigning a grade to it. Linn (1993) and Dunbar et al. (1991) for example pointed to the high subjectivity in any marking process, which relies heavily on professional judgement. However, moderation can impart consistency, provided there is careful training of moderators and provision of 'scoring rubrics', the necessary conditions for minimising error variance. Caroline Gipps compares the reliability in assessment in two portfolio schemes and she validates the need for careful training and marking criteria for moderators (Gipps, 1994, p. 104)[4]. Moderation is important to establish reliability or dependability of judgement:

> If we wish to be able to warrant assessment based conclusions without resorting to highly standardised procedures with all that this implies for poor validity we must ensure that teachers have common understandings of the criterion performance and the circumstances and contexts which elicit best performance.
>
> (ibid., p. 121)

Experience of moderation also develops the moderators' own practice, enabling exposure to and reflection on a variety and diversity of contexts and interpretations of grading (Koretz & Stecher, 1992, quoted in Gipps, 1994, p. 121).

Moderation can substantially support validity and reliability in ITET portfolio assessment. However, complete precision of grading is not 'fit for purpose'. In the case of portfolio assessment, validity relates to the domain of trust in the capacity of the professional judgement of assessors, moderators and portfolio creators themselves. For optimum validity we may substitute satisficing validity, using Herbert Simon's concept, which identifies the decision-making process in which one chooses a good enough option that is perhaps not the best.

Manageable Assessment Practices

An argument against portfolio assessment in general is the time required to go through each individual portfolio and the interviews to accompany them. However, solutions to this problem can be built into ITET programmes from the outset. A calendar of key reflection points around narratives and personal teaching statements can be developed across the course of the training period. Different focuses for each reflection point can be chosen, related to the stage of development in the training programme, so for example an ITET programme lasting an academic year may have four reflection points at which personal narratives and teaching statements can be used. These might correspond to the beginning of the course, midway through the first teaching placement; at the end of the first teaching placement and at the end of the course. The narratives and statements can be revisited by trainee and tutors as starting points for discussions and reflections. In this way, the material in the portfolio is gathered and 'assessed' throughout the period, leaving only key elements for the final assessment. The advantage here is that a key element of assessment resides in the professional judgement of the assessor. Mentors in school are the first port of call with the possibility of HEI tutors adding to this role. The qualities and skills required of mentors, which were established in Chapter 6, are evidenced here. In practice in most courses a developmental tutorial or mentoring session usually happens around specific points in the ITET programme. Generally, however, there is no specific reflective task as a focus. Often these individual tutorials revolve around drafting and finalising reports of practical teaching experience, or on the return of written, mainly academic assignments. These individual tutorials or mentor sessions could be extended to cover the elements of narrative and teacher statements added to the professional development portfolio.

Conclusion

Drawing on previous arguments for the importance of reflective practice this chapter has shown that accountability and quality assurance can be met on a model, which is not narrowly standards based, but still relates to external standards. Professional development portfolios can encompass the complexity of practice more subtly than mere aggregated descriptions of good teacher behaviour.

Perhaps we should reclaim some of the dimensions entailed in the term 'apprentice', a term that we have rejected because of its association with a view of professional practice as equivalent to the exercise of a set of transferable competencies. Maybe a term such as a 'Practiceship' might be useful to distinguish a professional learning period, which incorporates theoretical learning, in a university or equivalent, with practice learning, both of which are assessed. 'Practiceship' resonates with 'partnership' and relates to the professional training not only of teachers but also of nurses, doctors, lawyers and engineers among others. The medieval apprentice formally ended apprenticeship after serving a period of time and producing a piece of expert work, the masterpiece. The professional development portfolio could serve as an 'artefact', a visible record to carry forward into teaching. The analogy with apprenticeship breaks down here as the masterpiece represented the transition of novice to expert, the 'master craftsman', and traditionally apprenticeship lasted 7 years. Most teachers would claim that after a typical 1-year initial training they were hovering from novice to competent teacher. The portfolio would represent that stage of development and reflect change and development.

Notes

1. See also Stobart and Gipps, 1997; Watkins, 2001; Watkins and Carnell,2002;Davis, 1998, 1999.
2. See also Lyons, 1998; Turner, 2002.
3. See Golafshani, 2003, for a discussion of the applicability of the notions of reliability and validity in qualitative research.
4. The Pittsburgh portfolio programme used only external assessors who went through a rigorous training programme and there was a regular checking procedure, which led to re-training if acceptable judgements fell below a certain level. Inter-judge reliabilities here were at a consistently high level. The Vermont portfolio programme used teachers in the schools to carry out the rating with less rigorous training and checking procedures', which led to lower reliability levels. See Linn, 1993, and Dunbar et al., 1991, quoted by Gipps.

Chapter 9

Conclusion

Overview

Teaching is essentially a normative endeavour and the teacher's own character and habits, qualities and dispositions have a large role to play in the development of her knowledge and understanding. To teach is to engage with a set of practices, and be embedded in nested contexts, all of which affect the teacher's ability to teach well. Practical judgement is the bedrock of professional expertise. It develops through experience mediated through a process of well-grounded reflection, which can be aided to a significant extent by an expert mentor, given certain conditions. A model of teacher knowledge and understanding which forefronts the notion of practical judgement conceives of teaching as a profession, with autonomy as one of its goods. The teacher who exercises good judgement and professional expertise is an exemplary figure. Practical judgement has a connection with wisdom: it is bound up with virtues such as courage because

> the distinctive characteristic of practical knowledge, one which is so inherent that it cannot be eliminated, is the uncertainty which attends it. Of it we are compelled to say: act, but act at your peril. Judgement and belief regarding actions to be performed can never attain more than a precarious probability.
>
> (Dewey, 1960, p. 6)

Acknowledgment of uncertainty is a fruitful state as it opens the way for the unpredictable and complex interactions of a teacher's daily life in the classroom to become the material of review and critical reflection, to enable learning to develop in a meaningful way. Teachers who can cope with uncertainty may also have the disposition to critically evaluate educational policies and practices in order to decide on the value of their own practices and the relevance and appropriateness of any particular policy, strategy, pedagogical theory or curriculum initiative.

The story of ITET over the past 25 years is one of change from a conception of the teacher as a professional 'expert' capable of autonomous judgement, to one in which the teacher is closer to a technician of learning. It is a story of the increasingly centralised control of teachers, through prescriptive strategies and national curriculum, which is 'quality controlled' through high stakes assessment. The control discourse is an empiricist discourse. It talks of measurable outcomes (such as examination results) and targets (such as higher examination results). The discourse is driven by a quest for certainty about what improves teaching and learning. This is because the aims of education in this discourse are to raise achievement and achievement is defined in material terms, as gains in skills and verifiable knowledge, verification occurring through assessments, tests and examinations. It is the case that pupils do engage with Pastoral Social and Health Education Curriculum (PSHE), which has wider aims, and that there are considerations of how teachers should develop pupils' 'spiritual, moral, social and cultural' knowledge and understanding in the national curriculum (DfEE & QCA, 1999a). However, there is no compulsory assessment process for PSHE, and it therefore cannot be used in reporting or comparing pupil achievement. The control discourse is a standardisation discourse. Achievement is gauged through measurement. Levels are measured and computed and used to draw conclusions about a rise or fall in standards and to provide data on which to set targets for improvement in standards. For this reason we can call the control discourse 'a quest for certainty', using the title of Dewey's 1929 series of lectures on 'the relation of knowledge to action' (Dewey, 1960). It demonstrates the application of technical rationality.

The control discourse has tended to narrow the range of teaching methods and content currently used by trainee teachers, in my experience, and encouraged a climate of conformity. To teach daringly, something untried, 'inspired', is to expose oneself to the danger of

failure. Where Ofsted inspections have a model of what a good lesson is, it is often not judicious to take risks and to seek new ways
of working. As Dewey has pointed out 'practical doing or making;
these take effect in an uncertain future, and involve peril, the risk of
misadventure, frustration and failure' (ibid., p. 6).

It is important to admit that one's knowledge and understanding is
partial and open to modification through experience and reflection.
Flexibility seems to be an essential quality, and essential for well-
grounded reflection. We have seen that teaching is a complex practice
and that judgement is needed to choose between often competing
possible actions. If we can

> estimate more accurately the worth of things as signs, we can afford
> to exchange a loss of theoretical certitude for a gain in practical
> judgement ... What has been lost in the theoretical possibility of
> exact knowledge and exact prediction is more than compensated
> for by the fact that the knowing which occurs within nature involves
> possibility of direction of change.
>
> (ibid., p. 212)

Teachers also have to face personal disappointments, such as the
fact that their students may not want to learn. Burbules has defined
a 'tragic sense' that he believes good teachers need to develop:

> By accepting the inevitability of doubt and disappointment in much
> of what we do, the tragic sense also frees us to take these moments
> of failure as occasions for new learning. On the other hand, by
> stubbornly refusing to abandon hope in the face of cynicism, the
> tragic sense gives us a reason to care, to persist in our efforts.
> We could make our view of life simpler by adopting one view to
> the exclusion of the other (hope over an awareness of failure; cyn-
> icism over a sense of possibility), but ... either option makes us a
> worse educator – indeed, makes us a worse person.
>
> (Burbules et al., 1997, p. 65)[1]

The notion of 'the tragic sense' reminds us of the essential dispositional nature of teaching. This account has advocated reflection, inquiry, investigation and research into the wider practices of

teaching, which all help at a certain level. At times, however, teachers just need the grit to carry on. The ability to reflect and inquire one's way out of a difficult situation may well ride piggyback on the qualities of endurance and courage, among other virtues. ITET is limited in how far we can influence these dispositional aspects.

Implications for Future Development

Teachers need to engage in specific and focused reflective activities, as teachers developing an understanding and evaluation of their practice, and in some cases as researchers on that practice. Standards alone do not get at the nature of the practice or practices of teaching and tend to view teaching largely within a skills agenda. We can apply Barnett's view to ITET:

> higher education designed around skills is no higher education. It is the substitute of technique for insight; of strategic reason for communicative reason; and of behaviour for wisdom.
>
> (Barnett, 1994, p. 60)

ITET needs to work with a curriculum that enables practical judgement to develop and needs an assessment mechanism capable of evidencing teacher knowledge and understanding in its wider capacity and dispositional sense. A 'thin' version of the standards, as descriptors of some aspect of good teaching can be reconciled with a 'thick' version of reflective practice. This latter will have a well worked out, rigorous means of ensuring well-grounded reflection on the practice of teaching. Assessment needs to be capable of evidencing trainees' achievements of the QTS standards and their knowledge and understanding in the widest sense.

There are two main reasons why we ought to extend assessment to include practices such as the creation of teacher narrative and the use of reflective teaching statements, within a professional development portfolio process. First, creating such practices would reflect better the nature of teaching and the place of human agency than a model based solely on standards assessment. Secondly, such a conception would itself influence the way in which trainees developed, because formal learning towards a qualification is to a large extent assessment led. The strength of 'practiceship' is in its bringing together the elements of theory and practice, which enable trainees to develop their practical judgement. To compliment the work that goes on in partnership through 'practiceship' it is essential to have an ITET formation and assessment mechanism, which can account for and validate the development of practical judgement.

Note

1. See also Biesta (1994).

Appendix

Key Events in ITET in England, from 1944 to 1997

1944	Publication of the McNair Report
1963	Publication of the Robbins Report
1972	Publication of the James Report
1984	Establishment of Council for the Accreditation of Teacher Education (CATE)
1992/1993	Publication of Circular 14/93 (Partnership; School Centred Initial Teacher Training (SCITT)
1994	Establishment of the Teacher Training Agency
1997	National Training Curriculum Published with Standards for the Award of Qualified Teacher Status (QTS)

References

Abbott, J. (1994), *Learning Makes Sense: Recreating Education for a Changing Future*. Letchworth: Education 2000.

Alexander, R. and Whittaker, J. (1980), *Developments in PGCE Courses*. Leeds: The Teacher Education Study Group Society for Research into Higher Education.

Altman, R. (2002), *Gosford Park: Director's Commentary*. Capitol Films DVD.

Andreko, L. (1998), 'The case for the teacher portfolio: evaluation tool carries a wealth of professional information', National Staff Development Council, http://www.nsdc.org/library/publications/jsd/andrejko194.cfm (Accessed 19 March 2006).

Ash, A., Hall, D. and Raffo, C. (2004), 'Initial teacher training and the transition to teaching in urban schools', British Educational Research Association Conference, September 2004, Manchester, http://www.leeds.ac.uk/educol/documents/00003778.doc (Accessed 19 March 2006).

Assesment Reform Group (1999), *Assessment for Learning; Beyond the Black Box*. Cambridge: University of Cambridge School of Education.

—(2002), *Assessment for Learning: 10 Principles*. London: ARG.

Atherton, J. (2003), 'Learning and teaching: reflective practice (online) UK', http://www.dmu.ac.uk/~jamesa/learning/reflecti.htm (Accessed 26 March 2004).

ATL (2006), 'Position statement – personalised learning, ATL', http://www.atl.org.uk/atl_en/education/postition_statements/personalisation.asp (Accessed 20 July 2007).

Awbrey, J. and Awbrey, S. (1995), 'Interpretation as action: the risk of inquiry', http://www.shss.montclair.edu/inquiry/fall95/awbrey.html (Accessed 06 November 1999).

Ayer, A.J. (1952), *Language, Truth and Logic*. New York: Dover Publications.

Baier, A. (1986), 'Trust and anti-trust'. *Ethics*, 96, 231–60.

Bailey, T. (2002), 'On trust and philosophy', March 2002 http://www.bbc.co.uk/radio4/reith2002/, BBC and the Open University (Accessed 04 January 2006).

Barnett, R. (1994), *The Limits of Competence*. Buckingham: Open University Press.

Barrett, E., Whitty, G., Furlong, J., Galvin, C. and Barron, L. (1992), *Initial Teacher Education in England and Wales: A Topography*. London: Goldsmiths College.

Barrow, R. (1984), *Giving Teaching Back to Teachers: A Critical Introduction to Curriculum Theory*. Brighton: Wheatsheaf Books.

Barrow, R. (1986), 'The concept of curriculum design'. *Journal of Philosophy of Education*, 20(1), 73–80.

BBC (1999), 'Teachers threaten appraisal boycott', http://news.bbc.co.uk/education specials/green paper/1999; 26.03.1999: BBC (Accessed 10 March 2004).

—(2000), 'Teacher Appraisal has had limited impact on education', says Ofsted http://news.bbc.co.uk/1/hi/in_depth/education/2000/teachers_pay/838033.stm; 17.07.2000: BBC (Accessed 10 March 2004).

Beattie, M. (2000), 'Narratives of professional learning: becoming a teacher and learning to teach'. *Journal of Educational Inquiry*, 1(2), 1–23.

Beckett, D. (1998), 'Disembodied learning: how flexible delivery shoots higher education in the foot, well, sort of'. *Electronic Journal of Sociology*, 3(3), http://www.sociology.org/content/vol003.003/beckett.html (Accessed 16 February 2008).

Beishuizen, J., Hof, E., van Putten, C. and Bouwmeester, S. (2001), 'Students' and teachers' cognitions about good teachers'. *British Journal of Educational Psychology*, 71, 185–201.

Bengtsson, J. (1995), 'What is reflection? On reflection in the teaching profession and teacher education'. *Teachers and Teaching: Theory and Practice*, 1(1), 23–32.

Benn, C. and Simon, B. (1972), *Half Way There: Report on the British Comprehensive School Reform*. Harmondsworth: Penguin Books.

Benton, P. (1990), *The Oxford Internship Scheme*. London: Calouste Gulbenkian Foundation.

BERA (2001), 'BERA's response to the National Educational Research Forum's consultation paper'. *Research Intelligence*, 74, 11–19.

Berger, P. and Luckmann, T. (1967), *The Social Construction of Reality*. New York: Doubleday and Company.

Bernbaum, G. (1979), *Schooling in Decline*. London: Macmillan.

Bernstein, B. (1977), *Class Codes and Control*. London: Routledge.

Best, R. (2002), *Pastoral care and Personal Social Education: A review of UK research*. Southwell: BERA.

Biesta, G. (1994), 'Pragmatism as a pedagogy of communicative action'. *Studies in Philosophy and Education*, 13(3–4), 273–90.

Black, P. and Harrison, C. (2003), *Assessment for Learning: Putting It into Practice*. Milton Keynes: Open University Press.

Black, P., Harrison, C., Lee, C., Marshall, B. and Wiliam, D. (2002), *Working Inside the Black Box: Assessment for Learning in the Classroom*. London: King's College.

Black, P. and Wiliam, D. (1998), *Inside the Black Box: Raising Standards Through Classroom Assessment*. London: King's College.

Boisvert, R. (1988), *Dewey's Metaphysics*. New York: Fordham University Press.

Bok, S. (1978), *Lying: Moral Choice in Public and Private Life*. Hassocks: Harvester.

Bottery, M. (2004), *The Challenges of Educational Leadership: Values in a Globalized Age*. London: Paul Chapman.

Boud, D., Keogh, R. and Walker, D. (1985), *Reflection: Turning Experience into Learning*. London/New York: Kogan Page and Nicols Publishing Company.

Bradley, P., Nordheim, L., De La Harpe, D., Innvaer, S. and Thompson, C. (2005), 'A systematic review of qualitative literature on educational interventions for evidence-based practice'. *Learning in Health and Social Care*, 4(2), 89–109.

Bransford, J., Brown, A. and Cocking R. (2000), *How People Learn: Brain, Mind, Experience, and School Committee on Developments in the Science of Learning*. Washington, DC: National Academy Press.

Bridges, D. (2003), *Fiction Written Under Oath? Essays in Philosophy and Educational Research*. Amsterdam: Kluwer.

Broadfood, P. (1996) 'Assessment and learning: power or partnership?' in H. Goldstein and T. Lewis (eds), *Assessment: Problems, Developments and Statistical Issues: A Volume of Expert Contributions*. Chichester: John Wiley and Sons Ltd, pp. 21–35.

Bronowski, J. (1973), *The Ascent of Man*. London: BBC and Book Club Associates.

Bruner, J. (1983), *Child's Talk: Learning to Use Language*. New York: W.W. Norton & Co.

Bruns, A. (2005), 'The reflective practitioner', http://snurb.info/index.php?q=trackback/183 (Accessed 07 May 2005).

Buber, M. (1958), *I and Thou*. New York: Charles Scribner's Sons.

Burbules, N. (1997), 'Why practice doesn't make perfect', http://www.eduiuc.edu/facstaff/burbules/ncb/papers/perfect.html (Accessed 14 February 2000).

Burbules, N. and Hansen, T. (1997), *Teaching and Its Predicaments*. Boulder, CO: Westview Press.

Burke, J. (1989), *Competency Based Education and Training*. Lewes: Falmer Press.

Burns, M. and Pachler, N. (2004), 'Inquiry as stance: teacher professional learning and narrative'. *Teacher Development*, 8(3), 149–64.

Calderhead J. (1991), 'The nature and growth of knowledge in student teaching'. *Teaching and Teacher Education*, 7(5–6), 531–5.

Camden L.E.A. (1991), *Appraisal in Camden*. London: C.L.E.A.

Collaborative Action Research Network (CARN) (2005), http://www.did.stu.mmu.ac.uk/carn/ (site update 22 February 2005) (Accessed February 2006).

Carr, D. (1993a), 'Questions of competence'. *British Journal of Educational Studies*, 41, 253–71.

—(1993b), 'Guidelines for teacher training: the competency model'. *Scottish Educational Review*, 25(1), 17–25.

—(2003), 'Rival conceptions of practice in education and teaching'. *Journal of Philosophy of Education*, 37(2), 253–67.

Carr, W. (2006), 'Education without theory'. *British Journal of Educational Studies*, 54(2) 136–59.

Carr, W. and Kemmis, S. (1989), *Becoming Critical; Education, Knowledge and Action Research*. Lewes: Falmer Press.

Carter, B. and Sealey, A. (2000), 'Language, structure and agency: what can realist social theory offer to sociolinguistics?'. *Journal of Sociolinguistics*, 4(1), 3–20.

CATE. (1984), *Initial Teacher Training: Approval of Courses*. London: DES.

Chitty, C. (1990), 'Central control of the school curriculum, 1944–1987' in B. Moon (ed.), *New Curriculum National Curriculum*. London: Hodder & Stoughton, in association with The Open University, pp. 3–14.

Chomsky, N. (1965), *Aspects of the Theory of Syntax*. Cambridge Mass: MIT Press.

Cochran-Smith, M. and Lytle, S. (1993), *Inside/Outside: Teacher Research and Knowledge*. New York: Teachers College Press.

Collier, G. (1994), *Social Origins of Mental Ability*. New York: Wiley.

Connell, J. (1995), 'Reconstructing a modern definition of knowledge: a comparison of Toulmin and Dewey', http://www.eduiuc.edu/EPS/PES-Yearbook/95_docs/connell.html (Accessed 02 December 1999).

Constas, M. (1998), 'The changing nature of educational research and a critique of postmodernism'. *Educational Researcher*, 27(2), 26–33.

Cooper, H. (1998), *Synthesising Research: A Guide for Literature Reviews*, 3rd edn. Thousand Oaks, CA: Sage.

Corbett, A. (1968), *Much to Do About Education*. London: Council for Educational Advance.

Cordingley, P. (2000), 'Constructing and critiquing reflective practice', *Reflective Practice*, 7(2), 183–91.

Cordova, D. and Lepper, M. (1996), 'Intrinsic motivation and the process of learning: beneficial effects of contextualization, personalization, and choice'. *Journal of Educational Psychology*, 88, 715–30.

Corey, S. (1953), *Action Research to Improve School Practices*. New York: Teachers College Press.

Cox, C. and Boyson, R. (1971), *The Black Papers on Education*. London: Centre for Policy Studies.

Cox, C. and Dyson, A. (1970), 'An open letter to members of parliament', in B. Moon (ed.), *Judging Standards and Effectiveness in Education*. London: Hodder & Stoughton, in association with The Open University, pp. 3–17.

Crewe, E. and Young, J. (2002), *Bridging Research and Policy: Context, Evidence, Links*. London: Overseas Development Institute.

Daly, M. (2002), 'Commentary on "Experience and Sensations", http//:www.california.com/~mcmf/markateondewey.html, (Accessed 27 October 2004).

Daniels, J. (1970), 'Introduction', in C. Rubinstein. and D. Stoneman (eds), *Education for Democracy: Penguin Education Special*. Harmondsworth: Penguin Books, pp. 9–14.

Darling-Hammond, L. (2001), 'Teacher testing and the improvement of practice'. *Teaching Education*, 12(1), 11–34.

Davies, B. (1994), 'On the neglect of pedagogy in educational studies and its consequences'. *British Journal of In-service Education*, 20(1), 17–34.

Davies, P. (1999), 'What is evidenced-based education?' *British Journal of Educational Studies*, 47(2), 108–21.

—(2000), 'The relevance of systematic reviews to educational policy and practice'. *Oxford Review of Education*, 26, 365–78.

Davis, A. (1998), *The Limits of Educational Assessment*. Oxford: Blackwell.

—(1999), *Educational Assessment: A Critique of Current Policy*. Impact No. 1. London: Philosophy of Education Society of Great Britain.

Davis-Case, D. (2001), 'The reflective practitioner', http://www.consecol.org/vol5/iss2/art15/ Conservation Ecology 5(2): 15. online (Accessed 07 May 2005).

Demetrion, G. (2006), 'Dewey's logic as a methodological grounding point for practitioner-based inquiry', http://www.nald.ca/fulltext/dewey/Dewey.pdf National Adult Literacy Database: Canada (Accessed 25 January 2006).

DES (1967), *The Training of Teachers Regulations 1967*. London: HMSO.

—(1972), *Teacher Education and Training*. London: HMSO.

—(1975), *A Language for Life*. London: HMSO.

—(1976), *School Education in England: Problems and Initiatives. The Yellow Book*. London: HMSO.

—(1979), *Aspects of Secondary Education in England.A Survey by HM Inspectors of Schools*. London: HMSO.

—(1980), *PGCE in the Public Sector*. London: HMSO.

— (1981), *Teacher Training and the Secondary School*. London: HMSO.

Dewey, J. (1929), *The Sources of a Science of Education*. New York: Liveright Publishing Corp.

— (1939), *Theory of Valuation*. Chicago: University of Chicago Press.

—(1958), *Experience and Nature*, 2nd edn. New York: Dover Publications Inc.

—(1960), *The Quest for Certainty*. USA: Capricorn Editions.

—(1966), *Democracy and Experience*. New York: The Free Press.

—(1980), *The School and Society*. Carbondale: Southern Illinois University Press with Feffer & Simons, Inc.

—(1990), *The Later Works, 1925–1953 Volume 17: 1885–1953*. Carbondale: Southern Illinois University Press with Feffer & Simons, Inc.

—(1991), *Logic: The Theory of Inquiry*, Jo Ann Boydston (ed.). Carbondale: Southern Illinois University Press with Feffer & Simons, Inc.

DfE (1991), *The Education (School Teacher Appraisal) Regulations 1991*. Statutory Instrument 1991 No. 1511. London: HMSO.

DfE and Welsh Office. (1992), *Initial Teacher Training (Secondary Phase)*. Circular 9/92. London: HMSO.

—(1993), *Initial Teacher Training (Secondary Phase*. Circular 14/93. London: HMSO.

DfEE (1997), *Teaching: High Status, High Standards*. Circular 10/97. London: DfEE.

DfEE and QCA (1999a), *The National Curriculum*. London: DfEE & QCA.

—(1999b), *The Revised National Curriculum for 2000*. London: DfEE & QCA.

DfES (2001), 'Key stage 3 strategy', http://www.standards.dfes.gov.uk/keystage3 (Accessed 03March 2004).

—(2002a), *Evaluation of the Effectiveness of the Statutory Arrangements for the Induction of Newly Qualified Teachers*. Totterdell M., Heilbronn R.,

Bubb S., Jones C. Research Brief and Report, vol. 338. London: DfES.

—(2002b), *The Standards Framework*. London: DfES.

—(2003), *Key Stage 3 National Strategy: Framework for Teaching Modern Foreign Languages: Years 7, 8 and 9*. London: DfES.

—(2004a), *Every Child Matters: Change for Children*. London: LMSO.

—(2004b), *A National Conversation About Personalised Learning*. DfES/0919/2004. Norwich: HMSO.

—(2005a), *Youth Matters Green Paper.* London: LMSO.

—(2005b), 'Higher standards, better schools for all: more choice for parents and pupils'. CM6677, Norwich: HMSO. http://www.dfes.gov.uk/publications (Accessed 16 April 2007).

—(2006), 'Highlights: personalised learning', http://www.dfes. gov.uk/highlights/article13.shtml (accessed 17.04.07).

DfES and TTA (2002). *Qualifying to Teach: Standards for the Award of QTS*. London: TTA.

Dick, B. (2003), Papers on action research and related topics, http://www.scu.edu.au/schools/gcm/ar/arp/arphome.html Action Research resources (Accessed 29 January 2006).

Donovan, S., Bransford, J. and Pelligrino, J. (2000), *Committee on Learning Research and Educational Practice Commission on Behavioural and Social Sciences and Education*. Washington DC: National Academy Press.

Dreyfus H. and Dreyfus S. (1986), *Mind Over Machine: The Power of Human Intuition and Expertise in the Era of the Computer*. Oxford: Basil Blackwell.

DSEA (2005), 'Teacher as researcher', http://www.dsea.org/teachingtips/researcher.asp, Delaware State Education Association (Accessed 01 February 2006).

Dunbar, S., Daniel, K. and Hoover, H. (1991), 'Quality control in the development and use of performance assessments'. *Applied Measurement in Education*, 4(4), 289–303.

Dunne, J. (1993), *Back to the Rough Ground*. Notre Dame Indiana: University of Notre Dame Press.

— (2003), 'Arguing for teaching as a practice; a reply to Alasdair MacIntyre'. *Journal of Philosophy of Education*, 37(2), 353–71.

Earley, P. and Kinder, K. (1994), *Initiation Rites*. Slough: National Foundation for Educational Research.

Elliot, A. (1981), *Child Language*. Cambridge: Cambridge University Press.

Elliott, B. and Calderdale, J. (1995), 'Mentoring for teacher development', in T.A. Kerry and S. M. Kerry (eds), *Issues in Mentoring*. London: Routledge in association with The Open University.

Elliott, J. (1991), *Action Research for Educational Change*. Buckingham: Open University Press.

Emery, H. (1998), 'A national curriculum for the education and training of teachers: an English perspective'. *Journal of In-service Education*, 24(2), 283–91.

EmTech (2005) 'Action research', http://www.emtech.net/action-research.htm (Emerging Technologies) (Accessed 01 February 2006).

EPPI (2005), 'Research evidence in education', The Evidence for Policy and Practice Information and Co-ordinating Centre, http://eppi.ioe.ac.uk/EPPIWeb/home.aspx?page=/reel/intro.htm (Accessed 03 February 2006).

Eraut, M. (1994), *Developing Professional Knowledge and Competence*. Falmer Sussex: Falmer Press.

—(1995), 'Schön shock'. *Teachers and Teaching: Theory and Practice*, 1, 9–22.

Evans, J. (2000), 'Systematic reviews of education'. *Research Intelligence*, 73, 25–6.

Everton, T. (1992), 'Partnership in training: University of Leicester's new mode of teacher education'. *Cambridge Journal of Education*, 22, 143–55.

Ewbank, A. (2004), 'The teacher as researcher SIG', http://www.teacherasresearcher.org/. American Educational Research Association (Accessed 01 February 2006).

Fenstermacher, G. (1988), 'The place of science and epistemology in Schön's conception of reflective practice', in P. P. Grimmet and G.L. Erickson (eds), *Reflection in Teacher Education*. New York: Teachers College Press.

Filer, A. (2000), *Assessment; Social Practice and Social Product*. London and New York: Routledge Falmer.

Flew, A. (1982), 'Education fundamentals; The four Es', in C. Cox and J. Marks (eds), *The Right to Learn*, London: Centre for Policy Studies, pp. 17–26.

Fogel A., de Koeyer I., Bellagamba F. and Bell H. (2002), 'The dialogical self in the first two years of life', *Theory and Psychology*, 12(2), 191–205.

Freire, P. (1972), *Cultural Action for Freedom*. London: Penguin Books.

Furlong, J. (2002), 'Ideology and reform in teacher education in England'. *Educational Researcher*, 31(6), 23–5.

Furlong, V. and Hirst, P. (1988), *Initial Teacher Training and the Role of the School*. Milton Keynes: Open University Press.

Gadamer, H. G. (1975), *Truth and Method*. New York: The Continuing Publishing Corporation.

Gardner, P. (1996), 'Higher education and teacher training: a century of progress and promise', in R. Furlong and J. Smith (eds), *The Role of Higher Education in Initial Teacher Training*, London and Philadelphia: Kogan Page, pp. 35–50.

Garrison, J. (1997), *Dewey and Eros*. New York and London: Teachers College Press.

—(1999), 'Dangerous dualisms in Siegel's theory of critical thinking: a Deweyan pragmatist responds'. *Journal of Philosophy of Education*, 33(2), 213–32.

Garson, S., Heilbronn, R., Hill, B., Pomphrey, C., Willis, J. and Valentine, A. (1989), *World Languages Project*. London: Hodder & Stoughton.

Giddens, A. (1991), *Modernity and Self Identity*. Stanford: Stanford University Press.

Gillard, D. (2005, 'The Plowden Report', http://www.infedorg/schooling/plowden_report.htm. *The Encyclopaedia of Informal Education* (Accessed 20 February 2006).

Gilroy, P. (1993), 'Reflections on Schön: an epistemological critique and a practical alternative', in P. Gilroy and M. Smith (eds), *International Analyses of Teacher Education*. Abingdon: Carfax Publishing Company, pp. 125–42.

Ginsburg, M. and Gorostiaga, J. (2001), 'Relationships between theorists/researchers and policy makers/practitioners: rethinking the two-cultures thesis and the possibility of dialogue'. *Comparative Education Review*, 45(2), 173–96.

Gipps, C. (1994), *Beyond Testing: Towards a Theory of Educational Assessment*. London and Washington, DC: Falmer Press.

Goff, L., Colton, A. and Langer, G. (2000), 'Power of the portfolio', http://www.nsdc.org/library/publications/jsd/goff214.cfm, National Staff Development Council (Accessed 19 March 2006).

Goffman, E. (1971), *The Presentation of Self in Everyday Life*. London: Penguin.

Golafshani, M. (2003), 'Understanding reliability and validity in qualitative research'. *The Qualitative Report*, 8(4) December 2003, 597–607.

Goldstein, H. and Lewis, T. (eds) (1996), *Assessment: Problems, Developments and Statistical Issues*. Chichester, NY: Brisbane, Toronto, Singapore: John Wiley and Sons.

Goodman, K. (1987), *What's Whole in Whole Language?* Portsmouth, NH: Heinemann.

Goodson, I. (1990), 'Curriculum reform and curriculum theory: a case of historical amnesia', in B. Moon (ed.), *New Curriculum National Curriculum*. London: Hodder & Stoughton, in association with The Open University, pp. 47–55.

Graff, H. (1999), 'Interdisciplinary explorations in the study of children, adolescents and youth – for the past, present and future'. *Journal of American History*, 85(4), 1538–47.

Guba, E. and Lincoln, Y. (1989), *Fourth Generation Evaluation*. California: Sage.

Haager, D., Lee, O., McIntosh, R., Shay, J. and Schumm, S. (1993), 'Observations of students with learning disabilities in general education classrooms'. *Exceptional Children*. http://www.questia.com/PM.qst?a=o&d=5000239319 (Accessed 12 January 2006).

Hager, P. (2000), 'Know-how and workplace practical judgement'. *Journal of Philosophy of Education*, 34(2), 281–96.

Hammersley, M. (1997), 'Educational research and teaching: a response to David Hargreaves – Teacher Training Agency lecture'. *British Educational Research Journal*, 23(2), 141–61.

—(2001), 'Systematic reviews of research literatures: a "narrative" response to Evans & Benefield'. *British Educational Research Journal*, 27(5), 543–55.

—(2002), *Educational Research, Policymaking and Practice*. London: SAGE Publications for The Open University, UK.

—(2005), 'Should educational research be critical?' Paper given to Philosophy of Education Seminar, Institute of Education, University of London.

Handscombe, G. (2005), 'LEA as learning organisations: research engaged authority and schools', http://www.bera.ac.uk/pdfs/BERALGAlearningconfGraham.ppt, Essex LEA (Accessed 03 June 2006).

Hansen, D. (1997), 'Being a good influence', in N. Burbules and D. Hansen (eds), *Teaching and Its Predicaments*. Boulder, CO: Westview, pp. 163–73.

Hardin, R. (1993), 'The street-level epistemology of trust'. *Politics and Society*, 21, 505–29.

Hargreaves, A. (2003), *Teaching in the Knowledge Society*. Maidenhead Philadelphia: Open University Press.

Hargreaves, D. (1996), *Teaching as a research-based profession: possibilities and prospects, the TTA annual lecture*. London: Teacher Training Agency.

—(1998), *Creative Professionalism: The Role of Teachers in the Knowledge Society*. London: Demos.

Harré, R. (1977), 'The self in monodrama', in T. Mischel (ed.), *The Self: Psychological and Philosophical Issues*. Oxford: Basil Blackwell, pp. 274–91.

Hawkins, P. and Shohet, R. (1989), *Supervision in the Helping Professions*. Milton Keynes: The Open University.

Haynes, B. (2004), 'Is teaching a practice?' http://k1.ioe.ac.uk/pesgb/z/Haynes.pdf, Institute of Education, University of London for PESGB (Accessed 10 January 2006).

Hazzan, O. (2002), 'The reflective practitioner perspective in software engineering education'. *Journal of Systems and Software Archive*, 63 (3), 161–71, http://portal.acm.org/citation.cfm?id=771440 (Accessed 07 May 2005).

Heidegger, M. (1962), *Being and Time, Sein und Zeit*, 7th edn, J.A.R. Macquarrie, E. Trans. Oxford: Blackwell Publishers.

Heilbronn, R. (2000), 'The National Teacher Research Panel: teaching as evidence-based practice'. *Prospero*, 6 (3 and 4), 70–7.

Heilbronn, R. and Jones, C. (1997), *New Teachers in an Urban Comprehensive*. London: Trentham Books.

Heilbronn, R., Jones, C., Bubb, S. and Totterdell, M. (2002), 'School based induction tutors: a challenging role'. *School Leadership and Management*, 22(4), 371–87.

Henning-Stout, M. (1994), *Responsive Assessment: A New Way of Thinking About Learning*. San Francisco: Jossey Bass Publishers.

Hewett, S. (1971), *The Training of Teachers. A Factual Survey*. London: University of London Press.

Hewitt, J. (1976), *Self and society: a symbolic interactionist social psychology*. Boston, Allen and Bacon Inc.

Hextall, I. and Mahony, P. (2002), 'Consultation and the management of consent: standards for Qualified Teacher Status'. *British Educational Research Journal*, 26(3), 323–42.

Hickman, L. (1998), *Reading Dewey*. Bloomington: Indiana University Press.

Hiebert, J., Gallimore, R. and Stigler, J. (2002), 'A knowledge base for the teaching profession: what would it look like and how can we get one?' http://www.lessonlab.com/press/HiebertGallimore-Stigler2002.pdf. Lesson Lab Press (Accessed 08 February 2006).

Hillage, J. and Pearson R. (1998), *Excellence in Research on Schools*. London: Institute for Employment Studies.

Hirst, P. (1974), *Knowledge and the Curriculum*. London: Routledge & Kegan Paul.

—(1990), 'Internship: a view from outside', in P. Benton (ed.), *The Oxford Internship Scheme*. London: Calouste Gulbenkian Foundation, pp. 147–59.

—(1996), 'The demands of a professional practice and preparation for teaching', in J. Furlong and R. Furlong (eds), *The Role of Higher Education in Initial Teacher Training*. London: Kogan Page, pp. 166–78.

HMSO (1999), 'The Management of Health and Safety at Work Regulations 1999', http://www.opsi.gov.uk/si/si1999/19993242.htm (HMSO) (Accessed 06 February 2006).

Hogan, P. (2003), 'Teaching and learning as a way of life'. *Journal of Philosophy of Education*, 37(2), 207–25.

Holton, R. (1994), 'Deciding to trust, coming to believe'. *Australasia Journal of Philosophy*, 72, 63–76.

Houston, J. (1990), *Thesaurus of ERIC Descriptors*. Phoenix, Arizona: Oryx Press.

Hume, D. (1911), *A Treatise on Human Nature*. London: J.M. Dent & Sons Ltd.

Humes, W. and Bryce, T. (2003), 'Post-structuralism and policy research in education'. *Journal of Education Policy*, 18(2), 175–87.

Hursthouse, R. (2003), 'Virtue ethics'. *The Stanford Encyclopaedia of Philosophy* (Fall 2003 Edition), N. Edward Zalta (ed.), http://plato.stanford.edu/archives/fall2003/entries/ethics-virtue/ (Accessed 15 May 2006).

Hyland, T. (1993), 'Competence, knowledge and education'. *Journal of Philosophy of Education*, 27(1), 57–68.

Institute of Education (2004a), *Unpublished Account: Email Communication*. London: Institute of Education, University of London.

INTASC (2006), Florida State New Teachers' Assessment Instrument, New Teacher and Assessment Consortium (INTASC), http://www.fiu.edu/~edpsy/specedprofstand.htm. Interstate (Accessed 06 February 2006).

Jessup, G. (1991), *Outcomes: NVQs and the Emerging Model of Education and Training*. Lewes: The Falmer Press.

Johns, C. (2004), *Becoming a Reflective Practitioner*. London: Blackwell.

Jones, K. (1996), 'Trust as an affective attitude'. *Ethics*, 107, 4–25.

Kelly, M. and Beck T. (1995), 'Mentoring as a staff development activity', in T. Kerry and A. Mayes (eds), *Issues in Mentoring*. London: Routledge in association with the Open University, pp. 253–8.

Kemmis, S. (1993), 'Action research and social movement: a challenge for policy research'. *Education Policy Analysis Archives*, 1(1), http://epaa.asu.edu/epaa/v1n1.html (Accessed 30 January 2006).

Kerry, T. and Mayes, A. (eds) (1995), *Issues in Mentoring*. London: Routledge in association with the Open University.

Klenowski, V. (2002), *Developing Portfolios for Learning and Assessment: Processes and Principles*. London: Routledge Falmer.

Kogan, M. (1987), 'The Plowden Report twenty years on'. *Oxford Review of Education*, 13(1), 13–21.

Koretz, D and Stecher (1992), *The Vermont Portfolio Assessment Program: Interim Report*. Los Angeles, CA: CRESST, UCLA.

Kulp, C. (1992), *The End of Epistemology: Dewey and His Current Allies on the Spectator Theory of Knowledge*. Westport, CT: Greenwood Press.

Lambert D. (2005), 'Opinion piece why subjects really matter'. Geographical Association, http://www.geography.org.uk (Accessed 20 July 2007).

Lave, J. and Wenger, E. (1991), *Situated Learning: Legitimate Peripheral Participation*. New York: Cambridge University Press.

Lawlor, S. (1990), *Teachers Mistaught*. London: Centre for Policy Studies.

Levinas, E. (1969), *Totality and Infinity*. Translator Alphonso Lingis. Pittsburgh: Duquesne University Press.

Lewin, K. (1946), 'Action research and minority problems'. *Journal of Social Issues*, 2, 34–6.

Linn, R. (1993), 'Performance assessment: policy promises and technical measurement standards'. *Educational Researcher*, 23(9), 4–14.

Lipton, P. (1991), *Inference to the Best Explanation*. London: Routledge.

Lively, K. (1992), 'More states back new standards for what teachers must know and be able to do in classrooms'. *Chronicle of Higher Education*, 39(16), A20.

Luhmann, N. (1979), *Trust and Power*. Chichester: Wiley.

Lum, G. (1999), 'Where's the competence in competence-based education and training?' *Journal of Philosophy of Education*, 33(3), 403–18.

Lyons, N. (1998), *With Portfolio in Hand; Validating the New Teacher Professionalism*. New York: Teachers' College Press.

Mabry, L. (1997), *Evaluation and the Post-modern Dilemma*. Greenwich, CT: JAI Press Inc.

MacGilchrist, B., Myers, K. and Reed, J. (1997), *The Intelligent School*. London: Paul Chapman Publishing Ltd.

MacIntyre A. and Dunne, J. (2002), 'Alistair MacIntyre on education: in dialogue with Joseph Dunne'. *Journal of Philosophy of Education*, 36(1), 53–371.

Marland, M. (1975), *The Craft of the Classroom*. London: Heinemann Educational Books.

Martin, S. and Cloke, C. (2000), 'Standards for the Award of Qualified Teacher Status: reflections on assessment implications'. *Assessment & Evaluation in Higher Education*, 25(2), 183–90.

Martin, W. (1969), *Realism in Education*. New York: Evanston and London: Harper & Row.

Maynard T, and Furlong, J. (1995), 'Learning to teach and models of mentoring', in T. Kerry and A. Mayes (eds), *Issues in Mentoring*. London: Routledge in association with the Open University, pp. 10–24.

McCall, G. (1977), 'The social looking-glass: a sociological perspective on self-development', in T. Mischel (ed.), *The Self: Psychological and Philosophical Issues*. Oxford: Basil Blackwell, pp. 274–91.

McIntyre, D. (1990), 'Ideas and principles guiding the internship scheme', in P. Benton (ed.), *The Oxford Internship Scheme*. London: Calouste Gulbenkian Foundation, pp. 17–33.

McLaughlin, T. (1999), 'Beyond the reflective teacher'. *Educational Philosophy and Theory*, 31(1), 9–25.

—(2003), 'Teaching as a practice and communities of practice'. *Journal of Philosophy of Education*, 37(2), 339–53.

—(2004), 'Philosophy, values and schooling: principles and predicaments of teacher example', in W.A.H. Aiken, J. Haldanne (eds), *Philosophy and Its Public Role. Essays in Ethics, Politics, Society and Culture*. Exeter UK and Charlottesville USA: Imprint Academic, pp. 339–53.

McNair, A. (1944), *The McNair Report: Teachers and Youth Leaders*. London: HMSO.

McNamara, D. (1996), 'The university, the academic tradition, and education', in J.A.S. Furlong (ed.), *The Role of Higher Education in Initial Teacher Training*. London: Kogan Page, pp. 179–92.

McShane, R. (1999), 'S1306 sports pedagogy the reflective practitioner', http://www.glos.ac.uk/subjectsandcourses/undergraduatefields/si/descriptors/si306.cfm, University of Gloucester (Accessed 07 May 2005).

Mead, G. (1934), *Mind, Self and Society*. Chicago: University of Chicago Press.

Menter, I. and Whitehead, J. (1995), *Learning the Lessons: Reform in Initial Teacher Training*. Bristol: University of the West of England and the National Union of Teachers.

Millins, P. (1971), 'The Department of Education and Science', in S. Hewett (ed.), *The Training of Teachers. A Factual Survey*. London: University of London Press, pp. 27–41.

Mischel, T. (1977), *The Self: Psychological and Philosophical Issues*. Oxford: Basil Blackwell.

Mitchell, R. (2000), 'Applied linguistics and evidence-based classroom practice: the case of foreign language grammar pedagogy'. *Applied Linguistics*, 21(3), 281–303.

—(2003), 'Rethinking the concept of progression in the National Curriculum for modern foreign languages: a research perspective'. *Language Learning Journal*, 27, 15–23.

Mitchell, R. and Myles, F. (1998), *Second Language Learning Theories*. London: Arnold.

Moore, A. (2004), *The Good Teacher*. London and New York: RoutledgeFalmer.

Moore, A. and Ash, A. (2002), 'Reflective practice in beginning teachers: helps, hindrances and the role of the critical other', British Educational Research Association (University of Exeter), http://www.leeds.ac.uk/educol/ (Accessed 03 February 2006).

Naigles, L. (2002), 'Form is easy, meaning is hard: resolving a paradox in early child language'. *Cognition*, 86, 157–99.

NCSL (2006), 'An overview of the summary report findings: special issue on personalised learning', Spring 2006, http://www.ncsl.org.uk National College of School Leadership (Accessed 18 April 2006).

NCVQ (1991), *NCVQ: Criteria for National Vocational Qualifications*. London: National Council for Vocational Qualifications.

NERF (2003), 'National Educational Research Forum: quality of educational research – sub-group report', http://www.nerf-uk.org/word/quality_report.doc?version=1. British Educational Research Association (Accessed 03 February 2006).

Newman, J. (2003), 'Educating as inquiry; a teacher action research site', http://www.lupinworks.com/ar/index.html. Literacy and Learning (Accessed 01February 2006).

Newman, S. (1999), 'Constructing and critiquing reflective practice'. *Educational Action Research*, 7(1) 145–63.

Newsom, J. (1963), *The Newsom Reports*. London: Central Advisory Council for Education (England).

Noddings, N. (2003), 'Is teaching a practice? *Journal of Philosophy of Education*, 37(2), 241–53.

Noel, J. (1999), 'On the varieties of phronesis'. *Educational Philosophy and Theory*, 31(3), 289.

Noels, K., Clément, R. and Pelletier, L. (1999), 'Perceptions of teachers' communicative style and students' intrinsic and extrinsic motivation'. *The Modern Language Journal*, 83, 23–4.

N. Ireland Working Group (1992), *Working Group for the Review of Initial Teacher Training in Northern Ireland Competences: Report of the Working Group 1*. Belfast: N. Ireland Working Group.

Novak, J. and Gowin, D. (1984), *Learning How to Learn*. Cambridge: Cambridge University Press.

Ofsted (1997), 'The Annual Report of Her Majesty's Inspectors of Schools', http://www.archive.official-documents.co.uk/document/hoc/129/129–02.htm. Ofsted (Accessed 15 March 2006).

O'Hear, A. (1988), *Who Teaches the Teachers?* London: Social Affairs Unit.

Oliver, C. and Aggleton, P. (2002), 'Mentoring for professional development in health promotion: a review of issues raised by recent research'. *Journal of Health Education*, 102(1), 32–8.

O'Neill, O. (2002), 'The philosophy of trust, a background to the Reith Lectures', 2002. http://www.bbc.co.uk/radio4/reith2002/, BBC and the Open University (Accessed 04 January 2006).

Open University (1994), *Postgraduate Certificate in Education mentors' materials*. Milton Keynes: Open University.

Pachler, N. (2005), 'Editorial: Reflecting education', 1(1), http://www.reflectingeducation.net/index.php/reflecting/article/view/5/9. Reflecting Education (Accessed 07 January 2006).

Paludan, J. P. (2006), *Personalised learning 2025, Schooling for Tomorrow: Personalising Education*. Paris: OECD Publishing. http://www.cifs.dk/scripts/artikel.asp?lng=2&id=1385 (Accessed 10 July 2007).

Paprgyris, A. and Poulymenakou, G. (2004), 'Acting and learning in virtual communities: the case of massively multiplayer online role playing games', http://www.eltrun.aueb.gr. Athens University of Economics and Business (Accessed 01 March 2006).

Patrick, H. (1986), 'From Cross to CATE: the universities and teacher education over the past century'. *Oxford Review of Education*, 12(3), 243–61.

Patrick, H., Bernbaum, G. and Reid, K. (1982), *The Structure and Process of Initial Teacher Education Within Universities in England and Wales.* Leicester: University of Leicester School of Education.

Perkins, M. (1952), 'Notes on the pragmatic theory of truth'. *The Journal of Philosophy*, 49(18), 573–87.

Peters, R. and White, J. (1969), 'The philosopher's contribution to educational research'. *Educational Philosophy and Theory*, 1, 1–15.

Peters, R. (1965), 'Education as initiation', in R. Archimbault (ed.), *Philosophical Analysis and Education*. London: Routledge & Kegan Paul, pp. 87–111.

Peters, R. (1966), *Ethics and Education*. London: George Allen & Unwin Ltd.

Plowden (1966), *The Plowden Report*. London: Central Advisory Council for Education, England.

Polanyi, M. (1969), *Knowing and Being*. London: Routledge and Kegan Paul.

Pollard, A. and James, M. (eds) (2004), *Personalised Learning: A Commentary by the teaching and Learning Research Programme: Autumn 2004.* London: ESRC.

Popper, K. (1972), *The Logic of Scientific Discovery*. New York: Harper-Collins.

Pring, R. (1996), 'Just dessert', in J. Furlong and R. Smith (eds), *The Role of Higher Education in Initial Teacher Training*. London and Philadelphia: Kogan Page, pp. 8–22.

Pring, R. (2000a), 'The false dualisms of educational research'. *Journal of Philosophy of Education*, 34(2), 247–60.

Pring, R. (2000b), *Philosophy of Educational Research*. London: Continuum.

Pring, R. (2001), 'The virtues and vices of an educational researcher'. *Journal of Philosophy of Education*, 35(3), 407–21.

QCA (2005), 'Assessment for learning', http://www.qca.org.uk/7659.html. QCA (Accessed 17 January 2006).

Quarantelli, E. and Cooper, J. (1966), 'Self-conceptions and others: a further test of Meadian hypotheses'. *Sociological Quarterly*, 7, 281–97.

Quine, W. (1969), *Ontological Relativity and Other Essays*. New York: Columbia University Press.

Ratner, J. (1939), *Intelligence in the Modern World: John Dewey's Philosophy*. New York: The Modern Library.

Reynolds, B. (1965), *Learning and Teaching in the Practice of Social Work* (2nd edn). New York: Russell and Russell.

Reynolds, D. (1998), *Improving the quality of teaching: Better Teachers, Better Schools: Lecture For The Teacher Training Agency*. London: TTA.

Reynolds, M. (1999), 'Standards and professional practice: the TTA and initial teacher training'. *British Journal of Educational Studies*, 47(3), 247–60.

Richards, M. (1974), *The Integration of a Child into a Social World*. London: Cambridge University Press.

Robertson, J.S. (1971), 'Voluntary colleges', in S. Hewett (ed.), *The Training of Teachers: a factual survey*. London: University of London Press, pp. 42–55.

Rockwell, T. (2001), 'Experience and sensation, Sellars and Dewey on the non-cognitive aspects of mental life'. *Education and Culture: the Journal of the John Dewey Society*, Winter 2001. www.california.com/~mcmf/index.html (Accessed 27 October 2004).

Rogers C. (2002), 'Defining reflection: another look at John Dewey and reflective thinking', http://www.tcrecord.org. *Teachers College Record 104: 842–66*. ID Number: 10890 (Accessed 1 March 2004).

Rorty, R. (1982), *Consequences of Pragmatism*. Brighton Sussex: The Harvester Press.

Roth, R. (1989), 'Preparing the reflective practitioner: transforming the apprentice through the dialectic'. *Journal of Teacher Education*, 40(2), 31–5.

Ryan, R. and Deci, E. (2000a), 'Intrinsic and extrinsic motivations: classic definitions and new directions'. *Contemporary Educational Psychology*, 25(1), 56–67.

—(2000b), 'Self-determination theory and the facilitation of intrinsic motivation, social development, and well-being'. *American Psychologist*, 55(1), 68–78.

Ryle, G. (1949), *The Concept of Mind*. Chicago: The University of Chicago Press.

—(1963), *The Concept of Mind*. Harmondsworth, Middlesex: Penguin Books.

—(1974), 'Intelligence and logic of the nature-nurture issue: reply to J.P. White'. *Proceedings of the Philosophy of Education Society*, 8(1), 52–60.

Sartre, J. (1938), *La Nausée*. Paris, Gallimard.

Schall, E. (1997), 'Notes from a reflective practitioner of innovation', in A. Altshuler, R. Behn (eds), *Innovation in American Government: Challenges, Opportunities, and Dilemmas*. http://govleaders.org/schall.htm. Brookings Institution Press (Accessed 07 May 2005).

Scheffler, I. (1974), *Four Pragmatists*. New York: Routledge & Kegan Paul.

Schön, D. (1971), 'Implementing programs of social and technological change'. *Technological Review*, 73(4), 47–51.

—(1983), *The Reflective Practitioner*. London: Temple Smith.

—(1987), *Educating the Reflective Practitioner*. San Francisco CA: Jossey-Bass Publishers.

—(Summer 1992), 'The theory of inquiry: Dewey's legacy to education'. *Curriculum Inquiry*, 22(2), 119–39.

Schwab, J.J. (1969), 'The practical: a language for curriculum'. *School Review*, 78(1), 1–23.

Shusterman, R. (1994), 'Dewey on experience: foundation or reconstruction?' *The Philosophical Forum* 26(2), 127–48.

Siegel, H. (2001), 'Dangerous dualisms or murky monism?' *Journal of Philosophy of Education*, 35(4), 577–94.

Simons, H. (2003), 'Evidence-based practice: panacea or promise?' *Research Papers in Education*, 18(4), 303–11.

Skemp, R. (1979), *Intelligence, learning, and action: a foundation for theory and practice in education*. Chichester, England: Wiley.

Slavin, R. (1986), 'Best-evidence synthesis: an alternative to meta-analytic and traditional reviews'. *Educational Researcher*, 15(9), 5–11.

Slembrouck, S. (2004), 'What is meant by "discourse analysis"?' http://bank.rug.ac.be/da/da.htm (Accessed 08 January 2006).

Smith, R. (1992), 'Theory as an entitlement to understanding'. *Cambridge Journal of Education*, 22(3), 387–98.

—(1999), 'Paths of judgement: the revival of practical wisdom'. *Educational Philosophy and Theory*, 31(3), 327–40.

—(2003), 'Unfinished business: education without necessity'. *Teaching in Higher Education*, 8(4), 477–91.

—(2006), 'On diffidence: the moral psychology of self-belief'. *Journal of Philosophy of Education*, 40, 51–62.

Snowdon, P. (2003), *Knowing how and knowing that: Presidential Address to the Aristotelian Society*. Paper presented at meeting held in Senate House. University of London: Monday 13 October 2003.

Spindler, J. and Biott, C. (2000), 'Target setting in the induction of newly qualified teachers: emerging colleagueship in a context of performance management'. *Educational Research*, 42(3), 275–85.

Springer Science and Business Media (1992), *Motivation and Emotion*. (Historical Archive), 3 September, pp. 165–85.

Stengel, B. (1998), 'Dewey on methods', http:www.eduiuc.edu/EPS/PES-yearbook/1998/stengel.html. *PES Yearbook* (Accessed 27 November 2004).

Stenhouse, L. (1975), *Introduction to Curriculum Research and Development*. London: Heinemann Education.

—(1980), 'Curriculum research and the art of the teacher'. *Study of Society*, 14–15.

—(1983), *Authority, Education and Emancipation*. London: Heinemann.

Stephenson, J. (2000), *Improving schools; improving teachers: supporting educators in times of change*. Presentation to AERA Conference, April 2000 (New Orleans).

Sternberg, R. (1990), *Metaphors of Mind*. Cambridge: Cambridge University Press.

Stevenson, T. and Lennie, J. (1992), 'Empowering school students in developing strategies to increase bicycle helmet wearing'. *Health Education Research*, 7(4) 555–66.

Stobart, G. and Gipps, C. (1997), *Assessment: A Teacher's Guide to the Issues*. 3rd edn. London: Hodder & Stoughton.

Stubbs, M. (1983), *Discourse Analysis: The Sociolinguistic Analysis of Natural Language*. Oxford: Blackwell.

Surrey County Council and Roehampton University (1993), *The New Teacher Competency Profile*. Surrey: SES.

Swenson, D. (1999), 'The reflective practitioner', http://www.css.edu/users/dswenson/web/TWAssoc/reflectivepractitioner2.html. David Swenson (Accessed 07 May 2005).

Taylor, C. (1989), *Sources of the Self: The Making of the Modern Identity*. Cambridge: Cambridge University Press.

Taylor, C. and White, S. (2000) *Practising reflexivity in health and welfare: Making knowledge*. Buckingham, UK: Open University Press.

TDA (2005a), 'Improving teacher quality', http://www.standards.dfes.gov.uk/otherresources/publications/teamwork/reflect/quality/. Teacher Development Agency (Accessed 12 January 2006).

TDA (2005b) 'Career Entry Development Profile: preparing for your teaching career', http://www.tda.gov.uk/upload/resources/pdf/c/cedpdividers.pdf Teacher Development Agency (Accessed 19 March 2006).

—(2007), 'Professional standards for teachers', http://www.tda.gov.uk/teachers/professionalstandards/downloads.aspx. Teacher Development Agency (Accessed 19 July 2007).

Thomas, J. (1990), *British Universities and Teacher Education*. London: The Falmer Press.

Thompson, M. (1997), *Professional Ethics and the Teacher: Towards a General Teaching Council*. Stoke on Trent, Trentham Books.

—(1992), Do 27 Competences Make a Teacher? *Education Review*, 6(2), 4–8.

Thrupp, M. (2001), 'Sociological and political concerns about school effectiveness research: time for a new research agenda'. *School Effectiveness and School Improvement*, 12(1), 7–40.

Tiles, J. (1992), *John Dewey: Critical Assessments*, vol. 4. London: Routledge.

Tooley, J. and Darby, D. (1998), *Educational Research: An OFSTED Critique*. London: Ofsted.

Torode, B. (1976), 'The revelation of a theory of the social world as grammar', in R. Harré (ed.), *Life Sentences*. London: Wiley, pp. 87–97.

Totterdell, M. and Lambert, D. (1993), 'The professional formation of teachers: a case study in reconceptualising initial teacher training through an evolving model of partnership'. *Teacher Development*, 2(3), 351–71.

Toulmin, S. (1984), 'Introduction to The Quest for Certainty', in J. Boydston (ed.), *John Dewey, The Later Works*, vol. 4, 1929, Carbondale: Southern Illinois University Press, pp. 7–12.

—(1990), *Cosmopolis*. New York: The Free Press.

Trent, F. and Slade, M. (2001), 'Declining rates of achievement and retention: the perceptions of adolescent males', http://www.boyslighthouse.edu.au/pdf/decrates.pdf. Boys' Education Lighthouse Schools Programme Commonwealth of Australia 2003 (Accessed 12 January 2006).

Tschannenn-Moran, M. and Hoy, W. (2000), 'A multidisciplinary analysis of the nature, meaning and measurement of trust'. *Review of Educational Research*, 70(4), 547–93.

TTA (1998), *National Standards for Qualified Teacher Status*. London: TTA.

—(2001), *The Role of the Induction Tutor: Principles and Guidance*. TPU0696/11–01 London: TTA.

—(2003), *A Handbook of Guidance*. London: TTA.

—(2004), *Qualifying to Teach*. London: TTA.

Turner, J. (1990), 'The area training organisation', in J. Thomas (ed.), *British Universities and Teacher Education, a Century of Change*. London: The Falmer Press, pp. 39–57.

Turner, N. (2002), 'The evolution of portfolios in teacher education', http://www.usca.edu/essays/vol32002/turner.pdf. St. Mary's College, USCA (Accessed 01 January 2006).

Urban, K. (2005), 'A peaceful coexistence of epistemologies – philosophy from the constructivist's point of view'. *Kybernetes*, 34(1–2), 295–305.

van Manen, M. (1991), *The Tact of Teaching*. Alberta: The Althouse Press.

—(1995), 'On the epistemology of reflective practice'. *Teachers and Teaching: theory and practice*, 1(1), 33–50.

Vygotsky, L. (1978), *Mind in Society: The Development of Higher Psychological Processes*. Cambridge Mass: Harvard University Press.

Watkins, C. (2000), 'Feedback between teachers', in S. Askew (ed.), *Feedback for Learning*. London: Routledge, pp. 34–44.

—(Spring 2001), 'Learning about learning enhances performance'. *Research Matters*, NSIN, (13).

Watkins, C. and Carnell, E. (2002), 'Effective learning, revised edition'. *Research Matters* (17).

Wells, G. (2004), 'Action, talk and text: the case for dialogic inquiry', http://education.ucsc.edu/faculty/gwells/Files/Papers_Folder/ATT.htm' University of California, Santa Cruz (Accessed 04 January 2006).

Wenger, E. (1998), *Communities of Practice: Learning, Meaning and Identity*. Cambridge: Cambridge University Press.

Wentzel, K. (2002), 'Are effective teachers like good parents? teaching styles and student adjustment in early adolescence'. *Child Development*, 74(1), 287–301.

Wenzlaff (1998), 'Dispositions and portfolio development: is there a connection?' http://www.questia.com/PM.qst?a=o&d=5001358541. Project Innovation 2002 Gale Group (Accessed 19 March 2006).

White, J. (1990), 'Two National Curricula – Baker's and Stalin's: towards a liberal alternative,' in B. Moon (ed.), *New Curriculum National Curriculum*. London: Hodder & Stoughton, in association with The Open University, pp. 35–46.

White, P. (1996), *Civic Virtues and Public Schooling*. New York: Teachers' College Columbia University.

Whitehead, J. (1999), 'Appendix: Action research: how do I improve what I am doing?' http://www.bath.ac.uk/~edsajw/benword/bapp.DOC. University of Bath (Accessed 30 January 2006).

Whitty, G., Barrett, E., Barton, L., Furlong, J. and Galvin C. (1992), 'Initial teacher education in England and Wales: a survey of current practices and concerns'. *Cambridge Journal of Education*, 22(3), 293–306.

Whitty, G. and Willmott, E. (1991), 'Competence-based teacher education: approaches and issues'. *Cambridge Journal of Education*, 21(3), 309–18.

Wilson, J. (2003), 'The concept of education revisited'. *Journal of Philosophy of Education*, 37(1), 101–8.

Winch, C. (2000), *Education, work and social capital*. London: Routledge.

—(2006), *Education, Autonomy and Critical Thinking*. Abingdon, Oxon: Routledge.

Winch, C. and Gingell, J. (2004), *Philosophy & Educational Policy: A Critical Introduction*. London: Routledge Falmer.

Wittgenstein, L. (1974), *Philosophical Investigations*, 3rd edn, G. Anscombe, Trans. Oxford: Basil Blackwell.

Wright, N. (1983), 'Standards and the black papers', in B. Cosin and M. Hales (eds), *Education Policy and Society; Theoretical Perspectives*. London: Routledge & Kegan Paul, in association with The Open University, pp. 170–82.

Wright, N. and Bottery, M. (1997), 'Perceptions of professionalism by the mentors of student teachers'. *Journal of Education for Teaching: International Research and Pedagogy*, 23, 235–52.

Young, M., Ashby, D., Boaz, A. and Grayson, L. (2002), 'Social science and the evidence-based policy movement'. *Social Policy and Society*, 1(3), 216–24.

Zeichner, K. (1994), 'Research on teacher thinking and different views of reflective practice in teaching and teacher education', in I. Carlgren, G. Handal and S. Vaage (eds.), *Teachers Minds and Actions: Research on Teachers' Thinking and Practice*. Bristol, PA: Falmer Press.

Index